Karl Marx

Selected Writings in Sociology & Social Philosophy

These selected texts, many of them previously unpublished in the United States, illustrate the principal themes of Marx's work: the theories of history and ideology, the analysis of capitalism, his conception of a future classless society, and his theory of the state and revolution. These selections from his early writings reveal Marx liberating himself from the philosophical tradition of Hegel, and creating a science of society which strikingly anticipates modern sociology.

T. B. Bottomore is Reader in Sociology at the University of London.

Maximilien Rubel is Maitre de recherches at the Centre National de la Recherche Scientifique, (Paris).

Dr. Erich Fromm is the author of several books in individual psychology and social psychology including **The Art of Loving, Beyond the Chains of Illusion, Forgotten Language, May Man Prevail?,** and **Psychoanalysis and Religion.** In addition, he is well known as a scholar of the philosophy of Karl Marx and has written **Marx's Concept of Man.**

KARL MARX

SELECTED WRITINGS IN
SOCIOLOGY & SOCIAL PHILOSOPHY

Newly translated by T. B. Bottomore.

Edited, with an introduction and notes, by
Mr. Bottomore and Maximilien Rubel,
and with a foreword by Erich Fromm

McGRAW-HILL BOOK COMPANY
NEW YORK   TORONTO   LONDON

First McGraw-Hill Paperback Edition, 1964
ISBN 07-040672-3

PRINTED IN THE UNITED STATES OF AMERICA
121314151617 MUMU 765432

PREFACE

MARX was a social scientist, a political philosopher, and a revolutionary. His reputation as a scientist has suffered, to some extent, from the combination of these activities and still more from the historical vicissitudes of " Marxism " as a political ideology.

It has also suffered from ignorance of his work, much of which remained unpublished until recent years. It was only in 1927 that the first volume of the projected complete works of Marx and Engels was published by the Marx–Engels Institute in Moscow, under the direction of D. Riazanov. This, and the succeeding volumes, made available for the first time the definitive texts of Marx's writings prior to 1847.[1] These texts [2] are indispensable to any serious examination of Marx's work, not only for their direct contributions to social theory, but also for the indications which they give concerning the vast project of sociological analysis which Marx elaborated in his youth, and of which he was able to publish, or even to write, only a small part. In the light of these youthful plans, even the substantial volumes of *Capital* and of *Theories of Surplus Value* appear as fragments only of a much larger work which was

---

[1] *Marx–Engels Gesamtausgabe*, 1927 onwards (referred to hereafter as *MEGA*). The internal political struggles in the USSR led to the dismissal of the first director of the Institute, Riazanov (who "disappeared" in 1931), and have now apparently resulted in the abandonment of the project which Riazanov conceived and began to carry out, viz. the publication of the complete works of Marx and Engels. Of the forty-two volumes originally planned only twelve have been published.

[2] The most important to the sociologist are: *Kritik des Hegelschen Staatsrechts* (1843), *Ökonomische-Philosophische Manuskripte* (1844), *Exzerpthefte* (1844–47), *Die Deutsche Ideologie* (1845–46). These were published in full for the first time in the *MEGA*, Vol. I/1 (1927), and Vols. I/3, 5 and 6 (1932).

to have been devoted to a general analysis of social institutions.

A further difficulty confronts the English student of Marx, since many of these earlier writings are still untranslated.[1] The effects of this deficiency are apparent in even the best critical literature (in English) on Marx, which relies heavily upon a few well-known works—the *Communist Manifesto*, the *Preface* of 1859, and the first volume of *Capital*.   In the present selection of texts we have tried to restore the balance by including a large number of translations from these early writings.   We have not, however, confined our selection to the manuscripts prior to 1847.   We have chosen passages from the whole of Marx's known writings, with the exception of his correspondence, in an endeavour to present, in a reasonably small compass, the main features of his method, and the main conclusions of his research.   One reason for an extensive selection is that many of Marx's writings which have been translated are not well known, and that in some cases the existing translations are unsatisfactory.   Another, more important, reason is that Marx's ideas developed, and we have tried to display this evolution, for example, in his ideas about social class and about the organization of capitalist industry.

Our introduction is not intended as a detailed commentary on the texts.   In the first part we consider some

---

[1] The existing translations are:

German Ideology, Parts I and III, edited with an introduction by R. Pascal, London, Lawrence & Wishart, 1938. (There is an earlier translation of some passages in S. Hook, *From Hegel to Marx*, New York, 1936.)

Selected Essays, translated by H. J. Stenning, London, 1926; New York, International Publishers, 1926.

The article by H. F. Mins, "Marx's Doctoral Dissertation," in *Science and Society*, XII, No. 1, 1948, contains some translated passages but is mainly a commentary.

There is a useful survey of Marx's early writings, with summaries of some of the texts, in H. P. Adams, *Karl Marx in His Earlier Writings*, London, Allen & Unwin, 1940.

of the intellectual influences upon Marx and the part they played in the construction of his own theories. This leads us to an examination of Marx's conception of history and of historical method, and of the science which he was trying to found, and to an account of the relation between social analysis and social philosophy in his thought. In the second part we present a brief historical survey of the influence of Marx's theories upon later sociology.

T. B. B.

M. R.

Autumn 1955

PREFACE TO SECOND IMPRESSION

In this second impression we have taken the opportunity to correct some minor errors and to revise a few passages in the translations. Otherwise the book remains unchanged.

T. B. B.

April 1961   M. R.

TRANSLATOR'S PREFACE

THE passages from Marx's writings included in this book are for the most part newly translated, and many of them are translated into English for the first time. The main exceptions are the extracts from the *Communist Manifesto*, which are so familiar that it seemed improper to alter the text in any way. In this case I have used the English translation of 1888. Other exceptions are the passages which were originally written and published in English; these are the articles from the *New York Daily Tribune* and the text published here is taken from the files of that newspaper. In the case of the passages from *Capital*, Vol. I, I have made liberal use of the translation by Moore and Aveling published in 1887, but I have entirely revised it, using the German text of the *Volksausgabe*, published in 1932 for the *Marx–Engels–Lenin Institute*.

So far as the other texts are concerned, where previous English translations existed I have usually consulted them, especially where the German text was obscure. But the older translations are frequently stilted and sometimes inaccurate, and I have only rarely modified my own rendering. The more recent translations are a good deal better and it will be seen that my own version is, in some cases, not very different (e.g. in some of the passages from the *German Ideology*, Part I).

Each passage is followed by a reference, or references, to its source and to the edition used for the translation. The year of first publication of the passage, or of composition in those cases where Marx himself did not publish it, is also given.[1]

[1] Except where the writing extended over an indeterminate period of years, e.g. *Capital*, Vols. II and III.

The following abbreviations have been used in the references:

Article I	"Kritische Randglossen zu dem Artikel: Der König von Preussen und die Sozialreform. Von einem Preussen," in *Vorwärts*, August 7, 1844.
Article II	Ditto, in *Vorwärts*, August 10, 1844.
Capital I, II, III	The three volumes of *Capital*.
CGP	*Critique of the Gotha Programme.*
CM	*Communist Manifesto.*
EPM	*Economic and Philosophical Manuscripts.*
GI	*German Ideology.*
Grundrisse	*Grundrisse der Kritik der politischen Ökonomie (Rohentwurf).*
HF	*Die Heilige Familie.*
JF	"Zur Judenfrage," in *Deutsch-Französische Jahrbücher*, February, 1844.
KHR	"Zur Kritik der Hegelschen Rechtsphilosophie. Einleitung," in *Deutsch-Französische Jahrbücher*, February, 1844.
KHS	*Kritik des Hegelschen Staatsrechts.*
MEGA	*Marx–Engels Gesamtausgabe.* (This is followed by a reference to the section and volume, e.g. MEGA I/3. Volume I/1 is in two parts and the references therefore appear as I/1/1 and I/1/2.)
MK	"Die moralisierende Kritik und die kritisierende Moral. Beitrag zur Deutschen Kulturgeschichte. Gegen Carl Heinzen," in *Deutscher-Brüsseler Zeitung*, October 28–November 25, 1847.
NYDT	*New York Daily Tribune.*
Preface	Preface to *A Contribution to the Critique of Political Economy*.

PP   *Poverty of Philosophy.*

TM   *Theorien über den Mehrwert.* (The volume references I, II/1, II/2, III [three volumes in four] are to Karl Kautsky's edition, published 1905–10.)

VA, I, II,   The three volumes in four of the *Volks-*
III/1, III/2   *ausgabe* of *Capital*

WLC   *Wage Labour and Capital.*

18th Brumaire *The Eighteenth Brumaire of Louis Bonaparte.*

Information about the dates of composition, original publication, and English translations of Marx's principal writings, including those from which extracts are published here, will be found in the Selected Bibliography in the Appendix, page 259 *seq.*

T. B. B.

CONTENTS

FOREWORD

These *Selected Writings in Sociology and Social Philosophy* will help greatly to acquaint the American reader with the thought of Karl Marx. Such acquaintance is very much needed, for ignorance of—or misconceptions about—Marxist thought are almost as great as the frequency with which *Marx* or *"Marxism"* are mentioned. This ignorance has many reasons. In the English-speaking countries one reason is obvious. Many of the writings of the young Marx have not been translated until recently; some remain untranslated today. The second reason is that even in those countries where all of Marx's writings have been published, his thought was given a one-sided and distorted interpretation. All the emphasis was put on the economic aspect of his teaching, and little on the philosophical-humanist aspect. (That the most important philosophical writings of the young Marx, *The Economic and Philosophical Manuscripts*, were only discovered in 1932 did not help either, toward a better understanding of Marx the humanist philosopher.)

Paradoxically enough, in one respect the interpretation of Marx's thought was the same among the most radically opposed wings of Marxism, the right wing socialists (Revisionists), and the Communists. Much as they disagreed on the question of democracy and freedom, they did agree on the economic interpretation of Marx's teachings. They considered the essence of Marxist thought to be a purely economic one: the transformation of a system of private ownership of the means of production into a system of public ownership. The communists quite explicitly hold the view that their system is "socialist" because their industry and agriculture are in the hands of the state which, as they see it, is the same as their being the property of the working class.

This concept of socialism, however, is by no means the Marxist concept. Socialism, to Marx, meant a society which provides
the material basis for the full development of the individual,
for the unfolding of all his human powers, for his full independence. Man, for Marx, was the root and the goal of all
social evolution. The goal of human development, as Marx saw
it, was essentially the same as it was for the great humanists of
the Renaissance and of the Enlightenment, from Erasmus to
Spinoza and Goethe. There are, however, two important points
of difference between Marx and previous humanist thought.
The humanists of earlier centuries, whether within or outside
the Church, believed that man could be transformed by the
power of religious teaching and education alone; in addition
some believed that political changes would be required, particularly the substitution of democracy for the feudal and abso-
lutist state. Marx, on the other hand, was convinced that no
amount of education can help realize the ideals of humanism
unless the *practice* of life is changed in such a way that it is
conducive to the development of the full individuality of man.
The conditions for such development were seen by Marx in the
system of socialism, in which the freely cooperating citizens
would direct a planned and rational economic system, the aim
of which was not profit but use. Such a system would form the
material basis for personal freedom and independence, but it
would not be a system in which maximal and ever-increasing
consumption would be the aim.

The second point of difference between the earlier humanists
and Marx is related to the one just discussed—his theory of society. For Marx the basis of any society is its mode of production, which in turn depends on the given "productive forces",
techniques of production, climate, geography, human skills, etc.
These not only are the conditions for a certain mode of production, but also for property and class relations. Marx was the
first to develop a scientific analysis of social structure and
social evolution, which permits the understanding of past his-

tory as well as certain predictions of alternatives for the future. This theory of history was misunderstood, as was his concept of socialism—and by the same people. To some extent this misunderstanding was caused by the words "historical materialism" which Engels used in referring to Marx's theory. (Marx himself never spoke of historical materialism.) The word "materialism" was confused with the mechanical materialism of the physiologists of the nineteenth century, and also with the *moral* concept of materialism vs. idealism. With regard to the first confusion, the fact is that Marx was profoundly opposed to mechanical materialism. His "materialism" meant that one must start, not with man's ideas and man's consciousness, but with the real man and the real conditions of his life. With regard to materialism in a moral and spiritual sense, the confusion is rather ironical. Marx's main criticism of capitalism was precisely that it makes man a prisoner of material interests. Socialism for him was that social order which would liberate man from slavery to greed as well as to blind economic forces. For him, man should become a being who *is* much, rather than one who *has* much. The reproach from the capitalist side that Marx was a materialist for whom material satisfaction is the aim of life is precisely the opposite of Marx's teaching, and it is surprising indeed, that this reproach is made by people who emphasize that the wish for profit is the main incentive for work. The situation becomes even more confused if one considers that Soviet economy is, in practice, based on the same capitalist principle of monetary incentive for work, even while at the same time paying lip service to Marxism.

Socialism as a realization of humanism is still little known in the world. But the distortion of Marx's thought by Communism, reformist socialism and the conservative enemies of both, is slowly giving way to a new understanding of the real Marx. This new understanding, I believe, is part of a renaissance of humanism which is occurring today throughout the world, and in various ideological camps. There is a new humanism in the

Catholic Church, in the Protestant Church, among socialists, among scientists and philosophers. This renaissance of humanism is a reaction to the threat of man and humanity which we are becoming increasingly aware of. The threat is a double one: the threat to mankind's physical existence by nuclear war, and the threat to his spiritual existence by the increasing automatization, bureaucratization and alienation of man. Against this threat to man a new wave of humanist thought and feeling is moving. The representatives of the new humanism are still in the minority in their respective camps. Yet their voice is heard with ever-increasing clarity.

The authors of this book form part of this movement; they are among the most learned and most authentic socialist humanists, and this collection of writings will help to restore the picture of Marx's teaching to its proper place in the history of philosophy and social theory. But they are by no means alone. Except in the Soviet Union, where there is little fertile research on Marx, their position is shared by Marxist scholars in France, England, Italy, Australia, India, Japan, the United States, as well as in Poland, Yugoslavia, Hungary and Czechoslovakia.[1]

There is one more word to be added. A number of scholars, mostly inside the Soviet Union, but some also in the west, claim that while the young Marx was, indeed, a humanist, he was not yet a "Marxist". They claim that the writings of the Marx of 1844 were idealistic and metaphysical, and that the "mature" Marx, with his emphasis on economy, had outgrown the ideas of his earlier years. This view is shared neither by the authors, nor by many other Marx scholars, nor by myself. It is true that Marx changed his terminology; thus, for instance, he stopped using the term "the essence of man"; but he did not change the substance of his thought about man's nature; this holds specifically true for the concept of alienation

---

[1] A symposium on "Humanist Socialism" in which T. B. Bottomore and M. Rubel are participating will be published in 1964 by Doubleday & Co. Inc.

which is the key concept in the *Economic and Philosophical Manuscripts,* and this remained so until the end of Marx's life. Nothing could demonstrate this better than comparing a sentence written by the young Marx with a paragraph from his last work, the third volume of *Capital.* In the *German Ideology* Marx wrote: "man's own deed becomes an alien power opposed to him, which enslaves him instead of being controlled by him." And "This crystallization of social activity, this consolidation of what we ourselves produce into an objective power above us, growing out of our control, thwarting our expectations, bringing to naught our calculations, is one of the chief factors in historical development up till now." At the end of *Capital* III Marx wrote: "The realm of freedom only begins, in fact, where that labour which is determined by need and external purposes, ceases; it is therefore, by its very nature, outside the sphere of material production proper. Just as the savage must wrestle with Nature in order to satisfy his wants, to maintain and reproduce his life, so also must civilized man, and he must do it in all forms of society and under any possible mode of production. With his development the realm of natural necessity expands, because his wants increase, but at the same time the forces of production, by which these wants are satisfied, also increase. Freedom in this field cannot consist of anything else but the fact that socialized mankind, the associated producers, regulate their interchange with Nature rationally, bring it under their common control, instead of being ruled by it as by some blind power, and accomplish their task with the least expenditure of energy and under such conditions as are proper and worthy for human beings. Nevertheless, this always remains a realm of necessity. Beyond it begins that development of human potentiality for its own sake, the true realm of freedom, which however can only flourish upon that realm of necessity as its basis. The shortening of the working day is its fundamental prerequisite." [1]

[1] "Karl Marx, Selected Writings. . . ." by Bottomore and Rubel, page 254/5.

This paragraph represents the quintessence of Marx's thought: man can never transcend the realm of necessity which is that of material production. But he can achieve an optimum of freedom even in this realm of necessity by the fact that "the associated producers regulate their interchange with Nature rationally, bring it under their common control, instead of being ruled by it as by some blind power. . . ." Here we find the same concept of alienation and de-alienation as in the early writings. In the following sentence Marx says that such a social order is the basis for the "development of human potentiality for its own sake, the true realm of freedom." Marx, at the end of his life, could not have expressed more clearly the goals and values which inspired him from the days of his youth, and thus confirmed the unity of his work against all later attempts at dividing and distorting it.

Erich Fromm
January 1964

INTRODUCTION

I. MARX'S SOCIOLOGY AND SOCIAL PHILOSOPHY

Teachers and contemporaries

It is still a prevalent view that Marx remained, throughout his life, a disciple of Hegel, merely filling out with a more or less factual content the grandiose philosophy of history of his master. Marx, of course, grew up in the atmosphere of Hegel's philosophy, and used its technical vocabulary, especially in his early writings. He never abandoned his respect for certain aspects of the " system." But his own social theory had other intellectual sources besides Hegel and, as we should remember, it was also based upon empirical study of working-class life and movements.

At the beginning of 1858, when he resumed his scientific work after a long interruption, Marx wrote to Engels that a fortunate chance had brought to his attention Hegel's *Logik*, and that reading it had been extremely profitable, especially for the choice of a method of exposition of his work. He added: " If ever the leisure for such work returns, I should very much like to make intelligible to common human understanding (in a short work) the rational aspect of the method which Hegel discovered but at the same time mystified." [1]

Marx never found the time, in the remaining twenty-five years of his life, to do this. He contented himself with " flirting " with the Hegelian style in his exposition of the theory of value in *Capital*.[2] In his early writings, however,

---

[1] Marx to Engels, January 14, 1858.
[2] See Preface to the 2nd German edition (1873).

Marx had already criticized and rejected Hegel's political theory as it is expounded in the *Grundlinien der Philosophie des Rechts*. He had carefully analysed Hegel's political concepts and outlined a sociological theory of the State. His opposition to Hegel, at this time, was expressed in fervent praise of democracy, not of socialism, since he had not yet come into contact with the socialist movement.[1] He had written, in 1844, a long critique of Hegel's method. He praised Hegel's conception, expounded in the *Phänomenologie des Geistes*, of the origin and development of man. Hegel, in Marx's view, had understood that man creates himself, in a historical process, of which the motive force is human labour, or the practical activity of men living in society. " The outstanding thing in Hegel's *Phänomenologie* is that Hegel grasps the self-creation of man as a process . . .; and that he therefore grasps the nature of *labour* and conceives the object man . . . as the result of his own labour." [2]

But in Marx's opinion—and this is the crucial difference between the two thinkers—Hegel conceived labour only in an alienated form; as the activity of pure spirit. For him the historical process was a movement and conflict of abstract categories, of which real individuals are simply the playthings. Political and economic alienation, which Hegel nevertheless understood and described very well, is projected into the heaven of pure thought, and the philosopher sets himself up as witness, judge, and redeemer of the alienated world.

" The *Phänomenologie* is a concealed, unclear and mystifying criticism, but so far as it grasps the alienation of man . . . all the elements of criticism are contained in it, and are often presented and worked out in a manner which goes far beyond Hegel's own point of view." [2]

---

[1] See *KHS*, *MEGA* I/1/1, pp. 403–553. This manuscript was probably written between March and August 1843, and was not published until 1927.

[2] *EPM* (1844), *MEGA* I/3, p. 156.

Thus Marx, while criticizing Hegel's philosophy of history, accepted this conception of history as a process of the self-creation of man. It does not follow that Marx was himself a philosopher of history, or that he derived his conception of historical development exclusively from Hegel. The notion of the historical development of social institutions is to be found in much of the political and historical writing of the latter part of the eighteenth century,[1] mingled with early formulations of the idea of progress, and may be regarded as the beginning of a separation of historical sociology from the philosophy of history. It has been argued, however, that Hegel gave to this idea of development a particular aspect by emphasizing the struggle of opposites— i.e. the dialectical movement—and that in Marx's social theory an analogous feature, the conflict of classes, occupies a prominent, even primordial, place. It is implied, therefore, that Marx, whether or not he was a philosopher of history, in the strict sense, was at any rate indebted to Hegel for one of his essential theories, which is thus represented as a philosophical rather than a sociological construction. But this resemblance seems slender evidence for asserting that such was in fact the genesis of Marx's theory of class struggle, particularly as Marx himself gave a different account; in a well-known letter he wrote:

". . . No credit is due to me for discovering the existence of classes in modern society, nor yet the struggle between them. Long before me bourgeois historians had described the historical development of this struggle of the classes

[1] See particularly the Scottish historians; Adam Ferguson, *Essay on the History of Civil Society*, 1767 (which was translated into German, and which probably influenced Hegel in his own discussion of "die bürgerliche Gesellschaft"), and John Millar, *The Origin of the Distinction of Ranks*, 1771, 4th edn. 1806; and in France, S. N. H. Linguet, *Théorie des lois civiles*, 1767, and the writings of Saint-Simon (discussed later). Marx was very familiar with the work of the Scottish historians and of Saint-Simon and the historians influenced by him, and he ranked them much higher than Hegel and his disciples in the historical field.

and bourgeois economists the economic anatomy of the classes." [1]

The effect of Hegel was much more that of provoking Marx to a general criticism and complete rejection of German historiography as it then existed.

A much more important part in Marx's thought was played by the Hegelian idea of " alienation " (*Entfremdung*). This concept was fundamental in the Hegelian account of mind, both in Hegel's own philosophy (in the *Phänomeno-logie*), and in a radically altered form in the work of the " Young Hegelians." By " alienation " the latter meant a condition in which man's own powers appeared as self-subsistent forces or entities controlling his actions. Thus Feuerbach made use of the notion of alienation in his study of Christianity: [2] he set out to show that the essence of religion was the essence of man himself projected outside himself and reified or personified. The powers and capacities attributed to the gods were in fact man's own powers and capacities; the divine law was nothing but the law of man's own nature.

Marx, as he indicated in his *Theses on Feuerbach*, started from the position Feuerbach had reached. The problem of alienation dominates all his writings, but no longer as a philosophical issue (i.e. a dispute about the essence of man). Alienation is examined as a social phenomenon. - Marx asks: in what circumstances do men project their own powers, their own values, upon hypothetical, superhuman beings; what are the social causes of this phenomenon? It was only in this sense (as an ideology) that Marx discussed religion; and he thereby contributed to founding the

[1] Marx to Weydemeyer, March 5, 1852. It is all too easy to dis-cover the sources of Marx's theory without recourse to Hegel. Marx had only to read the works of contemporary historians (outside Ger-many) and to observe what was happening under his eyes, both of which he did.

[2] L. Feuerbach, *Das Wesen des Christentums*, 1841.

modern sociology of religion. But he also, and this is where he diverged most from Feuerbach, investigated other forms of alienation. In opposition to Hegel's deification of the State, he regarded the State (as an arbitrary, external power dominating society) as only another form of human alienation. And in his analysis of the economic structure of capitalism, he described wealth in the form of capital as another mode of alienation; the rule of capital was " the domination of living men by dead matter." [1] Here, as in the case of religious alienation, Marx asks the question : What are the social causes of these phenomena? How does it happen that human beings project upon outside objects, upon reified abstractions, those powers which are truly their own—that, for example, they consider the State as a power which organizes society, when it is in fact the structure of society which gives rise to the State, or that they regard wealth in the form of capital, which is a creation of social labour (the labour of associated men), as an independent, active force, which " employs " human beings? [2]

It followed from Hegel's conception of labour as " spiritual labour," and of alienation as a purely spiritual phenomenon, that the dialectical process of " sublimation," by which alienation was overcome, took place only on the level of abstract thought and left unchanged the existing social

[1] See Part III, Section IV, pp. 167–77.

[2] Marx's concepts of ' false consciousness ' and ' ideology ' are related to the concept of ' alienation.' False consciousness is the consciousness of individuals in a condition of alienation, and ideology is the system of beliefs produced by such a false consciousness. Later, of course, Marx used the term ' ideology ' in different senses; e.g. in one sense, to mean a deliberately misleading system of ideas. For recent discussions of Marx's concept of ' alienation,' see: Jean Hyppolite, " De la structure du *Capital* et de quelques présuppositions philosophiques de l'oeuvre de Marx " in *Bulletin de la Société française de Philosophie*, Oct.–Dec. 1948 (reprinted in *Etudes sur Marx et Hegel*, Paris 1955) ; H. Popitz, *Der entfremdete Mensch*, Basle 1953; K. Löwith, "Man's self-alienation in the early writings of Marx," in *Social Research*, Summer 1954; H. B. Acton, *The Illusion of the Epoch*, London 1955.

institutions. According to Hegel, abstract right is sublimated in morality, morality is sublimated in the family,
the family is sublimated in civil society, civil society is
sublimated in the State, and finally the State is sublimated
in world history. But this whole dialectical process, which
Hegel expounds in the *Philosophie des Rechts*, leaves intact
the real social institutions, the family, civil society, and the
State. Marx opposed to this imaginative reconstruction
the idea of a real transformation of society, whose moral
aspect would be the re-acquisition by man of his natural
qualities, a rehabilitation of himself as a social being
liberated from enslaving alienations.

Hegel's theory took no account of real social phenomena,
and the philosopher was able to explain neither their
origins, nor their development, nor their disappearance.
Inevitably, he appeared to Marx as a kind of thaumaturge
who, with the aid of a magical formula called " negation of
the negation," succeeded as he willed in posing or deposing,
creating or destroying, conserving or abolishing, the social
creations of men. " The whole of Hegel's *Logik* is therefore
a demonstration that abstract thought is nothing in itself,
that the absolute idea is nothing in itself, and that only
Nature *is* something." [1] Hegel separated the act of thought
from the human subject, and turned this subject into a
predicate of the hypostatized thought. It is evident, Marx
comments, that " if man does not exist, his manifestation of
life cannot be human, and thought, therefore, could not be
grasped as a manifestation of the life of man, as a human,
natural subject, with eyes and ears etc., living in society, in
the world and in Nature." [2]

This, briefly, was the stage which Marx had reached in
his analysis at the moment when he was preparing to furnish,
" in various independent books, a critique of law, morals,

---

[1] *EPM* (1844), *MEGA* I/3, p. 169.   [2] Ibid., p. 170.

politics, etc. . . . and finally in a special work, the inter-relations of the whole, the relation between the different parts and a critique of the speculative treatment of this material." [1] But this encyclopædic work which Marx, then twenty-six years old, intended to compose in the course of his career, was never, in fact, completed. Only fragments of it were written, and even the *Critique of Political Economy* (the sub-title of *Capital*) is no more than an unfinished intro-duction.

Though it may be conceded that in his early writings Marx was a vigorous critic of Hegel, it is often argued that *Capital* represents a return to the Hegelian dialectic. It is clear that in certain chapters Marx deliberately imitated, and even parodied, the Hegelian *style*.[2] But he himself later took the opportunity of discussing his alleged " Hegel-ianism," and said that though he had passed through the school of the " great thinker," he had nevertheless over-turned and demystified the dialectic, while extracting its rational core.[3] Marx distinguished the manner of exposition from the method of research, and was concerned to empha-size the strictly empirical character of his own method:

" Of course the method of presentation must differ formally from the method of investigation. The aim of investigation is to appropriate the matter in detail, to analyse its various developmental forms, and to trace the inner connections between these forms. Not until this preliminary work has been effected can the movement as it really is be suitably described. If the description prove successful, if the life of the subject-matter be reflected on the ideal plane, then it may appear as if we had before us nothing more than an ideal construction.

" My own dialectical method is not only fundamentally

---

[1] *EPM* (1844), *MEGA* I/3, p. 33.

[2] This " flirtation " with Hegel's style is still more evident in the manuscripts written in 1857–58 which were the first drafts of *Capital*. See Karl Marx, *Grundrisse der Kritik der politischen Ökonomie (Rohentwurf)*.

[3] Preface to the 2nd edition of *Capital*, 1873.

different from the Hegelian dialectical method, but is its direct opposite. For Hegel, the thought process (which he actually transforms into an independent subject, giving to it the name of " idea ") is the demiurge (creator) of the real; and for him the real is only the outward manifestation of the idea. In my view, on the other hand, the ideal is nothing other than the material when it has been transposed and translated inside the human head." [1]

Marx's intention was to produce an empirical work, by considering " the development of the economic structure of society as a natural historical process," and by studying the " social antagonisms which arise from the natural laws of capitalist production." Marx compared himself with the physicist who studies the processes of Nature where they appear " in the most pragmatic form and least affected by disturbing influences," and he selected the whole of England as a laboratory in which to study the capitalist mode of production and " the relations of production and inter-course corresponding to it." But he was clearly aware that, since " in the analysis of economic forms neither the microscope nor chemical reagents can be used," they had to be replaced, in sociological analysis, by the power of abstraction, in order to discern, and to make statements about, the " pure events " of the social processes. For " contemporary society is not a fixed crystal, but an organism which is capable of transformation and which is continually apprehended in the process of transformation."

In any case, an examination of the structure of *Capital* will reveal that only a small part is written in what might be considered a Hegelian style. It is, for the most part, a presentation and analysis of sociological and historical data. In fact, *Capital* is, among other things, one of the earliest, and still one of the most valuable, works of social history conceived in a sociological manner, i.e. as the history of social institutions. It is a scientific work but at the same

[1] Preface to the 2nd edition of *Capital*, 1873.

time a moral indictment. In form and content it expresses Marx's pragmatic conception of science.

It is our contention, therefore, that Marx was indebted to Hegel for a different set of ideas than that which is usually mentioned. He was, from the beginning, an opponent of Hegel's political theory and of his philosophy of history. His criticism, in his early writings, shows very strongly the influence of other thinkers, and especially of Saint-Simon.[1]

There is some evidence for the view that Marx came under Saint-Simonian influence even before he began to study the Hegelian philosophy. Saint-Simon's disciples were extremely active in Germany,[2] and the Saint-Simonian doctrines gained so many adherents in the Moselle region that the archbishop was obliged to issue a special warning against this new heresy. At the time when Marx was completing his high-school studies in Trier, a Saint-Simonian propagandist was living in the town, Ludwig Gall, who published in 1835 a pamphlet on " The Privileged Classes and the Working Classes." Marx's father, and the head-master of his school, both belonged to a literary society of which Gall was also a member and which in 1834, because of its "liberal tendencies," attracted the attention of the police.[3] Moreover, when Marx went to the University of Berlin in 1837 he attended the lecture course of Eduard Gans, who was an enthusiastic Saint-Simonian.

Thus there were ample opportunities for Marx to become

---

[1] See the interesting article by Georges Gurvitch, " La sociologie du jeune Marx," which is reprinted as Chapter 10 of his *La vocation actuelle de la sociologie*, Paris, 1951.

[2] E. M. Butler, *The Saint-Simonian Religion in Germany*, 1926. This discusses only a limited period of the Saint-Simonian influence.

[3] B. Nicolaievsky and O. Maenchen-Helfen, *Karl Marx : Man and Fighter*, 1936, pp. 9 *seq.* See also Maxim Kovalevsky, "Two lives " (K. Marx and H. Spencer) in *Vestnik Evropy*, LX, 1909. Kovalevsky recalls in these reminiscences that Marx spoke of his father-in-law, Ludwig von Westphalen, as an enthusiastic disciple of Saint-Simon.

acquainted with the Saint-Simonian doctrines even before he studied Hegel. The first person to propagate Saint-Simonian ideas in the Rhineland was Marx's friend, Moses Hess, who was one of the editors of the *Rheinische Zeitung* in 1842. It was probably Hess also who brought to Marx's notice Lorenz von Stein's book *Sozialismus und Kommunismus des heutigen Frankreichs* (1842), which he reviewed in the *Rheinische Zeitung*. L. von Stein had drawn attention to the claims of the French socialists to base their doctrines on a science of society, and had set himself up as the spokesman in Germany of this new science in opposition to the existing *Staatswissenschaften*.

That Marx was, at least by 1846, very familiar with Saint-Simonian writing is evident from his detailed critical attack upon Karl Grün in the *German Ideology*.[1] The influence of Saint-Simon upon his own ideas is apparent from textual comparisons.[2] In the first place, there is in both writers the same emphasis upon industry, upon society as a workshop in which man produces spiritual as well as material products, and it is probable that Marx's immediately critical attitude to Hegel's concept of labour as purely spiritual labour, sprang from his early reading of Saint-Simon. Secondly, there is the conception of the relation between society and the State, that the State is (in certain circumstances) an obstacle to the development of industrial society, but also, that society (in particular the economic structure of society) is the basis of the State. Saint-Simon expressed this by saying, " La forme du gouvernement n'est qu'une forme et la constitution de la propriété est le fond; donc c'est cette constitution qui sert véritablement de base à l'édifice social " (*L'Industrie*).

Another element in Marx's social theory, English political economy, came considerably later. Marx himself gave an account of his studies up to 1843, and confessed his ignorance

---

[1] *MEGA* I/5, pp. 479–495. [2] See G. Gurvitch op. cit.

in economic matters at that time, in the preface to his *Contribution to the Critique of Political Economy* :

" The subject of my professional studies was jurisprudence, which I pursued, however, in connection with and as secondary to, the study of philosophy and history. In 1842–43, as editor of the *Rheinische Zeitung* I found myself embarrassed at first when I had to take part in discussions concerning so-called material interests. The proceedings of the Rhine Diet in connection with forest thefts and the extreme subdivision of landed property; the official controversy about the condition of the Moselle peasants into which Herr von Schaper, at that time president of the Rhine Province, entered with the *Rheinische Zeitung*; finally, the debates on free trade and protection, gave me the first impulse to take up the study of economic questions. At the same time a weak, quasi-philosophic echo of French socialism and communism made itself heard in the *Rheinische Zeitung* in those days when good intentions ' to go ahead ' greatly outweighed knowledge of the facts. I declared myself against such botching but had to admit at once in a controversy with the *Allgemeine Augsburger Zeitung* that my previous studies did not allow me to hazard an independent judgment as to the merits of the French schools. When, therefore, the publishers of the *Rheinische Zeitung* conceived the illusion that by a less aggressive policy the paper could be saved from the death sentence pronounced upon it, I was glad to take that opportunity to retire from public life into my study.

" The first work undertaken for the solution of the question that troubled me was a critical revision of Hegel's *Philosophy of Right*; the introduction to this work appeared in the *Deutsch-Französische Jahrbücher*, published in Paris in 1844."

Thus Marx's first economic studies were made in 1843–45, during his exile in Paris, and they were continued during his stay in Brussels from 1845–48. The extraordinary range of these studies can be seen from the extracts and commentaries in Marx's *Notebooks*.[1] In the field of economics Marx

---

[1] Published in *MEGA* I/3, pp. 411–579, and *MEGA* I/6, pp. 597–620. Much of this material was later used in preparing what was to have been the fourth volume of *Capital*, and which was published by Kautsky as *Theorien über den Mehrwert* (1905–10).

became a very learned man, and though he was influenced above all by Ricardo, he also drew largely upon the work of other economists who had concerned themselves with the labour theory of value, and in particular those, such as Hodgskin and Bray, who had drawn socialist conclusions from the theory. He was also strongly influenced by the writings of those who had approached economics from a broadly sociological point of view, regarding the subject-matter of economics as the relationships between human individuals and groups in the process of production, e.g. Adam Smith's *Wealth of Nations* and Quesnay's *Tableau Economique*. The outcome of Marx's omnivorous reading and of his critical study of his predecessors was a systematic presentation of the labour theory of value, as a part of his sociological analysis. We are not here concerned with the economic aspect of Marx's theory as such. Its most important characteristic is that it forms part of a socio-logical analysis of economic systems. Marx, in treating the political economy of his time as an " ideology," was attempting to analyse the *social* relationships which, in his view, underlay the *economic* relationships expressed in values, prices etc. His economic writings are a continuation of his early analysis of human labour; they bear less resemblance to contemporary economics than to the contemporary sociological study of economic systems. For example, Marx's long discussion of productive and unproductive labour [1] is meaningless from the point of view of modern economic theory, but it makes a valuable contribution to the sociology of work. Schumpeter has emphasized one feature of this connection between economics and sociology:

". . . though Marx *defines* capitalism sociologically, i.e. by the institution of private control over means of produc-tion, the mechanics of capitalist society are provided by his

---

[1] In the manuscript *Theories of Surplus Value*. See the texts on pp. 157-60.

economic theory.   This economic theory is to show how the sociological data embodied in such conceptions as class, class interest, class behaviour, exchange between classes, work out through the medium of economic values, profits, wages, investment, etc., and how they generate precisely the economic process that will eventually break its own institutional framework and at the same time create the conditions for the emergence of another social world." [1]

It is perhaps curious, when one considers Marx's clear intention to found a science of society which would embrace and complete the existing special sciences, that he never used the term ' sociology ' in any of his writings, though his near contemporary, Comte, had put it into circulation. Probably the explanation lies in Marx's dislike of the " positive philosophy " and in his low opinion of Comte and his disciples.

Apparently, he had not read Comte before 1866.   The enthusiasm for Comte which became evident at that time in England and France, surprised and indeed annoyed him, and he began to study Comte's work, whose encyclopædic character at once impressed him.   But he judged it greatly inferior to Hegel's writing.[2]   Despite its anti-theological appearance, the positive philosophy seemed to him " profoundly rooted in Catholic soil." [3]   He scornfully remarked, in connection with one of Comte's English disciples, " Positive philosophy means ignorance of everything positive." [4]

Marx entirely rejected Comte's social doctrine.   He condemned, especially, its theological and sectarian spirit, and its prophetic frenzy, but without feeling the need to subject the theory as a whole to systematic criticism.

[1] J. Schumpeter, *Capitalism, Socialism, and Democracy*, New York, 1942, p. 20.

[2] Marx to Engels, July 7, 1866.

[3] See *Capital*, Vol. I, 1st ed., where Marx writes, " Compared with Hegel's *Encyclopædia*, Comte's synthesis is the work of a schoolboy and has only local significance."

[4] Marx to Engels, March 20, 1869.

Probably Marx judged Comte mainly from the activities of his disciples, and especially his French disciples, who wanted to make positivism *the* philosophy of the labour movement. His estimate of Comte suggests two reflections. The first is that his hostility to the positivists who wished to impose a particular philosophical doctrine upon the labour movement, brings into relief his own repudiation of philosophical speculations upon the course of history, and his rejection of ideologies, even in the form of a new " positivist " religion.[1] The second concerns the nature of the science which Marx was trying to bring into being. It certainly had affinities with sociology as Comte conceived the subject. But there were also great differences which seem to justify Marx's critical attitude. His own " science of society," which we have now to examine, is closer to the present concerns of sociology than is the theory which gave its name to the discipline.

Marx the scientist

Marx undoubtedly considered himself a scientist. But his conception of science was pragmatic,[2] and it was perhaps this which originated the myth of " scientific socialism." Engels certainly believed that Marx had transformed socialism from a Utopia into a science. In *Anti-Dühring*,

[1] Most Marxist writers have treated Marx and Comte as the authors of rival " systems." See for instance :

C. de Kelles-Krauz, " Comtismo e Marxismo," in *La scienza sociale*, October 1901.

Lucy Prenant, " Marx et Comte," in *A la lumière du marxisme*, Vol. 2, Editions Sociales, Paris, 1937, pp. 19–76.

Paul Laberenne, " Efficacité politique et sociale du positivisme et du marxisme," ibid., pp. 77–123.

[2] Paul Lafargue, in his " Souvenirs personnels " (published in *Neue Zeit*, 1890), quoted Marx's remark that : " Science should not be an egoistic pleasure. Those who are fortunate enough to be able to devote themselves to scientific work should be the first to apply their knowledge in the service of humanity."

which Marx read in manuscript,[1] Engels attributed to him
" two great discoveries "; " the materialist conception of
history and the revelation of the secret of capitalist production through surplus value."   With these discoveries, Engels
adds, " Socialism became a science.   The main thing now
was to work out all its details and relations."   Engels again
refers to " scientific socialism," in connection with the theory
of surplus value which, according to him, was first formulated
by Marx.

Engels did not indicate the scope of this new science.
He sometimes referred to Marxian socialism as a theory,[2] a
theory of which he says that it is not a dogma but the
exposition of a process of evolution,[3] that it is a " theory of
evolution." [4]

Marx does not seem to have objected to Engels' account,
but his own view was different.   He wished to give a
" scientific basis " to socialism, which he regarded, not as a
science, but as a social and political movement striving to
bring about a new, and better, system of human relations.
In a letter to Sorge,[5] Marx condemned the attempts of those
(disciples of Lassalle, or admirers of Dühring) who wished
to give socialism a " higher ideal orientation," " that is,
to replace the materialist basis (which requires serious
objective study if one is to use it) by a modern mythology,
with its goddesses of justice, freedom, equality and fraternity."   In a later passage of the same letter he criticizes
" Utopian socialism," which " in the period before
materialist-critical socialism had appeared contained the
latter in germ, but which now coming *post festum* can only be
foolish, insipid, and fundamentally reactionary."

Marx's attitude is made clearer in a number of earlier

[1] *Anti-Dühring*, Preface of 1889, *MEGA* (Sonderausgabe), p. 9.
[2] Engels to Sorge, November 29, 1886.
[3] Engels to Mrs Wischnewetsky, December 28, 1886.
[4] Engels to the same, January 27, 1887.
[5] October 19, 1877.

writings.   In the *Poverty of Philosophy* he refers to the socialists and communists as " the theorists of the working class " who no longer need, as did the Utopian thinkers, " to look for a science in their own minds; they have only to observe what is happening before their eyes and to make themselves its vehicle of expression."   Later, Marx refers to this science as a product of the historical movement, as a science which becomes revolutionary, having ceased to be doctrinaire; this science is represented by the theorists of the working class who consciously associate themselves with the historical movement.   In the *Communist Manifesto* Marx speaks of the " theoretical conclusions of the Communists," which " merely express, in general terms, actual relations springing from an existing class struggle, from a historical movement going on under our very eyes."   These are conclusions derived from the empirical study of historical and social facts, but not a new " scientific socialism."   At the most they constitute a science *of* socialism, an analysis of an existing socialist movement and of the conditions in which it develops.[1]

The nature of Marx's science appears more clearly from the account which he gave of his studies when, in 1857, he resumed the scientific work which he had begun in 1844 and which had been interrupted by political and journalistic activities.   It was the commercial crisis of 1857 which provided the incentive to resume his studies in political economy,[2] and the nature of the work which he then undertook can be examined in the recently published manuscripts of 1857–58.[3]   The plan and method of the work are outlined in an introduction begun in August

[1] The *aims* of the socialist movement are another matter; see pp. 27–8.

[2] Marx to Lassalle, December 21, 1857.

[3] See *Grundrisse der Kritik der politischen Ökonomie (Rohentwurf)*, Dietz Verlag, Berlin, 1953.   These manuscripts were first published in 1939 in Moscow.

1857 and first published by Kautsky in *Neue Zeit*, in 1903.

The plan which Marx adumbrates is not, in fact, that of a treatise on political economy, but of a much broader study of society, as is indicated by the themes which he proposes to treat:

1. The abstract characteristics common to all forms of society, taking into account their historical aspect.
2. The main constituent elements of the internal structure of bourgeois society, upon which the basic social classes rest, capital, wage labour, and landed property. Town and country. The three great social classes. The exchange between them. Circulation. Credit.
3. Crystallization of bourgeois society in the form of the State. The "unproductive" classes. Taxation. Public debt. Public credit. Population. Colonies. Emigration.
4. International relations of production. International division of labour. International exchange. Exports and imports. Exchange.
5. The world market and crises.

Though he later modified some features of this plan, Marx never entirely abandoned his intention of dealing with the themes which he had thus defined. Only illness and death prevented him from carrying out his project.[1]

The introduction defines the subject which Marx proposed to discuss as "material production," and goes on to specify in more detail, "individuals producing in society, and therefore a socially determined production by individuals, naturally constitute the starting point."

[1] In 1881, two years before his death, Marx replied to Kautsky, who had inquired about the possible publication of his complete works, that these works "must first be written in their entirety." K. Kautsky, *Aus der Frühzeit des Marxismus*, 1935, p. 53.

Marx expands Aristotle's definition of man: " Man is
in the most literal sense a *zoon politikon*, not merely a social
animal, but an animal which can develop into an individual
only in society." This definition has, at the same time,
an ethical significance. Marx postulates the individuality
and uniqueness of man as an end which can be attained
only in society liberated from material and spiritual con-
straints.

The introduction continues with a critical account of the
Hegelian method and with an examination of the concept of
" society." Here Marx sketches a critique of a school of
sociology which has still not entirely disappeared. " To
consider society as a single subject is to consider it wrongly,
speculatively." [1] In Marx's view, " society" refers to individuals in their interrelations or interactions. The most
important of these interactions, to him, were those taking
place in the sphere of " material production," or, in other
words, the social process of human labour.

" The result at which we arrive, is not that production,
distribution, exchange, and consumption are identical, but
that they are all elements of a totality, distinctions within
a unity. Production predominates. . . . From it, the process continually recommences . . . but there is interaction
between the various elements. This is the case in every
organic whole."

At no point in his discussion of material production does
Marx use such expressions as " in the last analysis," or
" ultimate factor." In these manuscripts he is far from ex-
pounding the kind of monist determinism from which Engels
found it difficult to extricate himself when, after Marx's
death, he was obliged to concede the deficiencies of the

---

[1] Cf. with the statement in the *Economic and Philosophical Manuscripts*:
" It is above all necessary to avoid postulating ' society ' once more as
an abstraction confronting the individual. The individual *is* a social
being."

materialist conception of history as (in his account) he and Marx had formulated it in their various writings.[1]

The synopsis of a later chapter contains the following headings, " Production. Means of production and relations of production. Relations of production and relations of intercourse. Forms of State and consciousness in relation to the relations of production and intercourse. Legal relations. Family relations." Here Marx wrote down a few brief notes on historiography and on the so-called *Kulturgeschichten* which are, fundamentally, nothing more than histories of religions and States. He sets out to discuss the " different varieties of historiography " up to his time, and begins by making a distinction between an ideal and a real historiography, between a so-called objective and a subjective (moralistic, philosophical) historiography. He proposes to refute the criticisms levelled against the " materialism " of his own conception. He intends to examine the " dialectic of the concepts ' productive force (means of production) ' and ' relation of production,' a dialectic whose limits are to be determined and which does not abolish the real distinction." He proposes to investigate the problem of the relation between material production and artistic production, to criticize the current notion of progress, and to examine the relation between the concepts of historical necessity and contingency, taking as his point of departure, " Natural determination; subjective and objective. Tribes, races, etc."

The student of Marx can only regret that this *magnum opus*, for which the manuscripts of 1857–58 were preliminary drafts, the first attempts to carry out the intellectual programme conceived in 1844, remained largely unwritten. For Marx

[1] See Engels to Mehring, July 14, 1893; Engels to Starkenburg January 25, 1894, " It is not that the economic situation is the cause, or is alone active, while everything else is only passive. Rather there is an interaction on the basis of the economic necessity which in the last analysis always prevails."

here undertook to analyse some of the most fundamental, and most severely criticized, concepts in his social theory, among them those of " productive force," "relations of production," " ideology," and " historical necessity." But the intention was never realized, and Marx's science has largely to be reconstructed from his manuscripts and his published works. It is clearly broader than the special social sciences which existed at that time, e.g. political economy. Marx was concerned with the general character-istics of social action, and with the historical varieties of social systems. His analysis of social systems has two distinctive features; first, the importance which he attaches to the relation between society and Nature,[1] and secondly, the emphasis which he lays upon historical change. These two aspects are themselves related, for Marx is largely con-cerned with the effects in human social history of the chang-ing relationships between man and Nature.

Marx's science, therefore, appears in the first place as the outcome of his critical opposition to German historio-graphy in general and to the Hegelian philosophy of history in particular. It was an attempt to construct a historical social science.

Marx's historical method and sociological concepts

Marx's method has usually been called " historical materialism." [2] This is misleading in so far as it attributes to Marx a philosophical intention which he did not have. He was not concerned either with the ontological problem

---

[1] In Marx's theory, society and Nature are regarded as parts of a single system. It is this conception which leads him to declare that "Natural science will one day incorporate the science of man, just as the science of man will one day incorporate natural science; there will be a single science." *EPM, MEGA*, I/3, p. 123.

[2] Marx himself never used the terms " historical materialism " and "dialectical materialism." The first comes from Engels and the second from Plekhanov.

of the relation of thought and being, or with problems of the theory of knowledge. Speculative philosophy of this kind was what Marx *rejected*, in order to substitute science for metaphysics in a new field of knowledge.[1]

Marx spoke simply of the "materialist basis" of his method of investigation. In his postscript to the second edition of *Capital*, he refers the reader to the preface to his *Contribution to the Critique of Political Economy* for a fuller explanation of his " materialism." An examination of this preface, which condenses into a few propositions the theory worked out fifteen years earlier in the Brussels and Paris manuscripts, shows that the term "material" is employed simply to designate the fundamental, primary conditions of human existence. The expressions used are "material life," "material conditions of life," "material productive forces," "modes of production of material life," "material transformation of the economic conditions of production," etc.

Marx's scientific work was, as we have said, in the first place a new historiography. His earliest and dominating interest was in historical change. From Hegel he derived the notion of the self-creation of man, but, in opposition to Hegel, he conceived this self-creation as a social development based upon the human mastery of Nature. He excluded from his account of historical change any reference to forces or agencies beyond those of human beings living and working in society. For this reason it is misleading to regard Marx as a philosopher of history. His intention, at least, was to give a scientific account of social change, and his principal criticism of Hegel and the Young Hegelians was that they were philosophers of history and not historians.[2]

If Marx has been called a philosopher of history, this is no

---

[1] This is evident, in particular, from the *Theses on Feuerbach*; see pp. 67–9 below.

[2] See especially, Part I, Sect. I, below, pp. 51–66.

doubt partly due to the commingling of ethical and scientific judgments in his work, but still more to the misconceptions of his historical method which have been spread by zealous but mistaken disciples. Marx himself replied to one critic in a document which illumines better than any other text his own conception of historical method.[1]

" He has to transform my sketch of the origins of capitalism in Western Europe into a historical-philosophical theory of a universal movement necessarily imposed upon all peoples, no matter what the historical circumstances in which they are placed, and which will lead, in the last resort, to an economic system in which the greatly increased productivity of social labour will make possible the harmonious development of man. But I must protest. He does me too much honour, and at the same time discredits me. Let us consider an example. In *Capital* I have referred on several occasions to the fate which overtook the plebeians in ancient Rome. They were originally independent peasants, cultivating their own plots of land. In the course of Roman history they were expropriated. The same development which separated them from their means of production and subsistence, also gave rise to large landed property and large financial capital. Thus, at a certain moment, there were on the one hand free men stripped of everything except their labour power, and on the other hand, the owners of all this accumulated wealth, ready to exploit their labour. But what happened? The Roman proletarians did not become wage earners, but an idle mob, more abject even than the erstwhile ' poor whites ' of the southern States of the USA. Beside them grew up a system of production which was not capitalist, but was based upon slavery. Thus we see that events of a striking similarity, but occurring in different historical contexts, produced quite different results. The key to these phenomena can be discovered quite easily by studying each of these developments separately, but we shall never succeed in understanding them if we rely upon the

[1] Unpublished reply (in French) to Mikhailovsky, who had asserted that according to Marx's " philosophical system " Russia, like every other nation, would be obliged to pass through a stage of capitalist development. Cf. Nicolai—On (pseudonym of N. Danielson), *Histoire du développement économique de la Russie depuis l'affranchissement des serfs,* Paris, 1902, p. 509.

passe partout of a historical-philosophical theory whose chief quality is that of being supra-historical." [1]

Marx's conception of historiography was genuinely new, though he was indebted for some of its elements to Saint-Simon, and in a lesser degree, to those writers who had produced histories of " civil society." Marx thought that the subject-matter of historiography should be much wider than it had traditionally been, particularly among German historians; it should extend beyond the spheres of religion, politics, literature, and art. In his conception, industry, the practical activity of man in all its aspects, was to be the principal object of study of psychology [2] and of historiography, both of them forming part of a more general science dealing with Nature and man.

At this point Marx's historiography becomes what is more properly called historical sociology. He was less concerned to trace particular lines of historical causation, than to elaborate a set of categories for analysing social systems, taking into account that all social systems are continually undergoing change. The principal themes of this sociology are briefly outlined in the *Preface* of 1859, which, as we have said, summarizes the conclusions which Marx had reached in the earlier, unpublished manuscripts. These themes are: (i) the economic structure of society, (ii) the ideological superstructure, (iii) social revolution, and (iv) the future of society.

It is not our intention, here, to embark on a general discussion of these themes, or of the various concepts which

---

[1] Cf. Marx's letter to Annenkov (December 28, 1846) in which he sets down his criticism of Proudhon, later expanded in the *Poverty of Philosophy*. Marx attacks Proudhon as a *philosopher of history* : " In short, this is old-fashioned Hegelianism, not history. It is not profane history, the history of men, but sacred history, the history of ideas. In his (Proudhon's) conception man is only an instrument, which the idea, or eternal reason, uses for its own development."

[2] Industry is " an open book of the human faculties." *EPM, MEGA* I/3, p. 121.

Marx employs in his treatment of them. Our main concern is to display the new elements which Marx contributed to social theory. The emphasis which he placed upon the economic structure of society was neither new nor surprising; it was a commonplace among historians and economists, as we have shown in discussing Marx's precursors. Marx's own contribution, in this sphere, was the context in which he discussed economic structure, the context of the historical development of human labour as the primary relation between man and Nature, and his attempt to classify human societies in terms of their economic systems.

A much more original contribution was Marx's analysis of the ideological superstructure, and of its relation to what he called the " real basis " of society, that is, the mode of production and the corresponding social relations. His assertion that " it is not the consciousness of men which determines their being, but on the contrary, their social being which determines their consciousness " is not a philosophical (epistemological) proposition, but a statement about the genesis of ideological constructions, law, politics, religion, art, and philosophy. It is these " ideological forms," according to Marx, which constitute the principal stumbling-block for scientific investigation, when they are considered in themselves, without taking into account the correlations which can be established between a certain stage of economic development and the various cultural products. In his view, correlations of this kind, between modes of production, class structure, and styles of thought or artistic creation, could, in many cases, be established without difficulty.

Marx was, in fact, one of the originators of the sociology of knowledge, though in his eyes it was primarily a critical theory, intended to prepare the way for the constitution of a rigorous social science. Those who have followed Marx in this field have generally claimed too much for the sociology of knowledge, but they have nevertheless made important contributions to the history of thought, and especially of political thought.[1]

The third theme, that of social revolution, has largely been neglected by sociologists and, for that matter, by other social scientists. Indeed, the whole problem of social change has received surprisingly little attention; only recently have sociologists, anthropologists and economists begun to study intensively one particular aspect of this problem, namely, the processes of social change in under-developed countries under the impact of Western technology. But it is curious, when one reflects upon the tremendous effects which revolutions have had upon human social organization, that no sociologist since Marx has thought it worth while either to analyse revolutionary movements or to attempt a comparative study of revolutions. The sociology of revolution has so far only one major contribution to record, that of Marx himself.

Finally, the fourth theme of Marx's sociological analysis is the future of human society. It is here that sociology and social philosophy become interwoven to produce a doctrine which is presented as being at the same time a body of scientific knowledge and a spur to political action.

Science and revolution

The combination of scientific analysis with moral judgments is by no means uncommon in the field of social studies. Marx is unusual, and his work is exceptionally interesting because, unlike any other major social thinker, he was the recognized leader, and subsequently the prophet, of an organized political movement.

The publication of his early writings has thrown new light

[1] See, for instance, the essay by K. Mannheim, "Conservative Thought," in *Essays on Sociology and Social Psychology*, London 1953.

upon this aspect of his intellectual development. These writings, especially of the period before his exile in Paris (October 1843), show that Marx became a socialist *before* and not *after* having conceived his sociological theory of history.

Marx's adherence to the socialist movement followed his definitive rejection of the political philosophy of Hegel and his disciples, a rejection which he expounded in an important though unfinished, critical work, which was not published until 1927, when it appeared under the title *Kritik des Hegelschen Staatsrechts*.[1]   Marx took this manuscript with him into exile.   Once settled in Paris, where he made contact with working-class groups, and thus with the socialist movement, he resumed his work, and wrote an introduction to his critique of Hegel's philosophy of right.[2]

This latter text is at the same time a moral declaration and a sketch of a sociology of human poverty.   Its Feuerbachian inspiration is evident, but Marx had already gone beyond an anthropological analysis of religion, and had adumbrated a critique of society.

" Man makes religion, religion does not make man. Religion is indeed man's self-consciousness and self-awareness as long as he has not found his feet in the universe. But man is not an abstract being, squatting outside the world. Man is the world of men, the State, and society.   This State, this society, produce religion which is an inverted world consciousness, because they are an inverted world.   Religion is the general theory of this world, its encyclopædic compendium, its logic in popular form, its spiritual *point d'honneur*, its enthusiasm, its moral sanction, its solemn complement, its general basis of consolation and justification. It is the fantastic realization of the human being inasmuch as the human being possesses no true reality.   The struggle against religion is therefore indirectly a struggle against that world whose spiritual aroma is religion.

" Religious suffering is at the same time an expression of real suffering and a protest against real suffering.   Religion

[1] *MEGA* I/1/1, pp. 403-553.   [2] Ibid., pp. 607 *seq.*

is the sigh of the oppressed creature, the sentiment of a heartless world, and the soul of soulless conditions.   It is the opium of the people.

" The abolition of religion, as the illusory happiness of men, is a demand for their real happiness.   The call to abandon their illusions about their condition is a call to abandon a condition which requires illusions.

". . . The immediate task is to unmask human alienation in its secular form, now that it has been unmasked in its sacred form.   Thus the criticism of heaven transforms itself into the criticism of earth, the criticism of religion into the criticism of law, and the criticism of theology into the criticism of politics."

Marx had therefore already formulated in 1843 an intellectual and practical programme, from which he never afterwards deviated.   His aim was to transform speculative philosophy into a critical social theory which would be of use to men overcome by misery.   Marx called these men the " proletariat," but he was still far from having worked out a sociological concept.   He had observed the Parisian proletariat and had before his eyes a picture of misery and revolt.   He realized that there was some connection between his own experience as a thinker and writer, whose free exercise of his profession had been forbidden by an authoritarian government, and the condition of the proletariat.   What connected them was *alienation*, the separation of man from himself and from his neighbours, the divorce between man as a citizen and man as a worker, the projection of the social forces of man on to an external power which is an incarnation of arbitrariness and injustice.   The alienation of man thus appeared as the fundamental evil of capitalist society.

This evil finds its embodiment in the proletarian.   The latter is a member of a " class in civil society, which is not a class of civil society, a class which is the dissolution of all classes, a sphere of society which has a universal character because its sufferings are universal, and which does not claim a particular redress because the wrong which is done

to it is not a particular wrong but wrong in general . . .
which claims no traditional status but only a human
status . . . a sphere, finally, which cannot emancipate
itself without emancipating itself from all the other spheres
of society, without therefore emancipating all these other
spheres. . . ."

In his later writings Marx took for granted the moral
ideals which he had acquired in his youth, and which
clearly derive from the materialist writers of the eighteenth
century as well as from Saint-Simon and Feuerbach.[1] His
aim, and this he regarded also as the aim of the socialist
movement, was a society in which men, liberated from the
" alienations " and " mediations " of capitalist society,
would be the masters of their own destiny, through their
understanding and control both of Nature and of their own
social relationships. This ideal was not peculiar to Marx;
it was characteristic of one prominent tendency in the nine-
teenth-century theories of progress. In England it was best
represented by L. T. Hobhouse, who held, just as strongly as
Marx, that the rational control of the environment, both
natural and social, is an intellectual and moral aim of the
highest importance for man.

Where Marx differed from other writers in this tradition
was in his failure to expound his implicit moral philosophy
and thus to become aware of the complexity of the issues
involved. Only in his earlier writings, and especially in
the *Economic and Philosophical Manuscripts*, did he give any
connected account of the moral commitment which directed
all his subsequent scientific activity.[2]

[1] See, for example, the passage from the *Heilige Familie*, on p. 243.
[2] It will be seen that many of the texts concerning future society,
in Part V of the present book, are taken from the manuscripts of 1844.
Marx's social philosophy, like his sociology, has to be reconstructed from
the available texts. The Marxist attempts to do this, e.g. Kautsky's
Die Ethik und die materialistische Geschichtsauffassung, have so far produced
only travesties. For a different attempt, see M. Rubel, *Pages choisies de
Karl Marx*, Paris, 1948.

II. THE INFLUENCE OF MARX'S SOCIOLOGICAL THOUGHT

MARX's theories, for a variety of reasons, remained for some time isolated from the social sciences as they were being developed in the universities. Their sociological relevance only began to be realized towards the end of the nineteenth century, when sociology itself was becoming established as a separate discipline. On the occasion of the first Congress of the *Institut International de Sociologie*, in 1894, Marx's social theory had a prominent place in the discussions, as a result of the contributions by M. Kovalevsky, E. Ferri, F. Tönnies, P. de Lilienfeld, C. de Kelles-Krauz, and others.[1] Thus, in a paper on the primitive forms of society in Russia, M. Kovalevsky referred to the methodology proposed by the Russian philosopher and sociologist P. Lavrov, whom Marx knew and esteemed.[2] According to Lavrov, sociology could be defined as the study of human solidarity in its historical phases and perspectives. In his view the primary causes of the transformations which human society undergoes are the changes which occur in the economic sphere: " This is what the disciples of this school call by the ill-chosen name, historical materialism."[3]

C. de Kelles-Krauz, in his paper, observed that Marx's theory provided the frame of reference required in order to correlate the social phenomena discovered by historical and statistical inquiry. E. Ferri, the Italian criminologist, in a paper entitled " Sociology and Socialism," also praised Marx's theory of economic determinism. " Scientific-socialism is simply the logical application of the postulates of Darwin and Spencer in the field of political economy

[1] See *Annales de l'Institut International de Sociologie* (ed. by René Worms), Vol. I, Paris, 1895.
[2] See the letters of Marx to Lavrov in *Perepiska K. Marksa i F. Engelsa Russkimi Politicheskimi deyatelyami*, Moscow, 1927, pp. 161 *et seq.*
[3] *Annales de l'Institut International de Sociologie*, op. cit., p. 35.

and sociology." [1] In Marx's sociological theory, law, morals, and politics are only epiphenomena of economics, and this theory, according to Ferri, is confirmed by the researches of A. Loria and Thorold Rogers.[2] Marx was not simply an economist; his real title to fame is the theory of economic determinism formulated in the preface of his *Contribution to the Critique of Political Economy*.[3]

About the same time there occurred the first attempt made in France to establish a connection between the theories of Marx and Durkheim. In a long critical review of *Les règles de la méthode sociologique*, Georges Sorel contrasted Durkheim's psychologism with what he considered the pragmatic and scientific approach of Marx.[4] He criticized Durkheim for basing his method on the study of " things in themselves," or essences, instead of concerning himself— as Marx had done, more in accord with the scientific spirit—with the relations between things. Sorel refused to accept Durkheim's thesis, according to which " the possibility of a sociological science is established by generalizing the principle of causality borrowed from the physical sciences." [5] According to Sorel, the sociologist is not concerned with real causes (in the sense of the physical

---

[1] *Annales de l'Institut International de Sociologie*, op. cit. p. 163.

[2] A. Loria, author of *La teoria economica delle constituzione politica*, 1886, had to some extent appropriated Marx's theory, not without deforming it, and had been criticized by Engels in the preface to Vol. III of *Capital*. Thorold Rogers, in his *Economic Interpretation of History*, 1888, based on lectures given in Oxford, does not mention Marx, nor is he really concerned with the " economic interpretation of history." His book is a contribution to economic history, and contains nothing either to confirm or refute Marx's theory.

[3] *Annales*, op. cit., p. 167. Ferri had already developed these ideas in his book *Socialisme et science positive (Darwin, Spencer, Marx)*, 1896 (Eng. trans. *Socialism and Positive Science*, 1905), where he expressed his satisfaction that the conspiracy of silence around Marx's social theory had now been broken.

[4] Georges Sorel, " Les théories de M. Durkheim," in *Le Devenir social*, No. 1 (April 1895) and No. 2 (May 1895), pp. 1 *et seq.* and pp. 148 *et seq.*   [5] Ibid., p. 9.

sciences) but only with the broad categories of change. Recalling and quoting Marx's ideas expressed in the *Misère de la philosophie*, Sorel praised the "materialist theory of sociology," according to which "the various systems, political, philosophical, religious, cannot be considered as independent, with their own particular foundations." Marx had emphasized "the necessity of positing beneath this whole superstructure, the economic relationships," [1] and had thus assigned to sociology its major field of investigation, the system of production and exchange. By concentrating his attention on the division of labour, Durkheim, who was hostile to socialism, had neglected in his study of society a primary factor—the conflict of classes.

Sorel had already published a number of works whose originality distinguished them from the productions of orthodox Marxists. [2] In his later work he was more and more inclined to oppose the conceptions of Marx himself to those of his disciples, not excepting Engels, and he was ultimately led to an extreme opposition to ideological Marxism as a whole.

Durkheim later examined in more detail Marx's theory, at least in the form which it took in the commentaries of A. Labriola.

[1] Op. cit., p. 153.

[2] Cf. in particular, *L'Ancienne et la nouvelle métaphysique*, 1893 (new edition by E. Berth, under the title *D'Aristote à Marx*, Paris 1935); *La fin du paganisme*, 1894 (new edition by the author under the title *La ruine du monde antique*, with sub-title *Conception matérialiste de l'histoire* Paris, 1901; 3rd ed., Paris, 1933); *La science de l'éducation*, 1896; *Vico*, 1896. In this latter essay Sorel, with great acuity, treats Marx as a continuator of Vico's thought. After 1898 Sorel took a more critical view of Marx and came increasingly into conflict with the orthodox Marxists. See, for this period, "La necessita e il fatalismo nel marxismo," in *Riforma Sociale* V–VIII, Turin, 1898 (Sorel defends Marx against the charge of fatalism, saying that Marx had emphasized the role of contingency in technological progress); *L'idea giuridica nel marxismo*, Palermo, 1899; "Marxismo e scienza sociale," in *Rivista di sociologia*, III/1, Rome January, 1899.

" I consider extremely fruitful [Durkheim wrote] this idea that social life should be explained, not by the notions of those who participate in it, but by more profound causes which are unperceived by consciousness, and I think also that these causes are to be sought mainly in the manner according to which the associated individuals are grouped. Only in this way, it seems to me, can history become a science, and sociology itself exist." [1]

But according to Durkheim the validity of this conception was in no way connected with the destiny of a political movement, since in any case he himself had arrived at this view before reading Marx, and the whole development of historiography and psychology in the last half-century had been towards this " objective " conception of history, which should not be identified with historical materialism.

Nevertheless, it is worth noting that it was under Durkheim's direction that the early volumes of the *Année sociologique* devoted a considerable amount of space to the discussion and critical examination of the sociology of Marx, and of his disciples and interpreters.[2] There were already in fact several university centres, particularly in Germany and Italy, in which a vigorous discussion of Marx's sociology was taking place. The first impulse had been given by Rudolf Stammler, the author of a lengthy volume entirely devoted to historical materialism and its application in the field of law.[3] One of the noteworthy features of this book is the considerable use made by Stammler of some

[1] E. Durkheim, review of A. Labriola, *Essais sur la conception matérialiste de l'histoire*, in *Revue philosophique*, December 1897, p. 648. G. Kagan has pointed out, in an article " Durkheim et Marx " in *Revue d'Histoire économique et sociale*, May, 1939 p. 235, that the two thinkers had in common a desire to establish sociology both as a theoretical science and as the basis of a rational policy.

[2] " The materialist conception of history is in favour; every page of the *Année sociologique* is an indication of this." R. Lapie, referring to A. Labriola, *Essais sur la conception matérialiste de l'histoire*, in *L'Année sociologique*, I, 1898, p. 271.

[3] R. Stammler, *Wirtschaft und Recht nach der materialistischen Geschichtsauffassung*, Leipzig, 1896.

of Marx's writings which at that time had been almost completely forgotten, among them the articles in the *Rheinische Zeitung* (1842) and in the *Deutsch-Französische Jahrbücher* (1844), and also the *Heilige Familie* (1845). Stammler was in addition well versed in the literature of the Marxist school, and he criticized a number of Engels' ambiguous references to spiritual phenomena as " reflections " or " copies " of economic phenomena, statements which had been presented as a faithful interpretation of Marx's thought. Stammler regretted that Marx's theories had no epistemological foundation, and he introduced a philosophical distinction between the "form" and the " matter " of social life, or, in other words, between juridical norms and economic activity, the former being, in his view, the condition and indispensable premise of the latter. Thus the principal thesis of historical materialism was inverted, since, according to Stammler, the social relations of production cannot exist outside a definite system of legal rules. From this point of view, the problem of social determinism (*Gesetzmässigkeit*) is equated with that of the creation of legal norms and rules which permeate, and constitute the framework of, all social existence. Having revised Marx's theory in this way, Stammler went on to expound his own "social teleology," based on the principles of Kantian morality,[1] which he opposed to fatalistic determinism.

Stammler's book was warmly received in the *Année sociologique*, where F. Simiand praised the author for having expounded in an objective manner the meaning and relevance of historical materialism and for having succeeded in " verifying a relationship postulated between economic life and social life." [2] Simiand found particularly noteworthy

---

[1] " A community of men who are able to exercise free will, such is the final and absolute end of social life." R. Stammler, op. cit., p. 575.

[2] F. Simiand, review in *L'Année sociologique*, I, 1898, pp. 488–97.

in Stammler's exposition " the distinction, in the economy . . . between what is purely technological, and what is economic, that is, a definition of economic phenomena in terms of social factors." [1]

Stammler's book found an early and perspicacious critic in B. Croce, who was a close student of the obscurities and contradictions of German philosophy,[2] but the major critical examination of its thesis only appeared several years later, in an article by Max Weber.[3]

By the end of the nineteenth century Marx's theories had become so widely known that his literary executors prepared new editions of many of his writings which had been forgotten or had gone out of print, and also published a number of hitherto unpublished manuscripts.[4] These new editions and posthumous publications made it possible to obtain a more complete view of the sociological content of Marx's

[1] Op. cit., p. 497.

[2] B. Croce (Eng. trans.). *Historical Materialism and the Economics of Karl Marx* with an introduction by A. D. Lindsay, 1913. This is a collection of essays published between 1895 and 1899. Chapter II which was originally published in 1898, discusses Stammler's book.

[3] Max Weber, " R. Stammler's 'Überwindung' der materialistischen Geschichtsauffassung," in *Archiv für Sozialwissenschaft und Sozialpolitik*, 1907. Reprinted in *Gesammelte Aufsätze zur Wissenschaftslehre*, Tübingen, 1922, pp. 291-359. Weber's criticism is less concerned with historical materialism as such, than with the incoherencies in which Stammler's own work (of which a new and virtually unchanged edition had just been published) abounds. From the side of Marxism, Stammler's work was criticized by Max Adler; " R. Stammler's Kritik der materialistischen Geschichtsauffassung." *Marxistische Probleme*, 1913, 5th ed., 1922, pp. 214 *et seq.*

[4] During Engels' lifetime there were new editions of *Misère de la Philosophie* (in German), *Lohnarbeit und Kapital, Enthüllungen über den Kommunistenprozess zu Köln*; while the manuscripts of *Kapital*, Vols. II and III, and of the *Thesen über Feuerbach* were published for the first time. After Engels' death there was a new edition of *Zur Kritik der politischen Ökonomie* (by K. Kautsky, 1897) and the first publication of *Value, Price and Profit* (by Eleanor Marx, 1898). The journal *Neue Zeit*, founded in 1883, published a number of Marx's lesser known writings, some of which also appeared in French translations in *L'Ere nouvelle* (from 1893) and in *Devenir social* (from 1895).

work, and stimulated renewed discussion among historians, philosophers, and sociologists, particularly after Engels' death, on the problems of the materialist conception of history. Thus, even before the publication of Stammler's book, there had been an exchange of views between French and Italian thinkers who sympathized in greater or lesser degree with the Marxist school. The influence of Sorel's writings in Italy, and the interest of university teachers such as Labriola, Croce, and Gentile, had produced a movement in favour of giving a new direction to historical and socio-logical studies on the lines of the general philosophical conceptions which Engels had formulated, in response to various critics, to remove a number of misunderstandings concerning " historical materialism." [1]

The writings of Labriola, after those of Sorel, show the increasingly favourable reception of Marx's thought.[2] " In Marx, ideas, temperament, political action, and thought were united." [3] Marx's personality exercised an attraction through a many-sided work which was difficult to classify in any of the existing scientific disciplines. It was able to arouse the interest of the historian as well as the sociologist, of the economist as well as the philosopher. Labriola's commentary emphasizes especially this unifying character of Marx's work, in which the divisions between tradition-ally separate disciplines were surmounted. "The various analytic disciplines which illustrate historical facts, have ended by bringing forth the need for a general social science,

[1] See especially Engels' letters to Schmidt (October 5 and 27, 1890, July 1, 1891), on the subject of the book by Paul Barth, *Die Geschichts-philosophie Hegels und der Hegelianer bis auf Marx und Hartmann*; to J. Bloch (September 21, 1890); to F. Mehring (July 14, 1893), and to Starkenburg (January 25, 1894). These letters were published by E. Bernstein under the title "Die Briefe von F. Engels über den Geltungsbereich der materialistischen Geschichtsauffassung," in *Doku-mente des Sozialismus*, Vol. II, 1903.

[2] A. Labriola, op. cit. (Eng. trans. *Essays on the Materialistic Conception of History*, 1908).   [3] Ibid., p. 53.

which will unify the different historical processes. The materialist theory is the culminating point of this unification." [1] Nevertheless, this unifying principle should not be employed, in Labriola's view, as an infallible talisman which could miraculously unveil the constitutive elements of the social system. " The underlying economic structure, which determines all the rest, is not a simple mechanism, from which institutions, laws, customs, thought, sentiments, ideologies emerge as automatic and mechanical effects. Between this underlying structure and all the rest, there is a complicated, often subtle and tortuous process of derivation and mediation, which may not always be discoverable." [2] Defining sociology briefly as " the science of social functions and variations," [3] Labriola presents Marx's contribution to this new field of knowledge as a series of discoveries which will enable man to become master of his own destiny and to give significance to his life.

Labriola's interpretation of Marx's historical method aroused considerable discussion. Charles Andler [4] criticized in particular the " quietism " of Labriola, against whose views he quoted the *Theses on Feuerbach* which Engels had discovered in one of Marx's notebooks and had published in 1888.[5] A similar position was taken by Labriola's compatriot, Gentile, who not only considered the *Theses on Feuerbach* the key to Marx's thought, but also attempted, setting out from these theses, to reconstruct the " philosophy of practice " (*praxis*) which, according to him, had been expounded in an unpublished manuscript.[6]

---

[1] Op. cit., pp. 149 *seq.*   [2] Ibid., p. 152 *seq.*   [3] Ibid., p. 180.

[4] Charles Andler " La conception matérialiste de l'histoire d'après M. Antonio Labriola," in *Revue de Métaphysique et de Morale*, 1897.

[5] F. Engels. Appendix to *Ludwig Feuerbach and the Outcome of Classical German Philosophy* (Eng. trans., 1934).

[6] G. Gentile, *La filosofia de Marx*, Pisa, 1899. The importance of the *Theses on Feuerbach* had been recognized earlier, by L. Weryho, *Marx als Philosoph*, Berne, 1894, and by A. von Wenckstern, *Marx*, Leipzig, 1896.

These controversies had reached a point, at the end of the nineteenth century, where it was common to speak of " the crisis of Marxism," a crisis both intellectual and political, since it coincided with the revisionist movement in the German Social Democratic Party.[1] It is interesting to observe the tremendous efforts made at this time to draw up a balance sheet of " the scientific situation of Marxism," utilizing an enormous bibliographical apparatus, devoted not only to Marx's own works but also to the already abundant literature of exegesis and criticism. T. G. Masaryk, at that time professor in the Czech University of Prague, produced a long work of analysis and criticism which contains many acute and subtle observations on Marx's sociological method and hypotheses.[2]

Nothing better reveals the international character of this discussion than the echo which it found in a country where any " Marxist " publication was likely to be suppressed by the censor; between 1895 and 1900, numerous periodicals and books published in Russia paid increasing attention to the subject of " scientific socialism." At the centre of this discussion were the ideas of the sociologist and journalist, N. K. Mikhailovsky, one of the most brilliant representatives of the *narodnitchestvo*, and well known for his fervent attachment to the primitive agricultural commune and to individualism.[3] Already during Marx's lifetime *Capital*

---

[1] The " crisis of Marxism " attracted the attention at the same time, 1898, of Sorel and of Masaryk. Cf. *Critica Sociale*, May 1, 1898, and *Revue internationale de sociologie*, July 1898. A year later Bernstein published his *Voraussetzungen des Sozialismus*, which contained a critique of the Hegelian residues in Marx's work, as well as a declaration of faith in favour of a practical programme of social reform as the way towards socialism.

[2] T. G. Masaryk, *Die philosophischen und soziologischen Grundlagen des Marxismus*, Vienna, 1899. In the same year appeared L. Woltmann's *Der historische Materialismus*, Düsseldorf, a criticism of Marx from the point of view of Kantian philosophy.

[3] On Mikhailovsky, Lavrov, Kareyev, Struve, and others, see J. F. Hecker, *Russian Sociology*, New York, 1915.

had aroused discussion both in Russia itself and among Russian *emigrés*, in which Mikhailovsky and others took part.[1]

During Engels' lifetime two representatives of Russian " Marxism " took part in the debate; Lenin and Plekhanov. Replying to some articles in which Mikhailovsky argued that Marx had nowhere systematically expounded his materialist conception of history, Lenin wrote a pamphlet in which he presented Marx as the founder of scientific sociology.[2] The theory outlined by Marx in 1859, in the preface to *Zur Kritik der politischen Ökonomie* was there presented as a simple " hypothesis," but it had raised sociology for the first time to the level of a science.[3] In the same period Plekhanov published (under the pseudonym of " Beltov "), his *Development of the Monist Conception of History*.[4] Under this cautious title the book was a defence of the " modern materialism " created by Marx, against the idealist and " Utopian " sociological school of Kareyev, Lavrov, Mikhailovsky, and others. Two years earlier one of the leading representatives of the Russian populist movement, the economist Danielson, the translator of *Capital*, had published a comprehensive sociological study of the Russian economy,[5] in which he sought to show that

---

[1] Marx himself wished to join in this discussion if one may judge from a letter which he intended to send to the editor of *Otetchestvennye Zapiski*, in reply to an article of Mikhailovsky which had appeared in October 1877. However Marx did not send his letter, which was only published after his death. Cf. N. Danielson, *Sketches of our Economy since the Emancipation of the Peasants* (1893, in Russian. French trans. *Histoire du développement économique de la Russie depuis l'affranchissement des serfs*, Paris 1902), and above, p. 22.

[2] Lenin, *What the Friends of the People Are* (1894, Eng. trans. in *Selected Works*).

[3] Ibid.

[4] G. V. Plekhanov, *In Defence of Materialism. The Development of the Monist View of History*. Eng. trans. by A. Rothstein, London, 1947. First published in St Petersburg in 1895.

[5] Danielson, op. cit.

capitalism had no future in Russia, and that the *obchtchina*, reorganized on the basis of modern technology, could become " the starting point of a new social development." [1] It was against Danielson and the whole populist school that Lenin wrote his book *The Development of Capitalism in Russia*.[2]

These were the first publications in which an attempt was made to use Marx's sociological categories in empirical research. Tugan-Baranovsky's *History of the Russian Factory*,[3] a study of the changes in the internal structure of the Russian factory under the influence of economic and social changes, represents the same tendency.

It was, however, principally in Germany that the sphere of general sociological theory was abandoned for empirical studies designed to test the application of Marx's hypotheses in particular areas of research. Engels had already set an example by the publication of *Der Ursprung der Familie, des Privateigentums und des Staates*,[4] in which he used the notes which Marx had made on L. H. Morgan's *Ancient Society*. H. Cunow pursued this line of research, without accepting all Engels' interpretations, in a series of anthropological studies which attracted the attention of Durkheim.[5] Though Durkheim expressed reservations about " economic

[1] Op. cit., p. 497. The phrase is quoted from Marx and Engels.

[2] Published in 1899, Eng. trans. in *Selected Works*.

[3] Published in St Petersburg in 1898. German trans. revised by the author, *Geschichte der Russischen Fabrik*, 1900.

[4] Published in Zürich, 1884; 4th rev. edn. 1891. Eng. trans. 1902; new trans. from 4th edn., 1940. There exists a lengthy manuscript of Marx's extracts and notes concerning Morgan's book which has been published, in a Russian translation, in *Arkhiv K. Marksa i F. Engelsa*, Vol. IX, 1941.

[5] H. Cunow, *Die soziale Verfassung des Inkareichs. Eine Untersuchung des altperuanischen Kommunismus*, Stuttgart, 1896. The book was reviewed by F. Lévy in the first volume of the *Année sociologique* (1898). The following year Durkheim reviewed Cunow's articles, published in the *Neue Zeit* in 1897, on " Die ökonomischen Grundlagen der Mutterherrschaft."

materialism," he followed closely the publications of the Marxist sociological school, and was a well-informed critic of them, as for example in the case of the book by E. Grosse, *Die Formen der Familie und die Formen der Wirtschaft.*[1]

Among the works of the Marxist school of sociology in other fields of research should be mentioned Kautsky's studies of the origins of Christianity, and of the French Revolution, and his contributions to political sociology.[2] The first application of Marxist sociology in the field of literary history was F. Mehring's *Lessing-Legende.*[3]

In Italy, also, Marx's theory stimulated a number of new researches. One of the most interesting is E. Ciccotti's study of slavery in the ancient world.[4] This is an attempt to show in detail that the history of antiquity confirmed Marx's hypothesis concerning the relation between changes in the mode of production and in the social structure as a whole. A wide knowledge of classical literature and of contemporary sources enabled Ciccotti to present a plausible and interesting analysis of the relations between the development of slavery in the Greek cities and in the Roman Empire and the decline of the ancient world.

In Britain during this period, as also later, sociologists paid little attention to Marx's theories, as may be seen

---

[1] See *L'Année sociologique*, Vol. I, 1898, pp. 319 *seq.* Durkheim considered that the inadequacy of the " economic materialist " conception was most evident in the study of the family.

[2] See in particular the articles " Die Entstehung des Christentums," in *Neue Zeit*, later expanded in *Der Ursprung des Christentums*, Stuttgart, 12th edn. 1922. " Die Klassengegensätze von 1789," in *Neue Zeit*, Vol. VIII, 1889; *Die Agrarfrage*, Stuttgart, 1899.

[3] First published in *Neue Zeit*, 1892, and later as a book, Stuttgart, 1893.

[4] E. Ciccotti, *Il tramonto delle schiavità*, Turin, 1899 (French trans. *Le déclin de l'esclavage antique*, Paris 1910). On the diffusion of Marxism in Italy see R. Michels, " Historisch-Kritische Einführung in die Geschichte des Marxismus in Italien," in *Archiv für Sozialwissenschaft und Sozialpolitik*, XXIX, 1907, pp. 189–262.

from the early papers of the *Sociological Society*, founded in 1903.[1] In the writings of Hobhouse, from 1893 to 1929, Marx is hardly mentioned, and never in any important context; e.g. in the study of social classes, or of property and economic systems. Only J. A. Hobson, among the earlier writers, showed, in his studies of modern capitalism, the influence of Marx.[2]

From the beginning of the twentieth century there was an increasingly detailed and thorough study of the sources, structure, and practical bearing of Marx's work.[3] The vast literature on Marx was still largely philosophical,[4] and much of it was concerned with the intellectual relationship between Hegel and Marx.[5] This question also aroused the interest of sociologists, and the 1900 Congress of the

---

[1] See *Sociological Papers*, Vols. I–III, 1905–7. There is no mention of Marx except in a brief communication from A. Loria. The major influence upon British sociology was that of Comte, through J. S. Mill, H. Spencer, the English Positivists and L. T. Hobhouse.

[2] See *The Evolution of Modern Capitalism*, 1894; and *Imperialism: a Study*, 1902.

[3] These discussions received a powerful stimulus from the publication of writings formerly unknown or completely forgotten; e.g. the publication of Marx's doctoral thesis and a new edition of *Die Heilige Familie*, both published by F. Mehring, *Aus dem literarischen Nachlass von K. Marx, F. Engels und F. Lassalle*, Stuttgart, 1902 (4 vols.). Subsequently E. Bernstein published fragments of *Die deutsche Ideologie* and K. Kautsky published the *Theorien über den Mehrwert*, (1905–10).

[4] Among the studies of this kind may be mentioned: Marianne Weber, *Fichte's Sozialismus und sein Verhältnis zur Marxschen Doktrin*, Tübingen, 1900; N. Berdyaev, "F. A. Lange und die Kritische Philosophie in ihren Beziehungen zum Sozialismus," in *Neue Zeit*, XVIII/2, 1900, pp. 132 seq.; K. Vorländer, *Kant und der Sozialismus*, Berlin 1900; E. Hammacher, *Das philosophisch-ökonomisch System des Marxismus*, Leipzig, 1909. Marx's ethical theory was vigorously debated in the columns of the *Neue Zeit*, especially between K. Kautsky and O. Bauer, after the publication of Kautsky's *Die Ethik und die materialistische Geschichtsauffassung*, Stuttgart, 1906. A similar controversy had taken place in France, from 1894, between J. Jaurès and P. Lafargue; cf. *Idéalisme et matérialisme dans la conception de l'histoire*. New ed., Paris, 1946.

[5] Among the more interesting books on this subject are J. Plenge, *Marx und Hegel*, Tübingen, 1911; and Sven Helander, *Marx und Hegel*, Jena, 1922 (trans. from the Swedish).

Institut International de Sociologie was entirely devoted to a discussion of " historical materialism." The Italian sociologist, Groppali, passing in review Marx's writings from the essays in the *Deutsch-Französische Jahrbücher* (1844) to the *Zur Kritik der politischen Ökonomie* (1859), declared that they revealed " the progressive emancipation of Marx's thought, its liberation from the shackles of Hegel's philosophy." [1] The " materialist conception of history," he contended, was not a metaphysical doctrine but an instrument for the interpretation and explanation of social life, whose validity Marx himself had put to the test in his historical and economic studies.

Outside the field of these philosophical and methodological disputes, economists, historians, and lawyers in France, Germany, and Austria were making valuable contributions to sociological research, drawing inspiration from the methods suggested by Marx. Among these studies may be mentioned those of Sée in economic history, of Hilferding in economics, of Renner in law, and of Max Weber in sociology.[2] Sée found the most satisfactory criteria of explanation of the development of the demesne and of classes, as of the general relations between lords and peasants, in economic phenomena, and particularly in the economic relations between property-owners and tenants.

[1] A. Groppali, "De la place que le matérialisme historique occupe dans la philosophie et la sociologie contemporaines" in *Annales de l'Institut International de Sociologie*, 1900–01, p. 201. Cf. also C. de Kelles-Krauz, "Qu'est-ce-que le matérialisme économique?" in ibid., pp. 49–92.

[2] Henri Sée, *Les classes rurales et le régime domanial en France au moyen âge*, Paris, 1901; R. Hilferding, "Böhm-Bawerks Marxkritik," in *Marx-Studien*, I, 1904, pp. 1–61; J. Karner (pseudonym of Karl Renner), "Die soziale Funktion der Rechtsinstitute," in *Marx-Studien*, I, 1904, pp. 65 *seq.* (A revised edition was published in 1928, and an English translation under the title *The Institutions of Private Law and their Social Function* appeared in 1949, with a long Introduction and notes by O. Kahn-Freund); Max Weber, "Die 'Objectivität' sozialwissenschaftlichen und sozialpolitischen Erkenntnis," in *Archiv für Sozialpolitik*, 1904 (reprinted in Weber, *Gesammelte Aufsätze zur Wissenschaftslehre*, 1922).

Hilferding countered the objections raised by Böhm-Bawerk against Marx's theory of value, by pointing out that Marx's analysis was sociological, and that behind the economic categories there are the relations between classes in the process of production. In the same way, for Renner, legal institutions have a double character, on the one hand as the expression of human relationships, and on the other hand as fictions which dissimulate their dependence upon economic institutions. Max Weber, on assuming, together with W. Sombart and E. Jaffé, the editorship of the *Archiv für Sozialwissenschaft und Sozialpolitik*, elaborated the programme and methodological principles of the review. This programme represented, within well-defined limits, an acceptance of the sociological conception of history as Marx had formulated it : in the research envisaged, emphasis was to be placed, not on economic phenomena as such, but on phenomena which, in relation to their economic context, have a distinctive significance and relevance. Though Weber expressed reservations about the " materialist " aspect of Marx's sociology, he agreed that " the analysis of social and cultural phenomena, from the particular aspect of their economic determination and relevance, is a scientific principle of the greatest fecundity." [1] Many of the studies published in the *Archiv* show the interest of its collaborators in Marx's sociology, and in particular, those of Georg Simmel, whose *Philosophie des Geldes* showed the influence of Marx's thought in its most fruitful aspect. [2] At the first German congress of sociology the discussion between Marxist and non-Marxist sociologists assumed a particularly interesting character in connection with the principal subject

[1] Max Weber, op. cit., p. 166. The whole of Weber's work can be regarded as a debate with Marx. Cf. A. Salomon, " German Sociology " in *Twentieth Century Sociology* (ed. G. Gurvitch and W. E. Moore); " Max Weber . . . became a sociologist in a long and intense dialogue with the ghost of Karl Marx."

[2] G. Simmel, *Philosophie des Geldes*, Leipzig, 1900.

of the congress, the problem of the relations between technology, the economic system, and civilization.[1] There was founded, in the same year, 1910, the first review in which the scientific study and criticism of Marxism had a special place.[2] From this time the study of Marx was able to proceed at a level above that of political controversy—but the First World War temporarily put an end to this systematic investigation.

Well before 1914 Marx's sociology had spread beyond Europe and had a marked influence upon the development of social theory in the USA. Many of the early American sociologists had studied in Europe (particularly in Germany) and had unavoidably come into contact with Marx's ideas. The influence of Marx is apparent especially in their analysis of social class.[3] A. W. Small, in particular, made a systematic study of Marx and of the theory of class conflict. But it is in the work of two of the greatest American sociologists, G. H. Mead [4] and Thorstein Veblen [5] that the influence of Marx is most apparent.

After the First World War there came into being a veritable school of Marxist sociology with its own variety of tendencies, often mutually antagonistic, and contrasting strongly with the quasi-unanimity of non-Marxist scholars

[1] Cf. *Verhandlungen des 1. Deutschen Soziologentages von 19–22 Oktober 1910 in Frankfurt a. M.*, Tübingen, 1911.

[2] *Archiv für Geschichte des Sozialismus und der Arbeiterbewegung.* The review was founded in 1910 by Carl Grünberg with the support of several internationally known students of Marx, among them D. Riazanov, G. Mayer and M. Nettlau.

[3] Cf. C. H. Page, *Class and American Sociology. From Ward to Ross*, New York, 1940.

[4] Mead was a close student of Marx's sociological theories; see, for instance, the chapter on "Karl Marx and Socialism" in his *Movements of Thought in the Nineteenth Century*, ed. M. H. Moore, Chicago 1936.

[5] Cf. especially, *The Theory of the Leisure Class* (1899); *The Theory of Business Enterprise* (1905); *The Socialist Economics of Karl Marx and his Followers* (1906–07) reprinted in *The Place of Science in Modern Civilization* (1919).

who were favourable to Marx's sociology.[1] A superficial survey of the period 1918–25, confined largely to European countries, shows that more than 500 fairly important works were published on the various themes of Marx's sociology.[2] It is probable that for the period 1926–33 the figures would be at least equal to those for the earlier period.[3] Thus by the early 1930's Marx's sociological thought had gained recognition in most of the important academic centres specializing in the social sciences.

In Germany, the " debate with Marx " continued to preoccupy sociologists. Besides stimulating sociological research in general, it gave rise to a new field of sociological inquiry, the sociology of knowledge, in the work of Lukács[4] Scheler [5] and Mannheim.[6] But this development came to

---

[1] Among the more important productions of the Marxist " School " were N. Bukharin, *Historical Materialism* ; *A System of Sociology* (first published Moscow 1921, Eng. trans. 1926) ; K. Kautsky, *Die materialistische Geschichtsauffassung*, Berlin 1927 ; M. Adler, *Lehrbuch der materialistischen Geschichtsauffassung: Soziologie des Marxismus*, Berlin, 1930–32. At a later period, a number of German sociologists, strongly influenced by Marx, and refugees from Nazism, continued in Paris the work which they had begun in Frankfurt, in the review *Zeitschrift für Sozialforschung* (1933–39). The collaborators in the review included C. Bouglé, R. Briffault, Duprat, E. Fromm, de Saussure, Marcuse, R. Aron, V. Young and A. Demangeon. Cf. also the studies of Marx's sociological theories by K. Mannheim, G. Salomon and others in *Jahrbuch für Soziologie* (Karlsruhe, 1925 onwards).

[2] Cf. *Marx–Engels Archiv*, Vols. I and II, which contain an impressive international bibliography of the literature on Marxism. For Germany alone the Marx–Engels Institute possessed more than seventy doctoral theses presented between 1920 and 1924 and concerned with Marxist subjects.

[3] After the dismissal of Riazanov from his post as Director of the Marx–Engels Institute the work which he had begun was suspended, and there is therefore no exact information on publications concerned with Marxism after 1930.

[4] G. Lukács, *Geschichte und Klassenbewusstsein*, 1923 and later writings in the field of literary history.

[5] M. Scheler, *Die Wissensformen und die Gesellschaft*, 1926.

[6] K. Mannheim, "Probleme einer Wissenssoziologie" in *Archiv für Sozialwissenschaft und Sozialpolitik*, Vol. 54, 1925 ; *Ideologie und Utopie*, 1929 (Expanded English version, *Ideology and Utopia*, 1936).

an end, in 1933, with the victory of Nazism. Since that time neither the sociology of knowledge, nor Max Weber's sociology, has been pursued in the context in which it originated, that of a critical examination of Marx's sociology and an attempt to revise and develop its main elements. This eclipse of German sociology coincided with the publication in the *MEGA* of Marx's early writings, which, as a result, were not seriously studied until after 1945.

Outside Germany, in the 1930's, while Marxism as a political ideology flourished, scientific interest in Marx's sociology waned. In France, it was economic historians such as H. Sée and E. Labrousse who showed the greatest interest. Sée had already published a study of historical materialism.[1] Labrousse began to publish, from 1933, his detailed researches on the influence of economic factors in the French Revolution.[2] In fact, the revival, or in some cases the first appearance, of interest in Marx's sociology, is a recent phenomenon. In the USA it was marked by the publication of J. Schumpeter's *Capitalism, Socialism and Democracy*,[3] the first part of which is devoted to a close examination of Marx's sociological theory, and concludes that " the so-called Economic Interpretation of History is doubtless one of the greatest individual achievements of sociology to this day." In Britain, K. R. Popper has recently presented a full-length critical study of Marx as a sociologist.[4] Some Marxist writers, for the most part historians, have taken up a number of sociological problems; for example, M. H. Dobb, in his *Studies in the Development of*

[1] H. Sée, *Matérialisme historique et interprétation économique de l'histoire*, 1927.

[2] E. Labrousse, *Esquisse du mouvement des prix et des revenus en France au XVIIIe siècle*, 1933; *La crise de l'économie française à la fin de l'ancien régime et au début de la Révolution*, 1943.

[3] New York 1942.

[4] K. R. Popper, *The Open Society and Its Enemies*, 1945, 2nd rev. edn. 1950, Part II.

Capitalism,[1] which discusses some problems of the genesis and development of capitalism. Like much orthodox Marxist writing, this book is more impressive in its treatment of historical problems than in its analysis of contemporary society.

The year 1948, the centenary of the publication of the *Communist Manifesto*, was an occasion for a number of sociologists and other social scientists to reconsider Marx's social theory. In France, the centenary was marked by the publication of a series of studies which emphasized Marx's contribution to sociology.[2] G. Gurvitch's illuminating study of Marx's early writings presents Marx as " the prince of sociologists," and argues strongly for orientating sociological research towards the problems which Marx delineated.[3] In England the centenary was marked by a new edition of the *Communist Manifesto*, published by the Labour Party, and with a long historical and critical Introduction by H. J. Laski. Discussing Marx's historical and sociological method, Laski observed that " No serious observer supposes that the materialist conception of history is free from difficulties or that it solves all the problems involved in historical interpretation. But no serious observer either can doubt that it has done more in the last hundred years to provide a major clue to the causes of social change than any other hypothesis that has been put forward." [4]

More recently, Jean Piaget, in his discussion of the nature of sociological thought,[5] has indicated the importance of

---

[1] 1946. See also the essays by various authors in J. Saville (ed.) *Democracy and the Labour Movement*, London 1954.

[2] See *Cahiers Internationaux de Sociologie*, III, 4, 1948; especially G. Gurvitch, " La sociologie du jeune Marx," H. Lefebvre, " Marxisme et sociologie," and A. Cuvillier, " Durkheim et Marx."

[3] G. Gurvitch, art. cit.

[4] H. J. Laski, *Communist Manifesto : Socialist Landmark*, 1948, Introduction, p. 74.

[5] Jean Piaget, *Introduction à l'épistémologie génétique*, Vol. III, Paris 1950.

Marx's work and especially of his theory of ideology; "The great merit of Marx is that he made a distinction, in social phenomena, between an effective basis and a superstructure which oscillates between symbolism and an adequate consciousness, in the same sense (and Marx himself explicitly says this) as psychology is obliged to make a distinction between actual behaviour and consciousness. . . . The social superstructure stands in the same relation to its basis as does the individual consciousness to behaviour; . . . "[1]

*   *   *

We have tried to indicate some of the more important writings in which Marx's sociological thought has been examined, criticized or used in empirical research. The outcome of the prolonged " debate with Marx " has become clearer with the maturity of sociology itself. A great deal of Marx's work is a permanent acquisition of sociological thought; the definition of the field of study, the analysis of the economic structure and its relations with other parts of the social structure, the theory of social classes, and the theory of ideology. But this incorporation of Marx's ideas entails the disappearance of a " Marxist " sociology. Modern sociology is not the sociology of Marx, any more than it is the sociology of Durkheim, or Weber, or Hobhouse. It is a science which has advanced some way towards freeing itself from the various philosophical systems in which it originated, and with which its founders were still embroiled.

[1] Op. cit., p. 249.

SELECTED TEXTS

Part One

METHODOLOGICAL FOUNDATIONS

I. THE MATERIALIST CONCEPTION OF HISTORY

I WAS led by my studies to the conclusion that legal relations as well as forms of State could neither be understood by themselves, nor explained by the so-called general progress of the human mind, but that they are rooted in the material conditions of life, which are summed up by Hegel after the fashion of the English and French writers of the eighteenth century under the name *civil society*, and that the anatomy of civil society is to be sought in political economy. The study of the latter which I had begun in Paris, I continued in Brussels where I had emigrated on account of an expulsion order issued by M. Guizot. The general conclusion at which I arrived and which, once reached, continued to serve as the guiding thread in my studies, may be formulated briefly as follows: In the social production which men carry on they enter into definite relations that are indispensable and independent of their will; these relations of production correspond to a definite stage of development of their material powers of production. The totality of these relations of production constitutes the economic structure of society—the real foundation, on which legal and political superstructures arise and to which definite forms of social consciousness correspond. The mode of production of material life determines the general character of the social, political and spiritual processes of life. It is not the consciousness of men that determines their being, but, on the contrary, their social being determines their consciousness. At a certain stage of their development, the material forces of production in society come in conflict with the existing relations of production, or—what is but a legal expression for the same thing—with the property

51

relations within which they had been at work before. From forms of development of the forces of production these relations turn into their fetters. Then occurs a period of social revolution. With the change of the economic foundation the entire immense superstructure is more or less rapidly transformed. In considering such transformations the distinction should always be made between the material transformation of the economic conditions of production which can be determined with the precision of natural science, and the legal, political, religious, æsthetic or philosophical—in short ideological, forms in which men become conscious of this conflict and fight it out. Just as our opinion of an individual is not based on what he thinks of himself, so can we not judge of such a period of transformation by its own consciousness; on the contrary, this consciousness must rather be explained from the contradictions of material life, from the existing conflict between the social forces of production and the relations of production. No social order ever disappears before all the productive forces for which there is room in it have been developed; and new, higher relations of production never appear before the material conditions of their existence have matured in the womb of the old society. Therefore, mankind always sets itself only such problems as it can solve; since, on closer examination, it will always be found that the problem itself arises only when the material conditions necessary for its solution already exist or are at least in the process of formation. In broad outline we can designate the Asiatic, the ancient, the feudal, and the modern bourgeois modes of production as progressive epochs in the economic formation of society. The bourgeois relations of production are the last antagonistic form of the social process of production; not in the sense of individual antagonisms, but of conflict arising from conditions surrounding the life of individuals in society. At the same time

the productive forces developing in the womb of bourgeois
society create the material conditions for the solution of
that antagonism. With this social formation, therefore,
the prehistory of human society comes to an end.

Preface (1859)

The premises from which we begin are not arbitrary
ones, not dogmas, but real premises from which abstraction
can be made only in the imagination. They are the real
individuals, their activity and their material conditions of
life, including those which they find already in existence and
those produced by their activity. These premises can thus
be established in a purely empirical way.

The first premise of all human history is, of course, the
existence of living human individuals. The first fact to be
established, therefore, is the physical constitution of these
individuals and their consequent relation to the rest of
Nature. Of course we cannot here investigate the actual
physical nature of man or the natural conditions in which
man finds himself—geological, oro-hydrographical, climatic
and so on. All historiography must begin from these
natural bases and their modification in the course of history
by men's activity.

Men can be distinguished from animals by consciousness,
by religion, or by anything one likes. They themselves
begin to distinguish themselves from animals as soon as they
begin to *produce* their means of subsistence, a step which is
determined by their physical constitution. In producing
their means of subsistence men indirectly produce their
actual material life.

The way in which men produce their means of subsistence
depends in the first place on the nature of the existing means
which they have to reproduce. This mode of production
should not be regarded simply as the reproduction of the

physical existence of individuals. (It is already a definite form of activity of these individuals, a definite way of expressing their life, a definite *mode of life*.) As individuals express their life, so they are. What they are, therefore, coincides with their production, with *what* they produce and with *how* they produce it. What individuals are, therefore, depends on the material conditions of their production.

GI (1845–6)
MEGA I/5, pp. 10–11

(This conception of history, therefore, rests on the exposition of the real process of production, starting out from the simple material production of life, and on the comprehension of the form of intercourse connected with and created by this mode of production, i.e. of civil society in its various stages as the basis of all history, and also in its action as the State.) From this starting point, it explains all the different theoretical productions and forms of consciousness, religion, philosophy, ethics, etc., and traces their origins and growth, by which means the matter can of course be displayed as a whole (and consequently, also the reciprocal action of these various sides on one another). Unlike the idealist view of history, it does not have to look for a category in each period, but remains constantly on the real ground of history; it does not explain practice from the idea but explains the formation of ideas from material practice, and accordingly comes to the conclusion that all the forms of and products of consciousness can be dissolved, not by intellectual criticism, not by resolution into " self-consciousness," or by transformation into " apparitions," " spectres," " fancies," etc., but only by the practical overthrow of the actual social relations which gave rise to this idealist humbug; that not criticism but revolution is the driving force of history, as well as of religion, philosophy, and all other types of theory. (It shows that history does not end by being resolved into " self-consciousness," as " spirit of the spirit," but that at each stage of history there is found a material result, a sum of productive forces, a historically created relation of individuals to Nature and to one another, which is handed down to each generation from its predecessors, a mass of productive forces, capital, and circumstances, which is indeed modified by the new generation but which also prescribes for it its conditions of life and gives it a definite development, a special character. It shows that circumstances make men just as much as men make circumstances.

This sum of productive forces, capital, and social forms of intercourse, which every individual and generation finds in existence as something given, is the real basis of what philosophers have conceived as " substance " and the " essence of man," and which they have deified or attacked. This real basis is not in the least disturbed, in its effects and influence on the development of men, by the fact that these philosophers, as " self-consciousness " and the " unique," revolt against it. These conditions of life, which different generations find in existence, also determine whether or not the periodically recurring revolutionary convulsion will be strong enough to overthrow the basis of the existing order. If the material elements of a total revolution, i.e. on the one hand, the available productive forces, and on the other, the formation of a revolutionary mass, which revolts not only against particular conditions of existing society but against the whole existing " production of life," the " total activity " on which it is based, are not present, then it is quite immaterial as far as practical development is concerned whether the *idea* of this revolution has been expressed a hundred times already, as is demonstrated by the history of communism.

The whole previous conception of history has either completely neglected this real basis of history or else has considered it a secondary matter without any connection with the course of history. Consequently, history has always to be written in accordance with an external standard; the real production of life appears as *a*historical, while what is historical appears as separated from ordinary life, as supra-terrestrial. (Thus the relation of man to Nature is excluded from history and in this way the antithesis between Nature and history is established.) The exponents of this conception of history have consequently only been able to see in history the political actions of princes and States, religious and all sorts of theoretical struggles, and in particular have been obliged to share in each historical epoch the *illusion of that epoch*. For instance, if an epoch imagines itself to be actuated by purely " political " or " religious " motives, although " religion " and " politics " are only forms of its true motives, the historian accepts this opinion. The " idea," the " conception " of these conditioned men about their real practice, is transformed into the sole determining, active force, which controls and determines their practice. When the crude form in which the division of labour emerges among the Indians and the Egyptians engenders the caste system in their State and religion, the historian believes that the caste system is the power which has pro-duced this crude social form. While the French and the English at least hold by the political illusion, which is moderately close to reality, the Germans move in the realm of " pure spirit," and make religious illusion the driving force of history.

The Hegelian philosophy of history is the last consequence, brought to its " purest expression," of all this German historiography, which is concerned, not with real, nor even with political, interests, but with pure thoughts, which inevitably appear . . . as a series of " thoughts " which devour one another and are finally swallowed up in " self-consciousness." . .

GI (1845–6)
MEGA I/5, pp. 27–9

Hegel's conception of history presupposes an *abstract* or *absolute spirit* which develops in such a way that humanity is nothing but a *mass* which more or less consciously bears it along. Within the framework of *empirical*, exoteric history, Hegel introduces the operation of a *speculative*, esoteric history. The history of humanity becomes the history of the *abstract* spirit of humanity, *a spirit above and beyond* the real man.

Concurrently with this Hegelian doctrine, there developed in France the theory of the *doctrinaires*, who proclaimed the *sovereignty of reason* in opposition to the *sovereignty of the people*, in order to exclude the masses and to rule *by themselves.* That is logical. From the moment that *real* human activity is only the activity of a *mass* of human individuals, *abstract universality*, reason, spirit, must receive an abstract expression which is completely represented by a few individuals. And according to his position and his imaginative power each individual will, or will not, regard himself as this representative " of *spirit.*"

Already with Hegel the *absolute spirit* of history has its materials in the *masses*, but only finds adequate expression in *philosophy*. But the philosopher appears merely as the instrument by which absolute spirit, which makes history, arrives at self consciousness after the historical movement has been completed. The philosopher's share in history is thus limited to this subsequent consciousness. The philosopher arrives *post festum.*

HF (1845)
MEGA I/3, p. 257

Just as, for the earlier teleological thinkers, plants existed only in order to be eaten by animals, and animals only in order to be eaten by man, so history exists only to satisfy the need for consuming theoretical nourishment, for demonstration. Man exists so that history shall exist, and history

exists so that truth can be revealed.) In this critically debased form there is repeated the old speculative wisdom,
according to which man and history exist so that *truth* can
become *conscious of itself*.

(*History* thus becomes, like *truth*, a separate entity, a metaphysical subject of which the real human individuals are
only mere representatives) That is why the " Critical
School "[1] makes use of such expressions as " History is not
mocked; history has made the greatest efforts; history has
been active; what is history's purpose?; history gives us
the final proof; history reveals truths," etc.

HF (1845)
MEGA I/3, pp. 250–1

We are now able to discover why Saint Max [2] gave to the
whole first part of his book the title *Man* and passed off
all his history of sorcerers, ghosts and knights as the history
of " *man*." (The ideas and thoughts of men were naturally
ideas and thoughts about themselves and their conditions,
about their consciousness of themselves or of Man, for it
was a consciousness not only of the individual person but
of the individual in relation to a whole society and of the
whole society in which men lived.) The conditions, independent of themselves, in which they produced their material
life, the forms of intercourse which necessarily accompanied
them, the personal and social relations thus given, had, in
so far as they were expressed in thought, to take the form of
ideal conditions and necessary relations) i.e. to find expression in consciousness as conditions arising out of the concept
of man, of human existence, of the nature of man, of man as

[1] Marx speaks sometimes of the "kritische Kritik," sometimes of the
"absolute Kritik," when referring to the group of "Young Hegelians"
which included Bauer, Strauss, and others. I have translated these
expressions in most places as " Critical School," which reads more
sensibly in English.
[2] Max Stirner.

such. What men and their social relations actually were appeared in consciousness as representations of man as such, of his modes of being, or of his exact determinations. When the ideologists had thus assumed that ideas and thoughts dominated past history, that the history of ideas was the whole of past history, when they had assumed that real conditions were modelled on man and his ideal conditions, i.e. upon his determinations, in short when they had made the history of the consciousness men have of themselves the basis of their real history, nothing was easier than to call the history of mind, of ideas, of the sacred, of representations, the history of " *man* " and to substitute this for real history.

> *GI* (1845–6)
> *MEGA* I/5, p. 165

Does the " Critical School " believe that it has arrived even at the *beginnings* of knowledge of historical reality, so long as it excludes from the historical process, the theoretical and practical relations of man to Nature, i.e. natural science and industry? Or does it claim to have really understood any historical period, without having understood, for example, the industry, the direct mode of production of life itself, of this period? At all events the spiritual, *theological* " critical criticism " takes account, or at least takes account in its imagination, only of the political, literary, and theological aspects of the principal historical events. Just as it separates thought from sense experience, mind from body, and itself from the world, so it separates history from natural science and industry, and sees the birthplace of history, not in vulgar material production on earth, but in the cloudy regions of heaven.

> *HF* (1845)
> *MEGA* I/3, p. 327

. . . we must begin by stating the first presupposition of all human existence, and therefore of all history, namely, that men must be in a position to live in order to be able to "make history." But life involves before everything else eating and drinking, a habitation, clothing and many other things. The first historical act is, therefore, the production of material life itself. This is indeed a historical act, a fundamental condition of all history, which today, as thousands of years ago, must be accomplished every day and every hour merely in order to sustain human life. Even when, as with Saint Bruno,[1] the world of sense is reduced to a minimum, to a stick, it presupposes the action of producing the stick. In any conception of history, therefore, the first requirement is to observe this basic fact in all its significance and all its implications and to give it its proper importance. The Germans, as is well known, have never done this, and they have never therefore had an *earthly* basis for history and consequently never a historian. The French and the English, even if they have conceived the relation of this fact with so-called history only in an extremely one-sided fashion, particularly as long as they remained entangled in political ideology, have nevertheless made the first attempts to give the writing of history a materialist basis, in so far as they were the first to write histories of civil society, of commerce and industry.

The second point is that as soon as it is satisfied, the first need itself, the action of satisfying and the instrument which has achieved this satisfaction, leads to new needs—and this production of new needs is the first historical act.

GI (1845–6)
MEGA I/5, pp. 17–18

[1] Bruno Bauer.

Let us admit, with M. Proudhon, that real history, history as temporal order, is the historical succession in which ideas, categories and principles have manifested themselves.

Each principle had its own century in which to reveal itself: the principle of authority, for instance, had the eleventh century, just as the principle of individualism had the eighteenth century. Accordingly, it was the century which belonged to the principle, and not the principle which belonged to the century. In other words, it was the principle which made history, and not history which made the principle. When further, in order to save the principles as well as history, we ask ourselves why a particular principle appeared in the eleventh or the eighteenth century rather than in any other, we are bound to study closely the men of the eleventh century and those of the eighteenth, to examine their respective needs, their productive forces, their mode of production, the raw materials of their production, and finally the relations of man to man which resulted from all these conditions of life. In making a thorough study of these questions, are we not presenting the real, profane history of men in every century, showing men to be at the same time the authors and the actors of their own drama? But from the moment that men are represented as the authors and actors of their own history, we arrive, by a roundabout route, at the real point of departure, for we have now abandoned the eternal principles from which at first we began.

PP (1847)
MEGA I/6, pp. 183-4

. . . men, who every day remake their own life, begin to make other men, to propagate their kind: the relation between man and wife, parents and children, *the family.* The family, which is at first the only social relationship, becomes later, when increased needs create new social

relations and the increased population new needs, a subordinate one (except in Germany), and must then be treated
and analysed according to the existing empirical data, not
according to the " concept of the family," as is the custom
in Germany. These three aspects of social activity, moreover, should not be conceived as three different stages, but
simply as three aspects or, to make it clear to the Germans,
three " moments," which have existed contemporaneously
since the dawn of history and since the first men, and which
still assert themselves in history today.

The production of life, both of one's own by labour and
of fresh life by procreation, appears at once as a double
relationship, on the one hand as a natural, on the other as
a social relationship. By social is meant the co-operation
of several individuals, no matter under what conditions, in
what manner or to what end. It follows from this, that a
determinate mode of production, or industrial stage, is
always bound up with a determinate mode of co-operation,
or social stage, and this mode of co-operation is itself a
" productive force." It also follows, that the mass of productive forces accessible to men determines the condition
of society, and that the " history of humanity " must therefore always be studied and treated in relation to the history
of industry and exchange.

GI (1845–6)
MEGA I/5, pp. 18–19

The economists have a singular way of proceeding. For
them there are only two kinds of institution, artificial and
natural. Feudal institutions are artificial, while those of
the bourgeoisie are natural. They resemble in this respect
the theologians, who likewise distinguish two kinds of
religion. Every religion other than their own is a human
invention, while their own emanates from God. In saying
that the existing relations—the relations of bourgeois pro-

duction—are natural, the economists assert that these are the relations in which wealth is created and the productive forces are developed in accordance with the laws of Nature. Consequently, these relations themselves are natural laws, independent of the influence of time. They are eternal laws which must always govern society. Thus there has been history, but there is no longer any history. There has been history, because there were feudal institutions, and because in these feudal institutions are to be found relations of production entirely different from those in bourgeois society, which latter none the less the economists wish to present as natural and therefore eternal.

PP (1847)
MEGA I/6, p. 188

Once man has been recognized as the essence, the basis of all human activity, and of every human relationship, only the " Critical School " is capable of inventing *new categories*, and (as it does) of re-transforming *man* into a category and indeed into the principle of a whole series of categories. In this way it takes the last way of escape which remains open to *theological* " inhumanism," pursued and tracked down. *History* does *nothing*; it " does *not* possess immense riches," it " does *not* fight battles." It is *men*, real, living men, who do all this, who possess things and fight battles. It is not " history " which uses men as a means of achieving—as if it were an individual person—*its* own ends. History is *nothing* but the activity of men in pursuit of their ends.

HF (1845)
MEGA I/3, p. 265

Darwin has aroused our interest in the history of natural technology, i.e. in the formation of the organs of plants and animals, as instruments of production for sustaining life.

Does not the history of the productive organs of man, of organs that are the material basis of all social organization, deserve equal attention? And would not such a history be easier to compile, since, as Vico says, human history differs from natural history in this respect, that we have made the former, but not the latter? Technology discloses man's mode of dealing with Nature, the process of production by which he sustains his life, and by which also his social relations, and the mental conceptions that flow from them, are formed. Any history of religion even, that fails to take account of this material basis, is uncritical. It is, in practice, much easier to discover by analysis the earthly core of the misty creations of religion, than, conversely, to infer from the actual relations of life at any period the corresponding "spiritualized" forms of those relations. But the latter method is the only materialistic, and therefore the only scientific one. The inadequacy of the abstract materialism of natural science, which leaves out of consideration the historical process, is at once evident from the abstract and ideological conceptions of its spokesmen, whenever they venture beyond the bounds of their own specialism.

Capital I (1867)
VA I, p. 389, footnote 89

(1) In the development of the productive forces a stage is reached where productive forces and means of intercourse are called into being which, under the existing relations, can only work mischief, and which are, therefore, no longer productive, but destructive, forces (machinery and money). Associated with this is the emergence of a class which has to bear all the burdens of society without enjoying its advantages, which is excluded from society and is forced into the most resolute opposition to all other classes; a class which comprises the majority of the members of society

and in which there develops a consciousness of the need for a fundamental revolution, the communist consciousness. This consciousness can, of course, also arise in other classes from the observation of the situation of this class.

(2) The conditions under which determinate productive forces can be used are also the conditions for the dominance of a determinate social class, whose social power, derived from its property ownership, invariably finds its *practical* and ideal expression in a particular form of the State. Consequently, every revolutionary struggle is directed against the class which has so far been dominant.

(3) In all former revolutions the form of activity was always left unaltered and it was only a question of redistributing this activity among different people, of introducing a new division of labour. The communist revolution, however, is directed against the former *mode* of activity, does away with *labour*, and abolishes all class rule along with the classes themselves, because it is effected by the class which no longer counts as a class in society, which is not recognized as a class, and which is the expression of the dissolution of all classes, nationalities, etc., within contemporary society.

(4) For the creation on a mass scale of this communist consciousness, as well as for the success of the cause itself, it is necessary for men themselves to be changed on a large scale, and this change can only occur in a practical movement, in a *revolution*. Revolution is necessary not only because the *ruling* class cannot be overthrown in any other way, but also because only in a revolution can *the class which overthrows it* rid itself of the accumulated rubbish of the past and become capable of reconstructing society.

GI (1845–6)
MEGA I/5, pp. 59–60

Just as the *economists* are the scientific representatives of the bourgeoisie, so the *socialists* and *communists* are the theorists of the proletariat. As long as the proletariat is not sufficiently developed to constitute itself into a class, as long therefore as the struggle of the proletariat with the bourgeoisie has not acquired a political character, and while the productive forces are not yet sufficiently developed, within bourgeois society itself, to give an indication of the material conditions necessary for the emancipation of the proletariat and the constitution of a new society, these theorists remain Utopians who, in order to remedy the distress of the oppressed classes, improvise systems and pursue a regenerative science. But as history continues, and as the struggle of the proletariat takes shape more clearly, they have no further need to look for a science in their own minds; they have only to observe what is happening before their eyes, and to make themselves its vehicle of expression. As long as they are looking for a science and only create systems, as long as they are at the beginning of the struggle, they see in poverty only poverty, without noticing its revolutionary and subversive aspect, which will overthrow the old society. But from this moment, the science produced by the historical movement, and which consciously associates itself with this movement, has ceased to be doctrinaire and has become revolutionary.

PP (1847)
MEGA I/6, p. 191

II. EXISTENCE AND CONSCIOUSNESS

I

THE chief defect of all previous materialism (including that of Feuerbach) is that things (*Gegenstand*), reality, the sensible world, are conceived only in the form of *objects* (*Objekt*) *of observation*, but not as *human sense activity*, not as *practical activity*, not subjectively. Hence, in opposition to materialism, the *active* side was developed abstractly by idealism, which of course does not know real sense activity as such. Feuerbach wants sensible objects really distinguished from the objects of thought, but he does not understand human activity itself as *objective* (*gegenständlich*) activity. Consequently, in *The Essence of Christianity*, he regards the theoretical attitude as the only genuine human attitude, while practical activity is apprehended only in its dirty Jewish manifestation. He therefore does not grasp the significance of " revolutionary," " practical-critical " activity.

II

The question whether human thinking can pretend to objective (*gegenständlich*) truth is not a theoretical but a *practical* question. Man must prove the truth, i.e. the reality and power, the " this-sidedness " of his thinking in practice. The dispute over the reality or non-reality of thinking that is isolated from practice is a purely *scholastic* question.

III

The materialist doctrine concerning the changing of circumstances and education forgets that circumstances are changed by men and that the educator must himself be educated. This doctrine has therefore to divide society into two parts, one of which is superior to society,

The coincidence of the changing of circumstances and of human activity or self-changing can only be grasped and rationally understood as revolutionary *practice*.

IV

Feuerbach sets out from the fact of religious self-alienation, the duplication of the world into a religious and a secular one. His work consists in resolving the religious world into its secular basis. But the fact that the secular basis deserts its own sphere and establishes an independent realm in the clouds, can only be explained by the cleavage and self-contradictions within this secular basis. The latter therefore, must itself be both understood in its contradictions and revolutionized in practice. Thus, for instance, once the earthly family is discovered to be the secret of the heavenly family the former must itself be destroyed in theory and in practice.

V

Feuerbach, not satisfied with *abstract thought*, wants *empirical observation*, but he does not conceive the sensible world as *practical*, human sense activity.

VI

Feuerbach resolves the essence of religion into the essence of *man*. But the essence of man is not an abstraction inherent in each particular individual. The real nature of man is the totality of social relations.

Feuerbach, who does not enter upon a criticism of this real nature, is therefore obliged:

1. to abstract from the historical process, to hypostatize the religious sentiment, and to postulate an abstract—*isolated*—human individual;

2. to conceive the nature of man only in terms of a " genus," as an inner and mute universal quality

which unites the many individuals in a purely natural (biological) way.

VII

Feuerbach therefore does not see that the "religious sentiment" is itself a social product, and that the abstract individual whom he analyses belongs to a particular form of society.

VIII

All social life is essentially *practical*. All the mysteries which lead theory towards mysticism find their rational solution in human practice and in the comprehension of this practice.

IX

The highest point attained by that materialism which only observes the world, i.e. which does not conceive sensuous existence as practical activity, is the observation of particular individuals and of civil society.

X

The standpoint of the old type of materialism is civil society; the standpoint of the new materialism is human society or social humanity.

XI

The philosophers have only *interpreted* the world in different ways; the point is to *change* it.

Theses on Feuerbach (1845) [1]
MEGA I/5, pp. 533-5

Feuerbach is the only one who has a *serious* and *critical* relation to Hegel's dialectic, who has made real discoveries in this field, and who has above all overcome the old philosophy. . . .

[1] The text published by Engels in 1888 differed slightly from the original as translated here.

The great achievement of Feuerbach is:

1. to have shown that philosophy is nothing more than religion brought into thought and developed by thought and that it is equally to be condemned as another form and mode of existence of human alienation;

2. to have founded *genuine materialism* and *positive science* by making the social relationship of " man to man " the basic principle of his theory;

3. to have opposed to the negation of the negation which claims to be the absolute positive, a self-subsistent principle positively founded on itself.

EPM (1844)
MEGA I/3, pp. 151-2

Sense experience (cf. Feuerbach) must be the basis of all science. Science is only *genuine* science when it proceeds from sense experience, in the two forms of *sense* perception and *sensuous* need, that is, only when it proceeds from Nature. The whole of history is a preparation for " *man* " to become an object of sense perception, and for the development of human needs (the needs of man as such). History itself is a *real* part of *natural history*, of the development of Nature into man. Natural science will one day incorporate the science of man, just as the science of man will incorporate natural science; there will be a *single* science.

EPM (1844)
MEGA I/3, p. 123

Only now, after having considered four " moments," four aspects of the original, historical relationships, do we find that man also possesses " consciousness." Even so, this is not an original, " pure " consciousness. From the outset " spirit " is cursed with the " burden " of matter, which appears in this case in the form of agitated layers of air, sounds, in short, of language. Language is as old as consciousness, language *is* practical consciousness, as it exists for other men, and thus as it first really exists for myself as well. Language, like consciousness, only arises from the need, the necessity, of intercourse with other men. Where a relationship exists, it exists for me; the animal has no " *relations* " with anything, has no relations at all. For the animal, its relation to others does not exist as a relation. Consciousness is therefore from the very beginning a social product, and remains so as long as men exist at all. Consciousness is at first, of course, merely an awareness of the *immediate* sensible environment and of the limited connection with other persons and things outside the individual who is becoming self-conscious. At the same time, it is a consciousness of Nature, which first appears to men as a completely alien, all-powerful and unassailable force, with which men's relations are purely animal and by which they are overawed like beasts; it is thus a purely animal consciousness of Nature (natural religion).

It is at once apparent that this natural religion, or this determinate behaviour towards Nature, is conditioned by the form of society and vice versa. Here, as everywhere, the identity of Nature and man appears, in that the limited relation of men to Nature determines their limited relation to each other, and their limited relation to each other determines their limited relation to Nature, just because scarcely any historical modification of Nature has yet occurred. On the other hand, there is man's consciousness of the necessity of associating with the individuals around him, and the beginning of his awareness that he is living in society at all. This beginning is as animal as social life itself at this stage. It is mere herd-consciousness, and man is only distinguished from sheep at this point, by the fact that for him consciousness takes the place of instinct, or that his instinct is a conscious one.

This sheep-like or tribal consciousness receives its further development and extension through increased productivity, the multiplication of needs, and, what underlies both of these, the increase of population. Along with these changes there is a development of the division of labour which was at first nothing but the division of labour in the sexual act, and then the division of labour which emerges spontaneously or " naturally " by virtue of natural abilities (e.g. physical strength), needs, accidents, etc., etc.

GI (1845–6)
MEGA I/5, pp. 19–21

It is only in a social context that subjectivism and objectivism, spiritualism and materialism, activity and passivity, cease to be antinomies, and thus cease to exist as such antinomies. The resolution of *theoretical* contradictions is possible only through *practical* means, only through the practical energy of man. Their resolution is by no means, therefore, the task only of the understanding, but is a *real* task of life, a task which *philosophy* was unable to accomplish precisely because it saw there a *purely* theoretical problem.

The history of *industry*, and industry as it *objectively* exists, is an *open book of the human faculties*, and a human *psychology* which can be directly apprehended. This history has not hitherto been conceived in relation to human *nature*, but only from a superficial utilitarian point of view, since, in the condition of alienation, it was only possible to conceive real human faculties, and *human species-action*, in the form of abstract human existence, that is, religion, or as history in a general and abstract form, politics, art and literature. *Everyday, material* industry, (. . .) shows us, in the form of *sensible, external and useful objects*, in an alienated form, *the essential human faculties* transformed into *objects*. No *psychology* for which this book, i.e. the most tangible and accessible part of history, remains closed, can become a *genuine* science with a real content. What is to be thought of a science which remains aloof from this enormous field of human work, of a science which does not recognize its own inadequacy, so long as such a great wealth of human activity means nothing to it, except perhaps what can be expressed in one word—" *need* " or " *common need*? "

The *natural sciences* have developed a tremendous activity and have assembled an ever-growing mass of data. But philosophy has remained aloof from these sciences just as they have remained aloof from philosophy. Their momentary *rapprochement* was only a *fantastic illusion*. There was a desire for union, but the power to effect it was lacking. Historiography itself only takes natural science incidentally into account, regarding it as a factor making for enlightenment, for practical utility, and for particular great discoveries. But the natural sciences have penetrated all the more *practically* into human life, through their transformation of industry. They have prepared the emancipation of humanity, even though their immediate effect may have been to accentuate the dehumanizing of man. *Industry* is the real historical relation of Nature, and thus of the natural sciences, to man. Consequently, if industry is conceived as an *exoteric* form of the realization of the *essential human faculties*, one is able to grasp also the *human* essence of Nature or the *natural* essence of man. The natural sciences will then abandon their abstract materialist, or rather, idealist, orientation, and will become the basis of a *human* science, just as they have already become—though in an alienated form—the basis of a really human life. *One* basis for life and another for *science* is *a priori* a falsehood. Nature, as it develops in human history, in the genesis of human society, is the *real* nature of man; thus Nature, as it develops through industry, though in an *alienated* form, is truly *anthropological* Nature.

EPM (1844)
MEGA I/3, pp. 121–2

The extent to which the solution of a theoretical problem is a task of practice, and is accomplished through practice, and the extent to which correct practice is the condition of a true and positive theory, is shown for example in the case of *fetishism*. The sense perception of a fetishist differs from that of a Greek, because his sensuous existence is different. The abstract hostility between sense and spirit is inevitable so long as the human sense for Nature, or the human meaning of Nature, that is, consequently, the *natural* sense *of man*, has not yet been produced through man's own labour.

EPM (1844)
MEGA I/3, pp. 133–4

The fact is, therefore, that determinate individuals, who are productively active in a definite way, enter into these determinate social and political relations. Empirical observation must, in each particular case, show empirically, and without any mystification or speculation, the connection of the social and political structure with production. The social structure and the State are continually evolving out of the life-process of determinate individuals, of individuals not as they may appear in their own or other people's imagination, but as they really are: i.e. as they act, produce their material life, and are occupied within determinate material limits, presuppositions and conditions, which are independent of their will.

The production of ideas, conceptions and consciousness is at first directly interwoven with the material activity and the material intercourse of men, the language of real life. Representation and thought, the mental intercourse of men, still appear at this stage as the direct emanation of their material behaviour. The same applies to mental production as it is expressed in the political, legal, moral, religious and metaphysical language of a people. Men are the producers of their conceptions, ideas, etc.,—real, active men, as they are conditioned by a determinate development of their productive forces, and of the intercourse which corresponds to these, up to its most extensive forms. Consciousness can never be anything else than conscious existence, and the existence of men is their actual life process. If in all ideology men and their circumstances appear upside down as in a *camera obscura*, this phenomenon arises from their historical life process just as the inversion of objects on the retina does from their physical life-process.

In direct contrast to German philosophy, which descends from heaven to earth, here we ascend from earth to heaven. That is to say, we do not set out from what men say, imagine, or conceive, nor from what has been said, thought, imagined, or conceived of men, in order to arrive at men in the flesh. We begin with real, active men, and from their real life-process show the development of the ideological reflexes and echoes of this life-process. The phantoms of the human brain also are necessary sublimates of men's material life-process, which can be empirically established and which is bound to material preconditions. Morality, religion, metaphysics, and other ideologies, and their corresponding forms of consciousness, no longer retain therefore their appearance of autonomous existence. They have no history, no development; it is men, who, in developing their material production and their material intercourse, change, along with this their real existence, their thinking and the products of their thinking. Life is not determined by consciousness, but consciousness by life. Those who adopt the first method of approach begin with consciousness, regarded as the living individual; those who adopt the second, which corresponds with real life, begin with the real living individuals themselves, and consider consciousness only as *their* consciousness.

This method of approach is not without presuppositions, but it begins with the real presuppositions and does not abandon them for a moment. Its premises are men, not in some imaginary condition of fulfilment or stability, but in their actual, empirically observable process of development under determinate conditions. As soon as this active life-process is delineated, history ceases to be a collection of dead facts as it is with the empiricists (themselves still abstract), or an illusory activity of illusory subjects, as with the idealists.

Where speculation ends—in real life—real, positive science, the representation of the practical activity and the practical process of development of men, begins. Phrase-making about consciousness ceases, and real knowledge has to take its place. When reality is depicted, philosophy as an independent activity loses its medium of existence. At the most its place can only be taken by a conspectus of the general results, which are derived from the consideration of the historical development of men. In themselves and detached from real history, these abstractions have not the least value. They can only serve to facilitate the arrange-ment of historical material, and to indicate the sequence of its separate layers. They do not in the least provide, as does philosophy, a recipe or schema, according to which the epochs of history can rightly be distinguished. On the contrary, the difficulties only begin when we set about the consideration and arrangement of the material, whether of a past epoch or of the present, and the representation of reality.

GI (1845-6)
MEGA I/5, pp. 15-17

Social activity and social mind by no means exist *only* in the form of activity or mind which is *manifestly social*. Never-theless, *social* activity and mind, that is, activity and mind which show themselves directly in a *real association* with other men, are realized everywhere where this *direct* expression of sociability is based on the nature of the activity or corresponds to the nature of mind.

Even when I carry out *scientific work*, etc., an activity which I can seldom conduct in direct association with other men— I perform a *social*, because *human*, act. It is not only the material of my activity—like the language itself which the thinker uses—which is given to me as a social product. My *own* existence *is* a social activity. For this reason, what I myself produce, I produce for society and with the consciousness of acting as a social being.

. . . It is above all necessary to avoid postulating " society " once more as an abstraction confronting the individual. The individual is a *social being*. The manifestation of his life—even when it does not appear directly in the form of a *social* manifestation, accomplished in association with other men,—is therefore a manifestation and affirmation of *social life*. Individual human life and species-[1] life are not *different* things even though the mode of existence of individual life is necessarily a more *particular* or more *general* mode of species-life, or that of species-life a more particular or more general mode of individual life. In his *species-consciousness* man confirms his real *social life*, and reproduces his real existence in thought, while conversely species-being confirms itself in species-consciousness, and exists for itself in its universality as a thinking being. Though man is a *unique* individual—and it is just his particularity which makes him an individual, a really *individual* social being—he is equally the *whole*, the ideal whole, the subjective existence of society as thought and experienced. He exists, in reality, as the representation and the real mind of social existence, and as the sum of human manifestation of life.

[1] The term " species " was used by Marx, following Feuerbach, to refer to man's awareness of his general human qualities, of belonging to the "human species".

Thought and being are indeed *distinct*, but they also form a *unity*.

EPM (1844)

MEGA I/3, pp. 116–17

The existing relations of production between individuals must necessarily express themselves also as political and legal relations. Within the division of labour these relations are bound to assume an independent existence *vis-à-vis* the individuals. In language, such relations can only be expressed as concepts. The fact that these universals and concepts are accepted as mysterious powers is a necessary consequence of the independent existence assumed by the real relations whose expression they are. Besides this acceptance in everyday consciousness, these universals are also given a special validity and further development by political scientists and jurists who, as a result of the division of labour, are assigned to the cult of these concepts, and who see in them, rather than in the relations of production, the true basis of actual property relations.

GI (1845–6)

MEGA I/5, p. 342

The ideas of the ruling class are, in every age, the ruling ideas : i.e. the class which is the dominant *material* force in society is at the same time its dominant *intellectual* force. The class which has the means of material production at its disposal, has control at the same time over the means of mental production, so that in consequence the ideas of those who lack the means of mental production are, in general, subject to it. The dominant ideas are nothing more than the ideal expression of the dominant material relationships, the dominant material relationships grasped as ideas, and thus of the relationships which make one class the ruling one; they are consequently the ideas of its dominance.

The individuals composing the ruling class possess among other things consciousness, and therefore think. In so far, therefore, as they rule as a class and determine the whole extent of an epoch, it is self-evident that they do this in their whole range and thus, among other things, rule also as thinkers, as producers of ideas, and regulate the production and distribution of the ideas of their age. Consequently their ideas are the ruling ideas of the age. For instance, in an age and in a country where royal power, aristocracy and the bourgeoisie are contending for domination and where, therefore, domination is shared, the doctrine of the separation of powers appears as the dominant idea and is enunciated as an " eternal law." The division of labour, which we saw earlier as one of the principal forces of history up to the present time, manifests itself also in the ruling class, as the division of mental and material labour, so that within this class one part appears as the thinkers of the class (its active conceptualizing ideologists, who make it their chief source of livelihood to develop and perfect the illusions of the class about itself), while the others have a more passive and receptive attitude to these ideas and illusions, because they are in reality the active members of this class and have less time to make up ideas and illusions about themselves. This cleavage within the ruling class may even develop into a certain opposition and hostility between the two parts, but in the event of a practical collision in which the class itself is endangered, it disappears of its own accord and with it also the illusion that the ruling ideas were not the ideas of the ruling class and had a power distinct from the power of this class. The existence of revolutionary ideas in a particular age presupposes the existence of a revolutionary class. . . .

If, in considering the course of history, we detach the ideas of the ruling class from the ruling class itself and attribute to them an independent existence, if we confine ourselves to saying that in a particular age these or those ideas were dominant, without paying attention to the conditions of production and the producers of these ideas, and if we thus ignore the individuals and the world conditions which are the source of the ideas, it is possible to say, for instance, that during the time that the aristocracy was dominant the concepts honour, loyalty, etc., were dominant; during the dominance of the bourgeoisie the concepts freedom, equality, etc. The ruling class itself in general imagines this to be the case. This conception of history which is common to all historians, particularly since the eighteenth century, will necessarily come up against the phenomenon that increasingly abstract ideas hold sway, i.e. ideas which increasingly take on the form of universality. For each new class which puts itself in the place of the one ruling before it, is compelled, simply in order to achieve its aims, to represent its interest as the common interest of all members of society, i.e. employing an ideal formula, to give its ideas the form of universality and to represent them as the only rational and universally valid ones. The class which makes a revolution appears from the beginning not as a class but as the representative of the whole of society, simply because it is opposed to a *class*. It appears as the whole mass of society confronting the single ruling class. It can do this because at the beginning its interest really is more closely connected with the common interest of all other non-ruling classes and has been unable under the constraint of the previously existing conditions to develop as the particular interest of a particular class. Its victory, therefore, also benefits many individuals of the other classes which are not achieving a dominant position, but only in so far as it now puts these individuals in a position to raise themselves into the ruling class. When the French bourgeoisie overthrew the rule of the aristocracy it thereby made it possible for many proletarians to raise themselves above the proletariat, but only in so far as they became bourgeois. Every new class, therefore, achieves its domination only on a broader basis than that of the previous ruling class. On the other hand, the opposition of the non-ruling class to the new ruling class later develops all the more sharply and profoundly. These two characteristics entail that the struggle to be waged against this new ruling class has as its object a more decisive and radical negation of the previous conditions of society than could have been accomplished by all previous classes which aspired to rule.

This whole semblance, that the rule of a certain class is only the rule of certain ideas, ends of its own accord naturally, as soon as class domination ceases to be the form of social organization : that is to say, as soon as it is no longer necessary to represent a particular interest as general or the " general interest " as ruling.

GI (1845–6)
MEGA I/5, pp. 35–7

The more the established form of intercourse in society, and thus the conditions of the ruling class, come into conflict with the developed productive forces, and the greater therefore is the dissension within the ruling class itself and between it and the subject class, the less veridical naturally becomes the consciousness which originates from and expresses this form of intercourse; i.e. it ceases to express it. The earlier conceptions of these relations of intercourse, in which the real individual interests were asserted as general interests, decline into mere idealizing phrases, conscious illusions and deliberate deceits. But the more they are condemned as falsehoods, and the less they satisfy the understanding, the more dogmatically they are asserted and the more deceitful, moralizing and spiritual becomes the language of established society.

GI (1845–6)
MEGA I/5, pp. 271–2

Just as little must one imagine that the democratic representatives are indeed all shopkeepers or enthusiastic champions of shopkeepers. According to their education and their individual position they may be as far apart as heaven from earth. What makes them representatives of the petty bourgeoisie is the fact that in their minds they do not get beyond the limits which the latter do not get beyond in life, that they are consequently driven, theoretically, to the same problems and solutions to which material interest and social position drive the latter practically. This is, in general, the relationship between the *political* and *literary representatives* of a class and the class they represent.

18th Brumaire (1852)

In order to study the connection between intellectual and material production it is above all essential to conceive the latter in its determined historical form and not as a general category. For example, there corresponds to the capitalist mode of production a type of intellectual production quite different from that which corresponded to the medieval mode of production. Unless material production itself is understood in its specific historical form, it is impossible to grasp the characteristics of the intellectual production which corresponds to it or the reciprocal action between the two.

TM I, p. 381

Man's reflections on the forms of social life, and consequently, also, his scientific analysis of these forms, take a course directly opposite to that of their actual historical development. He begins, *post festum*, with the finished results of the process of development. The characteristics that stamp products as commodities, and whose establishment is a necessary preliminary to the circulation of commodities, have already acquired the stability of natural features of social life, before men try to give an account, not of their historical character, since they are already regarded immutable, but of their meaning. Consequently it was only the analysis of commodity price that led to the determination of the magnitude of value, and only the common expression of all commodities in money that led to the establishment of their character as values. It is, however, just this ultimate money form of the world of commodities that actually conceals, instead of disclosing, the social character of individual labour, and the social relations between the individual producers. If I assert that coats or boots stand in a relation to linen, as the universal incarnation of abstract human labour, the absurdity of the statement is self-evident. But when the producers of coats and boots relate those articles to linen, or, what is the same thing, to gold or silver, as the universal equivalent, they express the relation between their own individual labour and the collective labour of society in the same absurd form.

These forms constitute the categories of bourgeois political economy. They are socially accepted, and thus objective forms of thought which express the productive relations of a definite, historically determined mode of production, viz. the production of commodities. The whole mystery of commodities, all the magic and sorcery that surrounds the products of labour as long as they take the form of commodities, vanishes, therefore, as soon as we pass to other forms of production.

Capital I (1867)
VA I, 81–2

Political economy has indeed analysed, however incompletely, value and its magnitude, and has discovered what lies beneath these forms. But it has never once asked the question why this content takes these forms, why labour is represented by the value of its product and labour time by the magnitude of that value. These formulæ, which bear stamped upon them in unmistakable letters, that they belong to a social structure in which the process of production dominates man, instead of being controlled by him, appear to the bourgeois intellect as much a self-evident natural necessity as productive labour itself. Hence forms of social production that preceded the bourgeois form, are treated by the bourgeoisie in much the same way as the Fathers of the Church treat pre-Christian religions.

Capital I (1867)
VA I, pp. 85–7

Thus, when men bring the products of their labour into relation with each other as values, it is not because they see in these articles the mere material receptacles of homogeneous human labour. Quite the contrary. Whenever, by an exchange, men equate as values their different products, by that very act, they also equate, as human labour, the different kinds of labour expended upon them. They are not aware of this, but they do it. Value, therefore, does not carry a label describing what it is. It is value, rather, that converts every product of labour into a social hieroglyph. Later on, men try to decipher the hieroglyph, to penetrate the secret of their own social products; for to stamp an object of utility as a value, is just as much a social product as is language. The recent scientific discovery, that the products of labour, so far as they are values, are but material expressions of the human labour spent in their production, marks, indeed, an epoch in the history of the development of the human race, but does not by any means dissipate the mist through which the social character of labour appears as an objective character of the products themselves. Thus, despite this discovery, what is true only for this particular form of production (commodity production), namely that the specific social character of the labour of independent producers, consists in the equivalence of every kind of labour, as human labour, and that it assumes in the product the form of value—this fact appears to those caught up in the relationships of commodity production as a final truth. In the same way, the scientific analysis of air into its component elements, left the atmosphere, as an experienced physical object, unchanged.

Capital I (1867)
VA I, pp. 79–80

Political economy, which as an independent science first sprang into being during the period of manufacture, views the social division of labour only from the standpoint of manufacture, and sees in it only the means of producing more commodities with a given quantity of labour, and, consequently, of cheapening commodities and speeding up the accumulation of capital. In striking contrast with this accentuation of quantity and exchange-value, is the attitude of the writers of classical antiquity, who are exclusively concerned with quality and use-value. In consequence of the separation of the social branches of production, commodities are better made, the various bents and talents of men select a suitable field, and without some concentration of effort no important results can be obtained anywhere. Hence both product and producer are improved by the division of labour. If the increase in the quantity produced is occasionally mentioned, this is only done with reference to the greater abundance of use-values. There is not a word alluding to exchange-value or to the cheapening of commodities. This standpoint of use-value alone is taken by Plato, who treats the division of labour as the foundation on which the division of society into classes is based, as well as by Xenophon, who with characteristic bourgeois instinct, approaches more nearly to division of labour within the workshop. Plato's *Republic*, in so far as division of labour is treated in it as the formative principle of the State, is merely the Athenian idealization of the Egyptian caste system. Egypt also served as the model of an industrial country for many of Plato's contemporaries, among others for Isocrates; and it continued to have this significance for the Greeks of the Roman Empire.

Capital I (1867)
VA I, pp. 383–6

It was, however, impossible for Aristotle to discover from the form of value itself that in the form of commodity values all labour is expressed as equivalent human labour, and consequently as labour of equal worth. Greek society was founded upon slavery, and had, therefore, for its natural basis, the inequality of men and of their labour powers. The secret of the expression of value, namely, that all kinds of labour are equal and equivalent because and so far as they are human labour in general, cannot be deciphered until the notion of human equality has already acquired the fixity of a popular prejudice. This, however, is possible only in a society in which the great mass of the products of labour takes the form of commodities, and in which, consequently, the dominant social relation is that between men as owners of commodities. Aristotle's genius is shown precisely by the fact that he discovered, in the expression of the value of commodities, a relation of equality. Only the historical limitations of the society in which he lived, prevented him from discovering the real nature of this equality.

Capital I (1867)
VA I, p. 65

Proudhon begins by taking his ideal of justice, of *justice éternelle*, from the juridical relations that correspond to the production of commodities: thereby, it may be noted, he proves, to the consolation of all good citizens, that the production of commodities is a form of production as everlasting as justice. Then he turns round and seeks to reform the actual production of commodities, and the actual legal system corresponding thereto, in accordance with this ideal. What opinion should we have of a chemist, who, instead of studying the actual laws of the molecular changes in the composition and decomposition of matter, and on that basis solving definite problems, claimed to regulate the composition and decomposition of matter by means of the " eternal ideas," of *naturalité* and *affinité*? Do we really know any more about "usury," when we say it contradicts *justice éternelle*, *équité éternelle*, *mutualité éternelle*, and other *vérités éternelles* than the Fathers of the Church did when they said it was incompatible with *grace éternelle*, *foi éternelle*, and *la volonté éternelle de Dieu*?

Capital I (1867)
VA I, pp. 90–1 footnote

III. SOCIETY, SOCIAL RELATIONS, AND THE ECONOMIC STRUCTURE

LABOUR is, in the first place, a process in which both man and Nature participate, and in which man of his own accord starts, regulates, and controls the material reactions between himself and Nature. He opposes himself to Nature as one of her own forces, setting in motion arms and legs, head and hands, the natural forces of his body, in order to appropriate Nature's productions in a form adapted to his own wants. By thus acting on the external world and changing it, he at the same time changes his own nature. He develops his slumbering powers and compels them to act in obedience to his sway. We are not now dealing with those primitive instinctive forms of labour that remind us of the mere animal. An immeasurable interval of time separates the state of things in which a man brings his labour-power to market for sale as a commodity, from that state in which human labour was still in its first instinctive stage. We presuppose labour in a form that stamps it as exclusively human. A spider conducts operations that resemble those of a weaver, and a bee puts to shame many an architect in the construction of her cells. But what distinguishes the worst architect from the best of bees is this, that the architect raises his structure in imagination before he erects it in reality. At the end of every labour-process, we get a result that already existed in the imagination of the labourer at its commencement. He not only effects a change of form in the material on which he works, but he also realizes a purpose of his own that gives the law to his *modus operandi*, and to which he must subordinate his will. And this subordination is no mere momentary act. Besides the exertion of the bodily organs, the process demands that, during the whole operation, the workman's will be steadily in consonance with his purpose. This means close attention. The less he is attracted by the nature of the work, and by the mode in which it is carried on, and the less, therefore, he enjoys it as something which gives play to his bodily and mental powers, the more close his attention is forced to be.

The elementary factors of the labour-process are :

1. the personal activity of man, i.e., the work itself,
2. the object of the work, and
3. its instruments.

The soil (and this, economically speaking, includes water) in the virgin state in which it supplies man with necessaries or the means of subsistence ready to hand, exists independently of him, and is the universal object of human labour. All those things which labour merely separates from immediate connection with their environment, are objects of labour spontaneously provided by Nature. Such are fish which we catch and take from their element, water ; timber which we fell in the virgin forest ; and ores which we extract from their veins. If, on the other hand, the object of labour has, so to say, been filtered through previous labour, we call it raw material; such is ore already extracted and ready for washing. All raw material is the object of labour, but not every object of labour is raw material; it can only become so after it has undergone some alteration by means of labour.

An instrument of labour is a thing, or a complex of things, which the labourer interposes between himself and the object of his labour, and which serves as the conductor of his activity. He makes use of the mechanical, physical, and chemical properties of some substances in order to make other substances subservient to his aims. Leaving out of consideration such ready-made means of subsistence as fruits, in gathering which a man's own limbs serve as the instruments of his labour, the first thing of which the labourer possesses himself is not the object of labour but its instrument. Thus Nature becomes one of the organs of his activity, one that he annexes to his own bodily organs, adding stature to himself in spite of the Bible. As the earth is his original larder, so too it is his original tool house. It supplies him, for instance, with stones for throwing, grinding, pressing, cutting, etc. The earth itself is an instrument of labour, but when used as such in agriculture implies a whole series of other instruments and a comparatively high development of labour. No sooner is the labour developed to some extent, than it requires specially prepared instruments. Thus in the oldest caves we find stone implements and weapons. In the earliest period of human history domesticated animals, i.e. animals which have been bred for the purpose, and have undergone modifications by means of labour, play the chief part as instruments of labour along with specially prepared stones, wood, bones, and shells. The use and fabrication of instruments of labour, although existing in the germ among certain species of animals, is specifically characteristic of the human labour-process, and Franklin therefore defines man as a " tool-making animal." Relics of by-gone instruments of labour possess the same importance for the investigation of extinct economic forms of society, as do fossil bones for understanding the structure of extinct species of animals. It is not the articles made, but how they are made, and with what instruments, that enables us to distinguish different economic epochs.

Capital I (1867)
VA I, pp. 185–8

Nature constructs no machines, no locomotives, railways, electric telegraphs, self-acting mules, etc. They are the products of human industry, natural materials transformed into instruments of the human domination of Nature, or of its activity in Nature. They are instruments of the human brain created by the human hand; they are the materialized power of knowledge. The development of fixed capital indicates the extent to which general social knowledge has become a direct force of production, and thus the extent to which the conditions of the social life process have been brought under the control of the general intellect and reconstructed in accordance with it. It shows to what degree the social forces of production are produced, not only in the form of knowledge, but also as direct instruments of social practice and of the real life-process.

Grundrisse (1857–8), p. 594

Society as a whole, like a workshop, has its division of labour. If the division of labour within a modern workshop were taken as a model to be applied to a whole society, the society best organized for the production of wealth would, without question, be that which had only a single entrepreneur in charge, apportioning the work to the various members of the community in accordance with a predetermined rule. But things are not at all like this. Whereas, in a modern workshop, the division of labour is regulated in detail by the authority of the entrepreneur, modern society has no other rule, and no other authority for apportioning work, than free competition.

Under the patriarchal system, under the caste system, and under the feudal guild system, there was a division of labour in society as a whole according to fixed rules. Were these rules established by a legislator? No. They were born, originally, from the conditions of material production and only much later were they established as laws. It is thus that these various forms of the division of labour became so many bases of social organization. As for the division of labour within the workshop, it was only very slightly developed in all these types of society.

PP (1847)
MEGA I/6, p. 198

The division of labour only becomes a real division from the moment when the distinction between material and mental labour appears. From this moment, consciousness *can* really imagine that it is something other than consciousness of existing practice, that it is *really* conceiving something without conceiving something *real*; from now on consciousness is in a position to emancipate itself from the world and to proceed to the formation of " pure " theory, theology, philosophy, ethics, etc. But even if this theory, theology, philosophy, ethics, etc., comes into contradiction with existing conditions, this can only occur as a result of the fact that the existing social relations have come into contradiction with the existing forces of production. Furthermore, this can also occur, in a particular national sphere of relations, through the appearance of the contradiction, not within the national sphere, but between this national consciousness and the practice of other nations, i.e. between the national and the general consciousness of a nation.

Furthermore, it is quite immaterial what consciousness starts to do on its own; we obtain from all this rubbish only the one conclusion, that these three factors, the forces of production, the condition of society, and consciousness, can and must come into contradiction with one another, because the *division of labour* implies the possibility, indeed the fact, that intellectual and material activity—enjoyment and labour, production and consumption—devolve on different individuals, and that the only possibility of their not coming into contradiction lies in the abolition, in its turn, of the division of labour. It is self-evident, moreover, that " spectres," " bonds," " the higher being," " concept," " scruple," are merely the idealistic, spiritual expressions, the conceptions apparently of the isolated individual, the representations of empirical fetters and barriers, within which the mode of production of life, and the form of intercourse connected with it, move.

GI (1845–6)
MEGA I/5, p. 21

The organization and division of labour varies according to the instruments of labour available. The hand mill implies a different division of labour from that of the steam mill. To begin with the division of labour in general, in order to arrive at a specific instrument of production —machinery—is therefore to fly in the face of history.

Machinery is no more an economic category than is the ox which draws the plough. Machinery is only a productive force. The modern workshop, which is based on the use of machinery, is a social relation of production, an economic category.

PP (1847)
MEGA I/6, p. 197

Truly comical is M. Bastiat, who imagines that the ancient Greeks and Romans lived by plunder alone. But when people live by plunder for centuries, there must always be something at hand for them to seize; the objects of plunder must continually be reproduced. It would thus appear that even Greeks and Romans had some process of production, consequently, an economy, which just as much constituted the material basis of their world as bourgeois economy constitutes that of our modern world. Or perhaps Bastiat means that a mode of production based on slavery is based on a system of plunder. In that case he treads on dangerous ground. If a giant thinker like Aristotle erred in his appreciation of slave labour, why should a dwarf economist like Bastiat be right in his appreciation of wage labour? I take this opportunity of briefly answering an objection made by a German paper in America, to my work, *Zur Kritik der Politischen Oekonomie*, 1859. In the estimation of that paper, my view that each special mode of production and the social relations corresponding to it, in short, " that the economic structure of society is the real basis on which the juridical and political superstructure is raised, and to which definite social forms of thought correspond "; and " that the mode of production of material life determines the general character of the social, political, and intellectual processes of life "—all this is very true for our own times, in which material interests predominate, but not for the Middle Ages, in which Catholicism, nor for Athens and Rome, where politics, reigned supreme. In the first place it seems curious for anyone to suppose that these well-worn phrases about the Middle Ages and the ancient world are unknown to anyone else. This much, however, is clear, that the Middle Ages could not *live* on Catholicism, nor the ancient world on politics. On the contrary, it is the mode in which they gained a livelihood that explains why in one case politics, and in the other Catholicism, played the chief part. For the rest, it requires but a slight acquaintance with the history of the Roman republic, for example, to be aware that its secret history is the history of its landed property. On the other hand, Don Quixote long ago paid the penalty for wrongly imagining that knight errantry was compatible with all economic forms of society.

Capital I (1867)
VA I, pp. 87–8

The economic categories are only the theoretical expressions, the abstractions, of the social relations of production. M. Proudhon, as a true philosopher, seeing things upside down, sees in the real relations only the incarnation of these principles, of these categories which slumbered (as M. Proudhon the philosopher once again informs us) in the bosom of the " impersonal reason of humanity."

M. Proudhon the economist has clearly understood that men make cloth, linen, silk-stuffs, in certain determinate relations of production. What he has not understood is that these determinate social relations are just as much produced by men as are cloth, linen, etc. Social relations are intimately connected with the forces of production. In acquiring new forces of production, men change their mode of production, their way of earning their living; they change all their social relations. The hand mill will give you a society with the feudal lord, the steam mill a society with the industrial capitalist.

The same men who establish social relations in conformity with their material power of production, also produce principles, laws, and categories in conformity with their social relations. Thus, these ideas and categories are no more eternal than the relations which they express. They are *historical and transient products*.

There is a continuous movement of growth of the productive forces, of destruction of social relations, of formation of ideas; nothing is immutable but the abstract movement— *mors immortalis*.

PP (1847)
MEGA I/6, pp. 179–80

In order to prove that all labour must leave a surplus, M. Proudhon personifies society; he transforms it into a *social being*, which is far from being a society of persons, since it has its own laws which have nothing to do with the individuals of which society is composed. It also has its " own intelligence " which is not the common intelligence of men but an intelligence lacking in common sense. M. Proudhon reproaches the economists with having failed to understand the personality of this collective being. We should like to quote against him the following passage by an American economist who reproaches his fellow economists with exactly the opposite error: "The moral entity, the grammatical being, called society, has been clothed with attributes which have no real existence except in the imagination of those who make a thing out of a word . . . that it is which has led to so many difficulties and to such deplorable mistakes in political economy." (Th. Cooper, *Lectures on the Elements of Political Economy*, Columbia, 1826.)

PP (1847)
MEGA I/6, p, 166

Nothing could be more erroneous than the manner in which society is considered in relation to economic conditions, both by the economists and by the socialists. For instance, Proudhon says in criticism of Bastiat, *La différence pour la société, entre capital et produit n'existe pas. Cette différence est toute subjective aux individus.* Thus it is precisely the social which he calls subjective, while he calls a subjective abstraction, society. The distinction between capital and product is precisely that the product, as capital, expresses a determinate relation which belongs to a particular historical form of society. The so-called consideration of the question from the social point of view simply amounts to overlooking the distinctions which express the social relations (the relations of civil society). Society is not merely an aggregate of individuals; it is the sum of the relations in which these individuals stand to one another. It is as though someone were to say that, from the point of view of society, slaves and citizens do not exist; they are all men. In fact, this is rather what they are outside society. Being a slave or a citizen is a socially determined relation between an individual A and an individual B. Individual A is not as such a slave. He is only a slave in and through society. What Proudhon says here about capital and product, means, in his doctrine, that from the standpoint of society there is no distinction between capitalists and workers. Whereas in fact this distinction only exists from the standpoint of society.

Grundrisse (1857–58), pp. 175–6

. . . the division of labour offers us the first example of how, as long as man remains in natural society, that is, as long as a cleavage exists between the particular and the common interest, as long therefore as activity is not voluntarily, but naturally, divided, man's own act becomes an alien power opposed to him, which enslaves him instead of being controlled by him. For as soon as the division of labour begins, each man has a particular, exclusive sphere of activity, which is forced upon him and from which he cannot escape. He is a hunter, a fisherman, a shepherd, or a critical critic, and must remain so if he does not want to lose his means of livelihood; whereas in communist society, where nobody has one exclusive sphere of activity but each can become accomplished in any branch he wishes, production as a whole is regulated by society, thus making it possible for me to do one thing today and another tomorrow, to hunt in the morning, fish in the afternoon, rear cattle in the evening, criticize after dinner, in accordance with my inclination, without ever becoming hunter, fisherman, shepherd or critic.

This crystallization of social activity, this consolidation of what we ourselves produce into an objective power over us, growing out of our control, thwarting our expectations, bringing to naught our calculations, is one of the chief factors in historical development up to the present. It is precisely as a result of this contradiction between the interest of the individual and that of the community, that the latter takes an independent form as the *State*, divorced from the real interests of individual and community, and at the same time as an illusory community life, but always on the real basis of the bonds existing in every family and tribal aggregate, such as consanguinity, language, division of labour on a larger scale, and other interests. It arises especially, as will be shown later, on the basis of social classes conditioned by the division of labour, which emerge in every aggregate of this kind, and of which one dominates all the others. It follows from this, that all the struggles within the State, the struggle between democracy, aristocracy and monarchy, the struggle for the franchise, etc., are merely the illusory forms in which the real struggles of the different classes with each other are fought out.

GI (1845–6)
MEGA I/5, pp. 22–3

The relations between different nations depend upon the extent to which each has developed its productive forces, the division of labour, and internal intercourse. This statement is generally accepted. Not only the relation of one nation to others, however, but also the whole internal structure of the nation itself depends on the stage of development reached by its production and its internal and external intercourse. The degree to which the productive forces of a nation are developed is most clearly shown by the extent of the division of labour. Each new productive force, so far as it is not merely a quantitative extension of productive forces already known (e.g. the cultivation of fresh land), results in a further development of the division of labour.

The division of labour within a nation brings about, in the first place, the separation of industrial and commercial from agricultural labour, and hence the separation of *town* and *country* and the opposition of their interests. Its further development leads to the separation of commercial from industrial labour. At the same time, through the division of labour, various new groups are developed, within these various branches, among the individuals co-operating in distinct kinds of work. The relative position of these groups is determined by the methods employed in agriculture, industry and commerce (patriarchalism, slavery, estates, classes). The same conditions are evident, with the development of intercourse, in the relations of different nations to each other.

> GI (1845–6)
> MEGA I/5, p. 11

The specific economic form in which unpaid surplus labour is pumped out of the direct producers, determines the relation of domination and servitude, as it emerges directly out of production itself and in its turn reacts upon production. Upon this basis, however, is founded the entire structure of the economic community, which grows up out of the conditions of production itself, and consequently its specific political form. It is always the direct relation between the masters of the conditions of production and the direct producers which reveals the innermost secret, the hidden foundation of the entire social edifice and therefore also of the political form of the relation between sovereignty and dependence, in short, of the particular form of the State. The form of this relation between masters and producers always necessarily corresponds to a definite stage in the development of the methods of work and consequently of the social productivity of labour. This does not prevent an economic basis which in its principal characteristics is the same, from manifesting infinite variations and gradations, owing to the effect of innumerable external circumstances, climatic and geographical influences, racial peculiarities, historical influences from the outside, etc. These variations can only be discovered by analysing these empirically given circumstances.

Capital III
VA III/2, pp. 841–2

Man himself is the basis of his material production, as of all production which he accomplishes. All circumstances, therefore, which affect man, the subject of production, have a greater or lesser influence upon all his functions and activities, including his functions and activities as the creator of material wealth, of commodities. In this sense, it can truly be asserted that all human relations and functions, however and wherever they manifest themselves, influence material production and have a more or less determining effect upon it.

TM I, pp. 388–9

It will be agreed that England is a *political* country. It will be agreed, further, that England is the *country of pauperism*; indeed, the term itself is of English origin. A study of England is, therefore, the surest way of becoming acquainted with the *relations* between *pauperism* and *politics*. In England the distress of the workers is not *partial*, but *universal*, not limited to the manufacturing districts, but spread over the countryside. The movements here are not just appearing; they have recurred at intervals for almost a century.

How then, does the *English* bourgeoisie and the government and press which are associated with it, regard *pauperism*? In so far as the English bourgeoisie blames politics for the existence of pauperism, the *Whig* accuses the *Tory*, while the *Tory* accuses the *Whig*, of being responsible for it. According to the Whig, the chief cause of pauperism is the monopoly exercised by the great landowners and the laws prohibiting the import of corn. According to the Tory, the whole evil springs from liberalism, from competition, and from the too greatly extended factory system. Neither of the parties regards politics in general as a cause, but each one only the policy of the other party; neither party even dreams of a reform of society.

The most convincing expression of English opinion on pauperism—we are still referring to the opinion of the English bourgeoisie and government—is English *political economy*, that is to say, the scientific reflection of English economic circumstances.

Art. I (1844)
MEGA I/3, pp. 8–9

Part Two

PRE-CAPITALIST SOCIETIES[1]

[1] In this Part we have chosen texts to illustrate Marx's analysis of pre-capitalist societies. Marx did, however, make a detailed analysis of such societies, under the title " Progressive epochs in the economic formation of society." (See *Grundrisse*, op. cit., pp. 375–413.)

I. FORMS OF PROPERTY AND MODES OF PRODUCTION

SINCE Robinson Crusoe's experiences are a favourite theme with political economists, let us take a look at him on his island. Moderate though he is, there are several needs he has to satisfy, and he must therefore do a little useful work of various sorts, such as making tools and furniture, taming goats, fishing and hunting. Of his prayers and the like we take no account, since they are a source of pleasure to him, and he looks upon them as so much recreation. In spite of the variety of his work, he knows that his labour, whatever its form, is but the activity of one and the same Robinson, and consequently, that it consists of nothing but different modes of human labour. Necessity itself compels him to apportion his time accurately between his different kinds of work. Whether one kind occupies a greater space in his general activity than another, depends on the difficulties, greater or less as the case may be, to be overcome in attaining the useful effect aimed at. This our friend Robinson soon learns by experience, and having rescued a watch, ledger, and pen and ink from the wreck, he begins, like a true-born Briton, to keep a set of books. His stock-book contains a list of the useful objects that he possesses, of the operations necessary for their production, and lastly, of the labour-time that definite quantities of those objects have, on an average, cost him. All the relations between Robinson and the objects that form this wealth of his own creation, are here so simple and clear as to be intelligible without exertion, even to Herr M. Wirth. And yet these relations contain all that is essential to the determination of value.

Let us now transport ourselves from Robinson's island bathed in light to the European Middle Ages shrouded in darkness. Here, instead of the independent man, we find everyone dependent, serfs and lords, vassals and suzerains, laymen and clergy. Personal dependence here characterizes the social relations of production just as much as it does the other spheres of life organized on the basis of that production. But for the very reason that personal dependence forms the basis of this society, there is no necessity for labour and its products to assume a fantastic form different from their reality. They take the shape, in the transactions of society, of services in kind and payments in kind. Here the particular and natural form of labour, and not, as in a society based on production of commodities, its general abstract form, is the immediate social form of labour. Compulsory labour is just as much measured by time, as commodity-producing labour; but every serf knows that what he expends in the service of his lord is a definite quantity of his own personal labour-power. The tithe to be rendered to the priest is more tangible than his blessing. No matter, then, what we may think of the masks in which men play their parts in this society, the social relations between individuals in the performance of their labour, appear at all events as their own personal relations, and are not disguised under the shape of social relations between the products of labour.

For an example of labour in common or directly associated labour, we have no occasion to go back to that spontaneously developed form which we find on the threshold of the history of all civilized races. We have one close at hand in the patriarchal industries of a peasant family, that produces corn, cattle, yarn, linen, and clothing for home use. These different articles are, from the point of view of the family, diverse products of its labour, but they are not interchangeable commodities. The different kinds of labour, such as tillage, cattle tending, spinning, weaving and making clothes, which result in the various products, are, in their natural form, social functions, because they are functions of the family, which has its own spontaneously developed division of labour just as much as a society based on the production of commodities. The distribution of the work within the family, and the regulation of the labour-time of the several members, depend upon differences of age and sex and upon natural conditions varying with the seasons. The labour-power of each individual operates in this case merely as a definite portion of the whole labour-power of the family, and consequently, the expenditure of individual labour-power as measured by its duration, appears here as a social determination of labour.

Capital I (1867)
VA I, pp. 82–4

For a society based upon the production of commodities, in which the producers in general enter into social relations with one another by treating their products as commodities and values, whereby they reduce their individual private labour to the standard of homogeneous human labour—for such a society, Christianity with its cult of the abstract individual, more especially in its bourgeois developments, Protestantism, Deism, etc., is the most appropriate form of religion. In the ancient Asiatic mode of production, in that of classical antiquity, etc., we find that the conversion of products into commodities, and therefore the conversion of men into producers of commodities, holds a subordinate place, which, however, increases in importance as the primitive communities approach nearer and nearer to their dissolution. Genuinely trading nations exist in the ancient world only in its interstices, like the gods of Epicurus, or like the Jews in the pores of Polish society. Those ancient social organisms of production are, as compared with bourgeois society, extremely simple and transparent. But they are founded either on the immature development of man individually, who has not yet severed the umbilical cord that unites him with his fellow men in a primitive tribal community, or upon direct relations of subjection. They are the result of a low level of development of the productive power of labour, and of the correspondingly limited relations between men within the sphere of material life, both between man and man, and between man and Nature. This material limitation is reflected in the ideal sphere, in the early natural and folk religions. The religious reflection of the real world can, in any case, only finally vanish, when the practical relations of everyday life offer to man none but perfectly intelligible and reasonable relations to his fellowmen and to Nature. The life-process of society, i.e. the process of material production, will not shed its mystical veil until it becomes the product of freely associated men, and is consciously regulated by them in accordance with a settled plan. This, however, requires a definite material basis or set of conditions of existence which are themselves the spontaneous product of a long and painful process of development.

Capital I (1867)
VA I, pp. 84–5

Being independent of each other, the labourers are *isolated persons*, who enter into relations with the capitalist, but not with one another. Their co-operation begins only with the labour process, but they have then ceased to belong to themselves. On entering that process, they become incorporated with capital. As co-operators, as members of a working organism, they are but special modes of existence of capital. Hence, the productive power developed by the labourer when working *in co-operation*, is the *productive power of capital*. This productive power of associated labour is developed gratuitously, whenever the workmen are placed under given conditions, and it is capital that places them under such conditions. Because this power costs capital nothing, and because, on the other hand, the labourer himself does not develop it before his labour belongs to capital, it appears as a power with which capital is endowed by Nature—a productive power that is immanent in capital.

The tremendous effects of simple co-operation are to be seen in the gigantic structures of the ancient Asiatics, Egyptians, Etruscans, etc. " It has happened in times past that these Oriental States after supplying the expense of their civil and military establishments have found themselves in possession of a surplus which they could apply to works of magnificence or utility,.and in the construction of these their command over the hands and arms of almost the entire non-agricultural population has produced stupendous monuments which still indicate their power. The teeming valley of the Nile . . . produced food for a swarming non-agricultural population, and this food, belonging to the monarch and the priesthood, afforded the means of erecting the mighty monuments which filled the land. . . . In moving the colossal statues and vast masses of which the transport creates wonder, human labour almost alone, was prodigally used. . . . The number of the labourers and the concentration of their efforts sufficed. We see mighty coral reefs rising from the depths of the ocean into islands and firm land, yet each individual depositor is puny, weak, and contemptible. The non-agricultural labourers of an Asiatic monarchy have little but their individual bodily exertions to bring to the task, but their number is their strength, and the power of directing these masses gave rise to the palaces and temples, the pyramids, and the armies of gigantic statues of which the remains astonish and perplex us. It is that confinement of the revenues which feed them, to one or a few hands, which makes such undertakings possible." [1]

[1] Quoted from R. Jones, *Textbook of Lectures on the Political Economy of Nations* (1852).

This power of Asiatic and Egyptian kings, Etruscan theo-crats, etc., has in modern society been transferred to the capitalist, whether he be an isolated, or as in joint-stock companies, a collective capitalist.

Capital I (1867)
VA I, pp. 349–50

Whereas, in a society with capitalist production, anarchy in the social division of labour and despotism in that of the workshop mutually condition one another, we find, on the contrary, in those earlier forms of society in which the separation of trades has been spontaneously developed, then crystallized, and finally made permanent by law, on the one hand, the picture of a planned and authoritarian organization of social labour and on the other, the entire exclusion or at all events a very slight or sporadic and accidental development of the division of labour within the workshop.

Those small and extremely ancient Indian communities, some of which have continued down to this day, are based on common ownership of the land, on the association of agriculture and handicrafts, and on an unalterable division of labour, which serves, whenever a new community is started, as a plan and scheme ready cut and dried. Occupy-ing areas of from 100 up to several thousand acres, each forms a self-sufficient productive entity. The greater part of the products is destined for direct use by the community itself, and does not take the form of commodities. Hence, production here is independent of that division of labour brought about, in Indian society as a whole, by means of the exchange of commodities. It is only the surplus products which become commodities, to a large extent through the State, into whose hands from time immemorial a certain quantity of these products has found its way in the shape of rent in kind. The constitution of these communities varies in different parts of India. In those of the simplest form, the land is tilled in common, and the produce divided among the members. At the same time, spinning and weaving are carried on in each family as subsidiary industries. Side by side with the masses thus occupied in the same kind of work, we find the " chief inhabitant," who is judge, policeman and tax-gatherer in one; the book-keeper who keeps the account of the tillage and registers everything relating thereto; another official, who prosecutes criminals, protects strangers travelling through, and escorts them to the next village; the boundary man, who guards the boundaries against neighbouring communities; the water-overseer, who distributes the water from the common tanks for irrigation; the Brahmin, who conducts the religious services; the schoolmaster, who on the sand teaches the children reading and writing; the calendar-Brahmin, or astrologer, who makes known the lucky or unlucky days for seed-time and harvest, and for every other kind of agri-cultural work; a smith and a carpenter, who make and repair all the agricultural implements; the potter, who makes all the pottery of the village; the barber, the washer-man, who washes clothes, the silversmith, here and there the poet, who in some communities replaces the silversmith, in others the schoolmaster. This dozen or so of individuals is maintained at the expense of the whole community. If the population increases, a new community is founded, on the pattern of the old one, on unoccupied land. The whole mechanism discloses a systematic division of labour; but a division like that in manufactures is impossible, since the smith and carpenter, etc., find an unchanging market, and at the most there may be, according to the size of the villages, two or three of each, instead of one. The law that regulates the division of labour in the community acts here with the irresistible authority of a law of Nature, while each indi-vidual artisan, the smith, the carpenter, and so on, conducts in his workshop all the operations of his handicraft in the traditional way, but independently, and without recognizing any authority over him. The simplicity of the organization for production in these self-sufficing communities that constantly reproduce themselves in the same form, and if destroyed, by chance, spring up again on the same spot and with the same name—this simplicity supplies the key to the secret of the *unchangeableness* of Asiatic *societies*, an unchangeableness in such striking contrast with the constant dissolution and refounding of Asiatic *States*, and the never-ceasing changes of dynasty. The structure of the economic elements of society remains untouched by the storm-clouds of the political sky.

Capital I (1867)
VA I, pp. 374–6

A ridiculous prejudice has recently obtained currency that common property in its primitive form is specifically a Slavonic, or even exclusively Russian form. It is the primitive form that we can show to have existed among Romans, Teutons, and Celts, and even to this day we find numerous examples, ruins though they be, in India. A closer study of Asiatic, and especially of Indian forms of common property, would show how the different forms of primitive common property give rise to different forms of its dissolution. Thus, for instance, the various original types of Roman and Teutonic private property can be traced from different forms of Indian common property.

Kritik, p. 9, footnote 1 (1859)

In the pre-capitalist stages of society commerce rules industry. In modern society it is the other way about. Of course commerce will have more or less strong repercussions on the societies between which it is carried on. It will subject production more and more to exchange value by making the satisfaction of needs and subsistence more dependent on the sale than on the immediate use of the products.

. . . The development of commerce and commercial capital brings about everywhere an orientation of production towards exchange values, increases its volume, multiplies and universalizes it, develops money into world money. Commerce therefore has everywhere more or less of a dissolving influence on the existing organization of production, which, in all its different forms is primarily oriented towards use value. The extent to which commerce brings about a dissolution of the old mode of production depends on the solidity and internal structure of the latter. The outcome of this process of dissolution, or in other words, what new mode of production will take the place of the old, does not depend on commerce but on the character of the old mode of production itself. In the ancient world commerce and the development of commercial capital always resulted in a slave economy, or sometimes, depending on the point of departure, it resulted simply in the transformation of a patriarchal slave system devoted to the production of direct means of subsistence into a similar system devoted to the production of surplus value. But in the modern world it results in the capitalist mode of production. It follows from this, that these consequences were determined by quite other circumstances than the development of commercial capital.

It follows from the nature of the case that as soon as town industry as such is separated from agricultural industry, its products are from the outset commodities and require for their sale the intervention of commerce. The dependence of commerce upon the development of the towns, and, on the other hand, the dependence of the towns upon commerce, are to that extent self-evident. However, the extent to which industrial development will keep step with this development depends upon quite other circumstances. Ancient Rome, in the later days of the republic, had already developed commercial capital more highly than it had ever existed in the ancient world, without any progress in the development of crafts, while in Corinth and in other Grecian towns of Europe and Asia Minor the development of commerce was accompanied by highly developed crafts. On the other hand, at the opposite extreme from the development of towns and its conditions, the trading spirit and the development of commerce are frequently found among unsettled nomadic peoples.

Capital III
VA III/1, pp. 362–4

II. ECONOMIC STRUCTURE, SOCIAL STRATI-
FICATION, AND POLITICAL SYSTEMS

THE various stages of development in the division of labour are just so many different forms of property; i.e. the stage reached in the division of labour also determines the relations of individuals to one another with respect to the materials, instruments and product of labour.

The first form of property is tribal property. It corresponds to an undeveloped stage of production in which a people lives by hunting and fishing, by cattle breeding, or, at the highest stage, by agriculture. In the latter case, a large area of uncultivated land is presupposed. The division of labour is, at this stage, still very elementary, and is no more than an extension of the natural division of labour occurring within the family. The social structure, therefore, is no more than an extension of the family, with patriarchal family chiefs, below them the members of the tribe, and finally slaves. The slavery which is latent in the family only develops gradually with the increase of population and of needs, and with the extension of external intercourse, either war or trade.

The second form is the communal and State property of antiquity, which results especially from the union of several tribes into a city, either by agreement or by conquest, and which is still accompanied by slavery. Alongside communal property, personal and, later also real, private property is already beginning to develop, but as an abnormal form subordinate to communal property. It is only as a community that the citizens hold power over their labouring slaves, and on this account alone, therefore, they are bound to the form of communal property. This is the communal private property of the active citizens, who are forced to continue in this natural form of association in face of their slaves. For this reason, the whole structure of society based on communal property, and with it the power of the people, decays in proportion as private real property develops. The division of labour is already more developed. We already find the opposition of town and country, later the opposition between those States which represent town interests and those which represent country interests, and within the towns themselves the opposition between industry and maritime commerce. The class relation between citizens and slaves is now completely developed.

This whole conception of history appears to be contradicted by the fact of conquest. Previously, force, war, pillage, slaughter, etc., have been postulated as the driving force of history. Here we must confine ourselves to the chief points, and therefore take only one striking example—the destruction of an old civilization by a barbarous people and the consequent formation of an entirely new social structure (Rome and the barbarians, feudalism and the Gauls, the Byzantine Empire and the Turks). For the conquering barbarians war itself is still, as already suggested above, a regular form of intercourse which is the more eagerly exploited as population increase necessitates new means of production to supersede the traditional, and for them the only possible, primitive mode of production. In Italy, however, the concentration of landed property (caused not only by indebtedness and forced sales but also by inheritance, since, as a result of loose living and the small number of marriages, the old families gradually died out and their possessions came into the hands of a few), and its conversion into grazing land (resulting from the importation of plundered and tribute corn and the consequent lack of demand for Italian corn, as well as from ordinary economic causes still operative today) had brought about the almost total disappearance of the free population. Even the slaves died out again and again and had continually to be replaced with new ones.   Slavery remained the basis of the whole productive system.   The plebeians, standing between the freemen and the slaves, never became more than a *Lumpenproletariat*.   Rome indeed never became more than a city; its connection with the provinces was almost exclusively political and could therefore easily be severed again by political events.

With the development of private property there appear for the first time the conditions which we shall rediscover, only on a more extensive scale, with modern private property.   On the one hand there is the concentration of private property, which began very early in Rome (as the agrarian law of Licinius indicates) and developed rapidly from the time of the civil wars and especially under the emperors; on the other hand, associated with this, the transformation of the plebeian small peasantry into a proletariat, which, however, owing to its intermediate position between propertied citizens and slaves, never achieved an independent development.

The third form is feudal or estates property.   If antiquity started out from the *town* and its little territory, the Middle Ages started out from the *country*.   This different starting point was determined by the sparseness of the population which was scattered over a large area and which received no important increase from the conquerors.   In contrast to Greece and Rome, therefore, feudal development begins in a much larger area, prepared by the Roman conquests and by the spread of agriculture associated with them.   The last centuries of the declining Roman Empire and its conquest by the barbarians destroyed a number of productive forces; agriculture had declined, industry had decayed for lack of markets, trade had died out or had been violently interrupted, and the rural and urban population had diminished.   These conditions and the mode of organization of the conquest determined by them gave rise, under the influence of the Teutonic military constitution, to feudal property. Like tribal and communal property it is also based on a community, but the directly producing class which confronts it is not, as in the case of the ancient community, the slaves, but the enserfed small peasantry. As soon as feudalism is fully developed the opposition to the towns reappears. The hierarchical system of landownership, and the armed bodies of retainers associated with it, gave the nobility power over the serfs. This feudal structure was, just as much as the communal property of antiquity, an association against a subject producing class, but the form of association and the relation to the direct producers were different because of the different conditions of production.

This feudal structure of landownership had its counterpart in the *towns* in the form of guild property, the feudal organization of trades. Here property consisted chiefly in the labour of each individual. The necessity for association against the organized robber nobility, the need for communal market-halls, in an age when the industrialist was at the same time a merchant, the growing competition of the escaped serfs swarming into the rising towns, the feudal structure of the whole country, combined to bring about the *guilds*. The gradually accumulated capital of individual craftsmen, and their stable numbers in an increasing population, gave rise to the relation of journeyman and apprentice, which brought into being in the towns a hierarchy similar to that in the country.

Thus, in the feudal period, the chief forms of property consisted on the one hand of landed property with serf labour chained to it, and on the other hand of individual labour with small capital commanding the labour of journeymen. The structure of both was determined by the narrow conditions of production—small-scale and primitive cultivation of the land, and handicraft industry. There was little division of labour in the heyday of feudalism. The opposition between town and country existed within each nation, and the division into estates was certainly strongly marked, but apart from the differentiation of princes, nobility, clergy and peasants in the country, and masters, journeymen, apprentices, and soon also the rabble of casual labourers, in the towns, no division of importance took place. In agriculture it was rendered difficult by the strip system and by the emergence of the cottage industry of the peasants themselves. In industry there was no division of labour at all within the various trades and very little between them. The separation of industry and commerce already existed in the older towns; in the newer ones it only developed later when the towns entered into mutual relations.

The grouping of larger territories into feudal kingdoms was a necessity for the landed nobility as well as for the towns. The organization of the ruling class, the nobility, had everywhere, therefore, a monarch at its head.

GI (1845–6)
MEGA I/5, pp. 11–15

Co-operation in the labour process, as we find it at the dawn of human development, among hunting peoples, or in the agriculture of Indian communities, is based, on the one hand, on common ownership of the means of production, and on the other hand, on the fact, that the individual has not yet severed the navel-string which attaches him to his tribe or community, any more than an individual bee has freed itself from connection with the hive. Such co-operation is distinguished from capitalistic co-operation by both of the above characteristics. The sporadic application of co-operation on a large scale in the ancient world, in the Middle Ages, and in modern colonies, is based on *direct* relations of dominion and servitude, principally on slavery. The capitalistic form, on the contrary, presupposes from the outset the free wage labourer who sells his labour-power to capital. Historically, however, this form developed in opposition to peasant agriculture and to independent handicrafts whether organized in guilds or not. In contrast with these, capitalistic co-operation does not appear as a particular historical form of co-operation, but rather, co-operation itself appears to be a historical form peculiar to, and a specifically distinguishing mark of, the capitalist process of production.

Capital I (1867)
VA I, p. 350

Now, in order distinctly to appreciate the usurpation subsequently carried out, we must first properly understand what the *Clan* meant. The *Clan* belonged to a form of social existence which, in the scale of historical development, stands a full degree below the feudal state; viz. the *patriarchal* state of society. " *Klaen,*" in Gaelic, means children. Every one of the usages and traditions of the Scottish Gaels reposes upon the supposition that the members of the *clan* belong to one and the same family. The " great man," the chieftain of the clan, is on one hand quite as arbitrary, on the other quite as confined in his power, by consanguinity, etc., as every father of a family. To the clan, to the family, belonged the district where it had established itself, exactly as, in Russia, the land occupied by a community of peasants belongs, not to the individual peasants, but to the community. Thus the district was the common property of the family. There could be no more question, under this system, of private property, in the modern sense of the word, than there could be of comparing the social existence of the members of the clan to that of individuals living in the midst of our modern society. The division and subdivision of the land corresponded to the military functions of the single members of the clan.   According to their military abilities, the chieftain entrusted to them the several allotments, cancelled or enlarged according to his pleasure the tenures of the individual officers, and these officers again distributed to their vassals and under-vassals every separate plot of land.   But the district at large always remained the property of the clan, and, however the claims of individuals might vary, the tenure remained the same; nor were the contributions for the common defence, or the tribute for the Laird, who at once was leader in battle and chief magistrate in peace, ever increased.   Upon the whole, every plot of land was cultivated by the same family, from generation to generation, under fixed imposts.   These imposts were insignificant, more a tribute by which the supremacy of the " great man " and of his officers was acknowledged, than a rent of land in a modern sense, or a source of revenue.   The officers directly subordinate to the " great man " were called " Taksmen," and the district entrusted to their care, " Tak."   Under them were placed inferior officers, at the head of every hamlet, and under these stood the peasantry.

Thus you see, the *Clan* is nothing but a family organized in a military manner, quite as little defined by laws, just as closely hemmed in by traditions, as any family.   But the land is the *property of the family*, in the midst of which differences of rank, in spite of consanguinity, do prevail as well as in all the ancient Asiatic family communities.

" The Duchess of Sutherland and Slavery "
NYDT February 9, 1853

The class struggles of the ancient world took the form chiefly of a contest between debtors and creditors, which in Rome ended in the ruin of the plebeian debtors, who were replaced with slaves.   In the Middle Ages the contest ended with the ruin of the feudal debtors, who lost their political power together with the economic basis on which it was established. Nevertheless, the money form, which is the form of the relation between debtor and creditor, here reflects only the deeper-lying antagonism between the economic conditions of existence of the classes in question.

Capital I (1867)
VA I, p. 141

The final result is therefore the abolition of the distinction between capitalist and landowner, so that broadly speaking there remain only two classes in the population, the working class and the capitalist class. This disposal of landed property and transformation of land into a commodity is the final ruin of the old aristocracy and the complete triumph of the aristocracy of money.

Romanticism sheds many sentimental tears over this event, but we cannot do so. Romanticism always confuses the infamy involved in this *disposal of land*, with the wholly reasonable, and within the system of private property, necessary and desirable consequences of the *disposal of landed property*. In the first place, feudal landed property is already essentially land which has been disposed of, alienated from men and now confronting them in the form of a few great lords.

Already in feudal landownership the ownership of the earth appears as an alien power ruling over men. The serf is the product of the land. In the same way the heir, the first-born son, belongs to the land. It inherits him. The rule of private property begins with the ownership of land, which is its basis. But in feudal landownership the lord *appears* at least as king of the land. In the same way there is the appearance of a more intimate connection between the owner and the land than is the case in the possession of mere *wealth*. Landed property takes on an individual character with its lord, has its own status, is knightly or baronial with him, has its privileges, its jurisdiction, its political rights, etc. It appears as the inorganic body of its lord. Hence the adage, *nulle terre sans maître*, in which the joint growth of lordship and landed property is expressed. The rule of landed property does not, therefore, appear as the direct rule of capital. Its dependants stand to it more in the relation in which they stand to their fatherland. It is a narrow kind of nationality.

Feudal landed property gives its name to its lord, as a kingdom gives its name to a king. His family history, the history of his house, etc., all this makes the landed property individual to him, makes it formally belong to a house, to a person. Similarly, the workers on the estate are not in the condition of *day labourers*, but are partly the property of the lord, as in the case of serfs, and partly stand to him in relations of respect, subordination and duty. His relation to them is therefore directly political, and has even an *agreeable* side. Customs and character differ from one estate to another and seem to be in harmony with the type of land, whereas later only a man's pocket, not his own character or individuality, draws him to an estate. Finally, the lord does not try to extract the maximum profit from his estate. He rather consumes what is there, and tranquilly leaves the care of producing it to the serfs and tenant farmers. That is the *aristocratic* condition of landownership which reflects a romantic *glory* upon its lords.

It is inevitable that this appearance should be abolished, that landed property, the *root* of private property, should be drawn completely into the movement of private property and *become a commodity*; that the rule of the property owner should appear as the naked rule of private property, of capital, dissociated from all political colouring; that the relation between property owner and worker should be limited to the economic relationship of exploiter and exploited; that all personal relationships between the property owner and his property should cease, and the latter become purely *material* wealth; that in place of the honourable marriage with the land there should be a marriage of interest, and the land as well as man himself sink to the level of an object of speculation. It is inevitable that the root of landed property, sordid self interest, should also appear in a cynical form. . . . Thereby the medieval adage, *nulle terre sans seigneur*, is replaced with a new adage, *l'argent n'a pas de maître*, which expresses the complete domination of living men by dead matter.

EPM (1844)
MEGA I/3, pp. 75–7

Part Three

SOCIOLOGY OF CAPITALISM

I. THE ORIGINS AND DEVELOPMENT OF CAPITALISM

From the serfs of the Middle Ages sprang the chartered burghers of the earliest towns. From these burgesses the first elements of the bourgeoisie were developed.

The discovery of America, the rounding of the Cape, opened up fresh ground for the rising bourgeoisie. The East-Indian and Chinese markets, the colonization of America, trade with the colonies, the increase in the means of exchange and in commodities generally, gave to commerce, to navigation, to industry, an impulse never before known, and thereby, to the revolutionary element in the tottering feudal society, a rapid development.

The feudal system of industry, in which industrial production was monopolized by closed guilds, now no longer sufficed for the growing wants of the new markets. The manufacturing system took its place. The guild-masters were pushed on one side by the manufacturing middle class; division of labour between the different corporate guilds vanished in the face of division of labour in each single workshop.

Meantime the markets kept ever growing, the demand ever rising. Even manufacture no longer sufficed. Thereupon, steam and machinery revolutionized industrial production. The place of manufacture was taken by the giant, modern industry, the place of the industrial middle class by industrial millionaires, the leaders of whole industrial armies, the modern bourgeois.

Modern industry has established the world market, for which the discovery of America paved the way. This market has given an immense development to commerce, to navigation, to communication by land. This development has, in its turn, reacted on the extension of industry;

and in proportion as industry, commerce, navigation, railways, extended, in the same proportion the bourgeoisie developed, increased its capital, and pushed into the background every class handed down from the Middle Ages.

We see, therefore, how the modern bourgeoisie is itself the product of a long course of development, of a series of revolutions in the modes of production and of exchange.

Each step in the development of the bourgeoisie was accompanied by a corresponding political advance of that class. An oppressed class under the sway of the feudal nobility, an armed and self-governing association in the medieval commune; here independent urban republic (as in Italy and Germany), there taxable " third estate " of the monarchy (as in France); afterwards, in the period of manufacture proper, serving either the semi-feudal or the absolute monarchy as a counterpoise against the nobility, and, in fact, cornerstone of the great monarchies in general —the bourgeoisie has at last, since the establishment of modern industry and of the world market, conquered for itself, in the modern representative State, exclusive political sway. The executive of the modern State is but a committee for managing the common affairs of the whole bourgeoisie.

CM (1848)
MEGA I/6, pp. 526–8

An indispensable condition for the establishment of manufacturing industry was the accumulation of capital, facilitated by the discovery of America and the importation of its precious metals.

It has been sufficiently proved that the increase in the means of exchange resulted, on the one hand, in a reduction of wages and rents, and on the other hand, in an increase in industrial profits. In other words, to the extent that the landowners and workers, the feudal lords and the common people, fell, so the capitalist class, the bourgeoisie, rose.

There were other circumstances which contributed at the same time to the development of manufacturing industry; the increase in the volume of goods put into circulation as trade reached the East Indies by way of the Cape of Good Hope, the colonial system, and the development of maritime trade.

Another point which has not received enough attention in the history of manufacturing industry is the disbanding of the numerous retainers of the feudal lords. The lower grades of these retainers became vagabonds before going into the workshops. The creation of workshops was preceded, in the fifteenth and sixteenth centuries, by almost universal vagabondage. Another powerful aid to the workshops was provided by the large numbers of peasants who, driven from the land by the conversion of fields into pastures, and by the progress of agriculture which reduced the number of hands needed for cultivation, flocked into the towns during whole centuries.

The expansion of the market, the accumulation of capital, the changes in the social position of different classes, a multitude of people who found themselves deprived of their source of income : these were so many historical conditions for the establishment of manufacture.

PP (1847)
MEGA I/6, pp. 199–200

There is no doubt—and it is precisely this fact which has led to many wrong conceptions—that the great revolutions which took place in commerce in the sixteenth and seventeenth centuries, concurrently with the geographical discoveries, and which stimulated the development of commercial capital, were among the principal factors in the transition from feudal to capitalist production. The sudden expansion of the world market, the multiplication of circulating commodities, the zeal displayed among the European nations in the race after the products of Asia and the treasures of America, the colonial system, all materially contributed to the destruction of the feudal barriers of production. Nevertheless, the modern mode of production, in its first period, the manufacturing period, developed only in places where the conditions for it had already been created in the Middle Ages. Compare, for instance, Holland with Portugal. When in the sixteenth, and to some extent still in the seventeenth, century, the sudden expansion of commerce and the creation of a new world market had an overwhelming influence on the overthrow of the old mode of production and on the rise of the capitalist one, this occurred on the basis of the already created capitalist mode of production. . . .

The transition from the feudal mode of production may take two different paths. The producer may become a merchant and capitalist, in opposition to agricultural natural economy and to the guild organized handicrafts of medieval town industry. This is the really revolutionary way. Or the merchant may take possession of production directly. While this way serves historically as a mode of transition—for example, the English clothier of the seventeenth century, who brings the weavers under his control, although they remain independent workers, by selling wool to them and buying cloth from them—nevertheless it cannot by itself do much for the overthrow of the old mode of production, which it rather preserves and uses as its basis. . . . This method is everywhere an obstacle to a real capitalist mode of production and declines with the development of the latter.

Capital III
VA III/1, pp. 364–6

For the conversion of his money into capital, therefore, the owner of money must find in the commodity market a free labourer, free in the double sense, that as a free man he can dispose of his labour-power as his own commodity, and that on the other hand he has no other commodity for sale, and lacks everything necessary for the realization of his labour-power.

The question why this free labourer confronts him in the market, has no interest for the owner of money, who regards the labour market as a branch of the general market for commodities. And for the present it interests us just as little. We observe the fact theoretically, as he does practically. One thing, however, is clear—Nature does not produce on the one side owners of money or commodities, and on the other men possessing nothing but their own labour-power. This relation has no natural basis, nor is its social basis one that is common to all historical periods. It is clearly the result of a past historical development, the product of many economic revolutions, of the extinction of a whole series of older forms of social production.

So, too, the economic categories, which we have already discussed, bear the stamp of history. Definite historical conditions are necessary that a product may become a commodity. It must not be produced as the immediate means of subsistence of the producer himself. Had we gone further, and inquired under what circumstances all, or even the majority of products take the form of commodities, we should have found that this can only happen with production of a very specific kind, capitalist production. Such an inquiry, however, would have been foreign to the analysis of commodities. The production and circulation of commodities can take place, although the great mass of the objects produced are intended for the immediate requirements of their producers, and are not turned into commodities, and although, therefore, social production is as yet a long way from being entirely dominated by exchange-value. The appearance of products as commodities presupposes such a development of the social division of labour, that the separation of use-value from exchange-value, a separation which first begins with barter, must already have been completed. But such a stage of development is common to many forms of society, which in other respects present the most varied historical features.

On the other hand, if we consider money, its existence implies a definite stage in the exchange of commodities. The particular functions of money, either as the mere equivalent of commodities, or as means of circulation, or means of payment, as hoard or as universal money, point, according to the extent and relative preponderance of the one function or the other, to very different stages in the process of social production. Yet we know by experience that a moderate degree of development of the circulation of commodities suffices for the appearance of all these functions. It is otherwise with capital. The historical conditions of its existence are by no means given with the mere circulation of money and commodities. It arises only when the owner of the means of production and subsistence meets in the market with the free labourer selling his labour-power. And this one historical condition comprises a whole stage of history. Capital, therefore, announces from its first appearance a new epoch in the process of social production.

Capital I (1867)
VA I, pp. 176–8

In themselves, money and commodities are no more capital than are the means of production and of subsistence. They have to be transformed into capital. But this transformation itself can only take place under certain circumstances, whose essential features are, that two very different kinds of commodity-possessors must come into contact; on the one hand, the owners of money, means of production, and means of subsistence, who are eager to increase the sum of values they possess, by buying other people's labour-power; on the other hand, free labourers, the sellers of their own labour-power, and therefore the sellers of labour. Free labourers, in the double sense that they themselves do not form part and parcel of the means of production, as in the case of slaves, bondsmen, etc., and that the means of production do not belong to them, as in the case of peasant-proprietors; they are, therefore, free from, unencumbered by, any means of production of their own. With this polarization of the market for commodities, the fundamental conditions of capitalist production are given. The capitalist system presupposes the complete separation of the labourers from all property in the means by which they can realize their labour. As soon as capitalist production is firmly established, it not only maintains this separation, but reproduces it on a continually extending scale. The process, therefore, that clears the way for the capitalist system, can be none other than the process which takes away from the labourer the possession of his means of production; a process that transforms, on the one hand, the social means of subsistence and of production into capital, on the other, the immediate producers into wage-labourers. The so-called primitive accumulation, therefore, is nothing else than the historical process of divorcing the producer from the means of production. It appears as primitive because it forms the prehistoric stage of capital and of the mode of production corresponding with it.

The economic structure of capitalist society has grown out of the economic structure of feudal society. The dissolution of the latter set free the elements of the former.

The immediate producer, the labourer, could only dispose of his own person after he had ceased to be attached to the soil and ceased to be the slave, serf, or bondman of another. To become a free seller of labour-power, who carries his commodity wherever he finds a market, he must further have escaped from the dominion of the guilds, from their rules for apprentices and journeymen, and from the impediments of their labour regulations. Hence, the historical movement which changes the producers into wage-workers, appears, on the one hand, as their emancipation from serfdom and from the fetters of the guilds, and this side alone exists for our bourgeois historians. But, on the other hand, these new freedmen became sellers of themselves only after they had been robbed of all their own means of production, and of all the guarantees of existence afforded by the old feudal arrangements. And the history of this, their expropriation, is written in the annals of mankind in letters of blood and fire.

The industrial capitalists, these new potentates, had on their part not only to displace the guild masters, but also the feudal lords, the possessors of the sources of wealth. In this aspect their conquest of social power appears as the fruit of a victorious struggle both against feudal lordship and its outrageous prerogatives, and against the guilds and the fetters they laid on the free development of production and the free exploitation of man by man. The knights of industry, however, only succeeded in supplanting the knights of the sword by making use of events for which they themselves were not responsible. They have risen by means as vile as those by which the Roman freed-man once made himself the master of his *patronus*.

The starting-point of the development that gave rise to the wage-labourer as well as to the capitalist, was the servitude of the labourer. The advance consisted in a change of form of this servitude, in the transformation of feudal exploitation into capitalist exploitation. To understand its course, we need not go back very far. Although we come across the first beginnings of capitalist production as early as the fourteenth or fifteenth century, sporadically, in certain towns of the Mediterranean, the capitalist era dates from the sixteenth century. Wherever it appears, the abolition of serfdom has been long effected, and the crowning glory of the Middle Ages, the sovereign self-governing towns, has long been on the wane.

In the history of primitive accumulation, all revolutions are epoch-making that act as levers for the capitalist class in course of formation; but, above all, those moments when great masses of men are suddenly and forcibly torn from their means of subsistence, and hurled as free and " unattached " proletarians on the labour market. The expropriation of the agricultural producer, of the peasant, his separation from the soil, is the basis of the whole process. The history of this expropriation, in different countries, assumes different aspects, and runs through its various phases in different orders of succession, and at different periods. In England alone, which we take as our example, has it the classical form.

Capital I (1867)
VA I, pp. 752-4

Whatever may be the social mode of production, workers and means of production always remain its principal elements. But so long as they remain separated, they are only potentially such elements. For production to take place at all they must be brought together. The particular way in which they are brought together, is the distinguishing feature of different economic periods in the organization of society. In the present case, the separation of the free worker from his means of production is the datum from which we begin, and we have seen in what manner, and under what conditions, these two elements have been brought together in the hands of the capitalist, namely, as the productive mode of existence of his capital. The actual process which combines the personal and material elements in commodities, the process of production, thus becomes itself a function of capital, a capitalist process of production, whose nature was analysed in detail in the first volume of this work. Every process of commodity production is at the same time a process of exploitation of labour power, but the capitalist mode of commodity production is the first to become an epoch-making mode of exploitation, which in the course of its historical development, by its organization of labour and its stupendous technical progress, transforms the whole economic structure of society and far surpasses all earlier periods.

Capital II
VA II, pp. 34–5

The bourgeoisie has through its exploitation of the world market given a cosmopolitan character to production and consumption in every country. To the great chagrin of reactionaries, it has drawn from under the feet of industry the national ground on which it stood. All old-established national industries have been destroyed or are daily being destroyed. They are dislodged by new industries, whose introduction becomes a life and death question for all civilized nations, by industries that no longer work up indigenous raw material, but raw material drawn from the remotest zones; industries whose products are consumed, not only at home, but in every quarter of the globe. In place of the old wants, satisfied by the production of the country, we find new wants, requiring for their satisfaction the products of distant lands and climes. In place of the old local and national seclusion and self-sufficiency, we have intercourse in every direction, universal interdependence of nations. And as in material, so also in intellectual production. The intellectual creations of individual nations become common property. National one-sidedness and narrow-mindedness become more and more impossible, and from the numerous national and local literatures there arises a world literature.

The bourgeoisie, by the rapid improvement of all instruments of production, by the immensely facilitated means of communication, draws all, even the most barbarian nations, into civilization. The cheap prices of its commodities are the heavy artillery with which it batters down all Chinese walls, with which it forces the barbarians intensely obstinate hatred of foreigners to capitulate. It compels all nations, on pain of extinction, to adopt the bourgeois mode of production; it compels them to introduce what it calls civilization into their midst, i.e. to become bourgeois themselves. In one word, it creates a world after its own image.

The bourgeoisie has subjected the country to the rule of the towns. It has created enormous cities, has greatly increased the urban population as compared with the rural, and has thus rescued a considerable part of the population from the idiocy of rural life. Just as it has made the country dependent on the towns, so it has made barbarian and semi-barbarian countries dependent on the civilized ones, nations of peasants on nations of bourgeois, the East on the West.

The bourgeoisie keeps more and more doing away with the scattered state of the population, of the means of production, and of property. It has agglomerated population, centralized means of production, and has concentrated property in a few hands. The necessary consequence of this was political centralization. Independent, or but loosely connected provinces, with separate interests, laws, governments and systems of taxation, became lumped together into one nation, with one government, one code of laws, one national class interest, one frontier and one customs tariff.

The bourgeoisie, during its rule of scarce one hundred

years, has created more massive and more colossal productive forces than have all preceding generations together.
Subjection of Nature's forces to man, machinery, application of chemistry to industry and agriculture, steam navigation, railways, electric telegraphs, clearing of whole con-
tinents for cultivation, canalization of rivers, whole popula-
tions conjured out of the ground—what earlier century had
even a presentiment that such productive forces slumbered
in the lap of social labour?

We see then: the means of production and of exchange,
on whose foundation the bourgeoisie built itself up, were
generated in feudal society. At a certain stage in the
development of these means of production and of exchange,
the conditions under which feudal society produced and
exchanged, the feudal organization of agriculture and
manufacturing industry, in one word, the feudal relations
of property became no longer compatible with the already
developed productive forces; they became so many fetters.
They had to be burst asunder; they were burst asunder.

Into their place stepped free competition, accompanied
by a social and political constitution adapted to it, and by
the economic and political sway of the bourgeois class.

A similar movement is going on before our own eyes.
Modern bourgeois society with its relations of production,
of exchange and of property, a society that has conjured
up such gigantic means of production and of exchange, is
like the sorcerer who is no longer able to control the powers
of the nether world whom he has called up by his spells.
For many a decade past the history of industry and commerce is but the history of the revolt of modern productive
forces against modern conditions of production, against the
property relations that are the conditions for the existence
of the bourgeoisie and of its rule.

CM (1848)
MEGA I/6, pp. 529–31

What does the primitive accumulation of capital, i.e. its historical genesis, resolve itself into? In so far as it is not a direct transformation of slaves and serfs into wage-labourers, and therefore a mere change of form, it only means the expropriation of the immediate producers, i.e. the dissolution of private property based on the labour of its owner.

Private property, as the antithesis to social, collective property, exists only where the means of labour and external conditions of labour belong to private individuals. But according as these private individuals are labourers or not labourers, private property has a different character. The innumerable shades, that it at first sight presents, correspond to the intermediate stages lying between these two extremes. The private property of the labourer in his means of production is the foundation of petty industry, and petty industry is an essential condition for the development of social production and of the free individuality of the labourer himself. Of course, this petty mode of production exists also under slavery, serfdom, and other states of dependence. But it flourishes, it lets loose its whole energy, it attains its full classical form, only where the labourer is the private owner of the means of labour which he uses; the peasant of the land which he cultivates, the artisan of the tool which he handles as a virtuoso. This mode of production presupposes parcelling out of the soil, and of the other means of production. As it excludes the concentration of these means of production, so also it excludes co-operation, division of labour within each separate process of production, the control over, and the productive application of, the forces of Nature by society, and the free development of the social productive powers. It is only compatible with a primitive and limited society and system of production. To perpetuate it would be, as Pecqueur rightly says, " to decree universal mediocrity." At a certain stage of develop-

ment it brings forth the material agencies for its own dissolution. From that moment new forces and new passions
spring up in the bosom of society; but the old social organization fetters them and keeps them down. It must be
annihilated; it is annihilated. Its annihilation, the transformation of the individualized and scattered means of
production into socially concentrated ones, of the pigmy
property of the many into the huge property of the few, the
expropriation of the great mass of the people from the soil,
from the means of subsistence, and from the means of
labour, this fearful and painful expropriation of the mass of
the people forms the prelude to the history of capital. It
comprises a series of forcible measures, of which we have
passed in review only those that have been epoch-making
as methods of the primitive accumulation of capital. The
expropriation of the immediate producers was accomplished
with merciless vandalism, and under the stimulus of
the most infamous, sordid, petty, and odious passions. Self-
earned private property that is based, so to say, on the
fusing together of the isolated, independent labouring-
individual with the conditions of his labour, is supplanted
by capitalist private property, which rests on exploitation
of the nominally free labour of others.

As soon as this process of transformation has sufficiently
decomposed the old society from top to bottom, as soon as
the labourers are turned into proletarians, and their means
of labour into capital, as soon as the capitalist mode of production stands on its own feet, then the further socialization
of labour and further transformation of the land and other
means of production into socially exploited and, therefore,
common means of production, as well as the further expropriation of private proprietors, takes a new form. That
which is now to be expropriated is no longer the labourer
working for himself, but the capitalist exploiting many
labourers. This expropriation is accomplished by the

action of the immanent laws of capitalist production itself, by the centralization of capital. One capitalist always kills many. Hand in hand with this centralization, this expropriation of many capitalists by few, develop, on an ever-extending scale, the co-operative form of the labour process, the conscious application of science, the planned exploitation of the earth, the transformation of the instruments of labour into instruments which can only be used in co-operative work, the economizing of all means of production by their use as the means of production of combined, socialized labour, the entanglement of all peoples in the net of the world-market, and with this, the international character of the capitalist system. Along with the constantly diminishing number of the magnates of capital, who usurp and monopolize all the advantages of this process of transformation, grows the mass of misery, oppression, slavery, degradation, and exploitation; but with this too grows the revolt of the working-class, a class always increasing in numbers, and disciplined, united, organized by the mechanism of the process of capitalist production itself. The monopoly of capital becomes a fetter upon the mode of production, which has sprung up and flourished along with, and under it. Centralization of the means of production and socialization of labour at last reach a point where they become incompatible with their capitalist integument. This integument is burst asunder. The knell of capitalist private property sounds. The expropriators are expropriated.

The capitalist mode of appropriation, the result of the capitalist mode of production, produces capitalist private property. This is the first negation of individual private property, as founded on the labour of the proprietor. But capitalist production begets, with the inexorability of a law of Nature, its own negation. It is the negation of negation. This does not re-establish private property for the producer, but gives him individual property based on the acquisitions of the capitalist era: i.e., on co-operation and the possession in common of the land and of the means of production which are produced by labour.

The transformation of scattered private property, arising from individual labour, into capitalist private property is, of course, a process incomparably more protracted, violent, and difficult, than the transformation of capitalist private property, which already is in fact based upon socialized production, into socialized property. In the former case, we had the expropriation of the mass of the people by a few usurpers; in the latter, we have the expropriation of a few usurpers by the mass of the people.

Capital I (1867)
VA, pp. 801–4

It is enough to mention the commercial crises that by their periodical return put on its trial, each time more threateningly, the existence of the entire bourgeois society. In these crises a great part not only of the existing products, but also of the previously created productive forces, are periodically destroyed. In these crises there breaks out an epidemic that, in all earlier epochs, would have seemed an absurdity—the epidemic of over-production. Society suddenly finds itself put back into a state of momentary barbarism; it appears as if a famine, a universal war of devastation had cut off the supply of every means of subsistence; industry and commerce seem to be destroyed. And why? Because there is too much civilization, too much means of subsistence, too much industry, too much commerce. The productive forces at the disposal of society no longer tend to further the development of the conditions of bourgeois property; on the contrary, they have become too powerful for these conditions, by which they are fettered, and so soon as they overcome these fetters, they bring disorder into the whole of bourgeois society, endanger the existence of bourgeois property. The conditions of bourgeois society are too narrow to comprise the wealth created by them. And how does the bourgeoisie get over these crises? On the one hand, by enforced destruction of a mass of productive forces; on the other, by the conquest of new markets, and by the more thorough exploitation of the old ones. That is to say, by paving the way for more extensive and more destructive crises, and by diminishing the means whereby crises are prevented.

CM (1848)
MEGA I/6, pp. 531–2

It is not the case that too much wealth is produced. But it is true that there is periodical over-production of wealth in its capitalist and self-contradictory form.

The limitations of the capitalist mode of production become apparent:

1. In the fact that the development of the productive power of labour establishes, in the falling rate of profit, a law which becomes, at a certain point, hostile to this mode of production itself and which can only be overcome by periodical crises.

2. In the fact that the expansion or contraction of production is decided by the appropriation of unpaid labour and by the proportion of this unpaid labour to materialized labour in general, or in the language of the capitalists, by profit and by the proportion of this profit to the employed capital, by a definite rate of profit, instead of being determined by the relation of production to social needs, to the needs of socially developed human beings. Consequently, the capitalist mode of production reaches its limits at a level of production which would be wholly inadequate in terms of

the second presupposition (production for needs). It comes to a standstill at a point determined by the production and realization of profit, not by the satisfaction of human needs.

Capital III
VA III/1, pp. 287–8

The real limitation upon capitalist production is *capital itself*. It is the fact that capital and its self-expansion are the beginning and end, the motive and aim of production; that production is regarded as production for *capital*, instead of the means of production being considered simply as means for extending the conditions of human life for the benefit of the *society* of producers. The limits within which the preservation and augmentation of the value of capital, which is based upon the expropriation and pauperization of the great mass of producers, must take place, are always conflicting with the methods of production which capital must employ to attain its ends. These methods lead directly towards an unlimited expansion of production, towards production for its own sake, towards an unconditional development of the productive forces of society. The means, the unconditional development of the productive forces of society, enter continually into conflict with the limited end, the self-expansion of the existing capital. Thus while the capitalist mode of production is one of the historical means by which the material forces of production are developed and by which the world market which they imply is created, it represents at the same time a perpetual contradiction between this historical task and the social relations of production which it establishes.

Capital III
VA III/1, pp. 278–9

The three principal aspects of capitalist production are:

1. The concentration of means of production into a few hands, as a result of which they are no longer the property of the direct producers but are transformed into social powers of production. It is true that they become, at first, the private property of capitalists. These are the trustees of bourgeois society, but they pocket the proceeds of their trusteeship.

2. The organization of labour itself as social labour, by co-operation, division of labour, and the union of labour with the natural sciences.

   From both sides the capitalist mode of production abolishes private property and private (individual) labour, though it does so in an antagonistic form.

3. The creation of a world market.

The immense productive power, relative to population, which develops under the capitalist mode of production and the increase, though not in the same proportion, of capital values (not only their material substance), which grow much more rapidly than the population, are in contradiction with with the basis of this immense productive power, a basis which is always shrinking in comparison with the growing mass of wealth. They are in contradiction also with the conditions under which capital increases its value. This is the cause of crises.

Capital III
VA III/1, pp. 295–6

The ultimate cause of all real crises is always the poverty and restricted consumption of the masses, in contrast with the tendency of capitalist production to develop the productive forces in such a way that only the absolute power of consumption of society would be their limit.

Capital III
VA III/2, p. 528

II. THE SOCIAL SYSTEM OF CAPITALISM

CAPITAL consists of raw materials, instruments of labour, and means of subsistence of all kinds, which are employed in producing new raw materials, new instruments of labour, and new means of subsistence. All these components of capital are created by labour, products of labour, *accumulated labour*. Accumulated labour that serves as a means to new production is capital. So say the economists.

What is a negro slave? A man of the black race. The one explanation is worthy of the other.

A negro is a negro. Only under certain conditions does he become a *slave*. A cotton-spinning machine is a machine for spinning cotton. Only under certain conditions does it become *capital*. Torn away from these conditions, it is as little capital as *gold* by itself is *money*, or as sugar is the *price* of sugar.

In the process of production, human beings do not only enter into a relation with Nature. They produce only by working together in a specific manner and by reciprocally exchanging their activities. In order to produce, they enter into definite connections and relations with one another, and only within these social connections and relations does their connection with Nature, i.e. production, take place.

These social relations between the producers, and the conditions under which they exchange their activities and share in the total act of production, will naturally vary according to the character of the means of production. With the discovery of a new instrument of warfare, the fire-arm, the whole internal organization of the army was necessarily altered, the relations within which individuals compose an army and can act as an army were transformed, and the relation of different armies to one another was likewise changed.

The social relations within which individuals produce, *the social relations of production, are altered, transformed, with the change and development of the material means of production, of the forces of production. The relations of production in their totality constitute what is called the social relations, society,* and, moreover, a society at a definite stage of historical development, a society with a unique and distinctive character. Ancient society, feudal society, bourgeois (or capitalist) society, are such totalities of relations of production, each of which denotes a particular stage of development in the history of mankind.

Capital also is a social relation of production. It is a *bourgeois relation of production*, a relation of production of bourgeois society. The means of subsistence, the instruments of labour, the raw materials, of which capital consists —have they not been produced and accumulated under given social conditions, within definite social relations? Are they not employed for new production, under given social conditions, within definite social relations? And does not just this definite social character stamp the products which serve for new production as *capital*?

Capital consists not only of means of subsistence, instruments of labour, and raw materials, not only of material products: it consists just as much of *exchange values*. All products of which it consists are *commodities*. Capital, consequently, is not only a sum of material products, it is a sum of commodities, of exchange values, of social magnitudes.

WLC (1849)
MEGA I/6, pp. 482–3

Capital therefore presupposes wage-labour; wage-labour presupposes capital. They condition each other; each brings the other into existence.

WLC (1849)
MEGA I/6, p. 485

How then does a sum of commodities, of exchange values, become capital?

By the fact that, as an independent social power, i.e. as the power of a *part of society*, it preserves itself and multiplies by *exchange with immediate, living labour-power*.

The existence of a class which possesses nothing but the ability to work is a necessary presupposition of capital.

It is only the dominion of past, accumulated, materialized labour over immediate living labour that transforms accumulated labour into capital.

Capital does not consist in the fact that accumulated labour serves living labour as a means for new production. It consists in the fact that living labour serves accumulated labour as the means of preserving and multiplying its exchange value.

What is it that takes place in the exchange between capitalist and wage-labourer?

The labourer receives means of subsistence in exchange for his labour-power; but the capitalist receives, in exchange for his means of subsistence, labour, the productive activity of the worker, the creative force by which the worker not only replaces what he consumes, but also gives to the accumulated labour a greater value than it previously possessed. The worker gets from the capitalist a portion of the existing means of subsistence. For what purpose do these means of subsistence serve him? For immediate consumption. But as soon as I consume means of subsistence, they are irrevocably lost to me, unless I employ the time during which these means sustain my life in producing new means of subsistence, in creating by my labour new values in place of the values lost in consumption. But it is just this noble reproductive power that the worker surrenders to the capitalist in exchange for means of subsistence received. Consequently, he has lost it for himself.

WLC (1849)
MEGA I/6, pp. 484–5

But does wage-labour create any property for the labourer? Not a bit. It creates capital, i.e. that kind of property which exploits wage-labour, and which cannot increase except upon condition of begetting a new supply of wage-labour for fresh exploitation. Property, in its present form, is based on the antagonism of capital and wage-labour. Let us examine both sides of this antagonism. To be a capitalist, is to have not only a purely personal, but a social, *status* in production. Capital is a collective product, and only by the united action of many members, nay, in the last resort, only by the united action of all members of society, can it be set in motion. Capital is therefore not a personal, it is a social power. When, therefore, capital is converted into common property, into the property of all members of society, personal property is not thereby transformed into social property. It is only the social character of the property that is changed. It loses its class character.

CM (1848)
MEGA I/6, p. 539

If, then, capitalist management has two aspects by reason of the twofold nature of the process of production itself,—which, on the one hand, is a social process for producing use-values, on the other, a process for creating surplus-value —in form it is despotic. As co-operation extends its scale, this despotism assumes particular forms. Just as, at first, the capitalist is relieved from manual labour so soon as his capital has reached that minimum amount with which real capitalist production begins, so now, he hands over the work of direct and constant supervision of the individual workman, and groups of workmen, to a special kind of wage-labourer. An industrial army of workmen, under the command of a capitalist, requires, like a real army, officers (managers), and sergeants (foremen, overlookers), who exercise authority on behalf of the capitalist during the labour process. The work of supervision becomes their established and exclusive function. When comparing the mode of production of independent peasants and artisans with production by slave labour, the political economist counts this labour of superintendence among the *faux frais* of production. But when considering the capitalist mode of production, he, on the contrary, treats the work of management made necessary by the co-operative character of the labour process as identical with the different work of control, necessitated by the capitalist character of that process and the conflict of interests between capitalist and labourer. It is not because he is an industrial manager that a man is a capitalist; on the contrary, he is an industrial manager because he is a capitalist. The management of industry is an attribute of capital, just as in feudal times the functions of general and judge were attributes of landed property.

Capital I (1867)
VA I, pp. 347–8

The labour of superintendence and management will naturally be required whenever the direct process of production assumes the form of a combined social process, and does not rest on the isolated labour of independent producers. It has, however, a twofold character.

On the one hand, all work in which many individuals co-operate, necessarily requires for the co-ordination and unity of the process a directing will, and functions which are not concerned with fragmentary operations but with the total activity of the workshop, similar to those of the conductor of an orchestra. This is a kind of productive labour which must be performed in every mode of co-operative production.

On the other hand, this labour of superintendence necessarily arises in all modes of production which are based on the antagonism between the worker as a direct producer and the owner of the means of production. The greater this antagonism the more important is the role played by superintendence. Hence it reaches its maximum in a slave system.[1] But it is indispensable also under the capitalist mode of production, since the process of production is at the same time the process by which the capitalist consumes the labour power of the worker. In the same way, in despotic States, the labour of superintendence and universal interference by the government comprises both the discharge of community affairs, the need for which arises in all societies, and the specific functions arising from the antagonism between the government and the mass of the people.

In the works of ancient writers, who have the slave system before their eyes, both sides of the labour of superintendence are as inseparably combined in theory as they were in practice. So it is, also, in the works of the modern economists, who regard the capitalist mode of production as an absolute mode of production. On the other hand, . . . the apologists of the modern slave system know how to utilize the labour of superintendence to justify slavery just as well as the other economists use it to justify the wage system. . . .

The labour of management and superintendence, not as a function resulting from the nature of all co-operative social labour, but as a consequence of the antagonism between the owner of means of production and the owner of mere labour-power (whether this labour-power is bought by buying the labourer himself, as it is under the slave system, or whether the labourer himself sells his labour-power so that the process of production is the process by which capital consumes his labour-power), as a function resulting from the servitude of the direct producers, has often been quoted in

[1] Marx here quotes, in a footnote, J. E. Cairnes, *The Slave Power*, 1862.

justification of this relation of servitude itself.   And exploitation, the appropriation of the unpaid labour of others, has quite as often been represented as the reward justly due to the owner of capital for his labour. . . .

Now the wage-labourer, like the slave, must have a master who will put him to work and rule him.   And once this relation of master and servant has been presupposed, it is quite proper to compel the wage-labourer to produce his own wages and also the wages of superintendence, a compensation for the labour of ruling and superintending him, " a just compensation for his master in return for the labour and talents devoted to ruling him and to making him useful to himself and to society." [1]

The labour of superintendence and management arising from the antagonistic character and the rule of capital over labour which all modes of production based on class antagonism have in common with the capitalist mode, is directly and inseparably connected, under the capitalist system also, with those particular productive functions which are entailed by all co-operative social labour of individuals. The wages of an *epitropos*, or *régisseur* as he used to be called in feudal France, are entirely differentiated from the profit, and assume the form of wages for skilled labour whenever the business is operated on a sufficiently large scale to warrant paying such a manager, although our industrial capitalists do not " attend to affairs of State or study philosophy " for all that.

It has already been remarked by Mr Ure [2] that the industrial managers, and not the industrial capitalists, are " the soul of our industrial system " . . . The capitalist mode of production itself has brought matters to such a

[1] Quoted from a speech reported in *New York Daily Tribune*, December 20, 1859.
[2] Andrew Ure (1778–1857) was a chemist and scientific author, who published in 1835 his *Philosophy of Manufactures*, concerned with the conditions of factory workers.

point that the labour of superintendence, entirely separated from the ownership of capital, walks the streets. It is therefore no longer necessary for the capitalist to perform the labour of superintendence himself. The conductor of an orchestra need not be the owner of the instruments of its members, nor is it part of his function as a conductor that he should have anything to do with the *wages* of the other musicians. The co-operative factories furnish the proof that the capitalist has become just as superfluous as a functionary in production as he himself, in his highest developed form, finds the large landowner superfluous. To the extent that the labour of the capitalist is not the purely capitalistic one arising from the process of production and ceasing with capital itself, to the extent that it is not limited to the function of exploiting the labour of others, to the extent that it arises from the social form of the labour process as a combination and co-operation of many for the purpose of bringing about a common result, to that extent it is just as independent of capital as that form itself, as soon as it has burst its capitalistic shell. . . .

The wages of management, both for the commercial and the industrial manager, are entirely separated from the profits of enterprise in the workers' co-operative factories as well as in capitalist joint-stock companies. The separation of the wages of management from the profits of enterprise which in other cases appears accidental, is here constant. In the co-operative factory the antagonistic character of the labour of superintendence disappears, since the manager is paid by the labourers instead of representing capital against them. The joint-stock companies in general, developed with the credit system, have a tendency to separate the function of management more and more from the ownership of capital, whether it be self owned or borrowed. In the same way, in the development of civil society the functions of judge and administrator are separated from feudal property whose prerogatives they were in feudal times. But as the mere owner of capital, the money capitalist is confronted by the investing capitalist, while money capital itself assumes a social character with the development of credit, being concentrated in banks and loaned by them instead of by its original owners, while on the other hand the mere manager, who has no title whatever to the capital whether by borrowing or otherwise, performs all the real functions of the investing capitalist as such; only the functionary remains and the capitalist disappears from the process of production as a superfluous person. . . .

On the basis of capitalist production a new swindle develops in joint-stock enterprises in connection with the wages of management. It consists in placing alongside and above the real manager a board of managers or directors for whom superintendence and management are in practice only a pretext for plundering the shareholders and enriching themselves.

Capital III
VA III/1, pp. 418–26

Manufacture, in fact, produces the skill of the specialized labourer, by reproducing, and systematically driving to an extreme within the workshop, the naturally developed differentiation of trades, which it found ready to hand in society at large. On the other hand, the conversion of subdivided work into the life-calling of an individual, corresponds to the tendency shown by earlier societies, to make trades hereditary; either to petrify them into castes, or whenever particular historical conditions give rise to individual variability incompatible with a caste system, to ossify them into guilds. Castes and guilds arise from the action of the same natural law that regulates the differentiation of plants and animals into species and sub-species, except that, when a certain degree of development has been reached, the hereditary nature of castes and the exclusiveness of guilds are decreed as a social law.

Capital I (1867)
VA I, pp. 355–6

This [1] is the abolition of the capitalist mode of production within capitalist production itself, a self-destructive contradiction which is prima facie only a phase of transition to a new form of production. It manifests its contradictory nature by its effects. It establishes a monopoly in certain spheres and thereby invites the intervention of the State. It reproduces a new aristocracy of finance, a new variety of parasites in the shape of promoters, speculators and merely nominal directors; a whole system of swindling and cheating by means of company promoting, stock jobbing, and speculation. It is private production without the control of private property.

Capital III
VA III/1, pp. 479–80

We have seen that the capitalist process of production is a historically determined form of the social process of production in general. This process is, on the one hand, a process by which the material requirements of human life are produced, and on the other hand, a process which takes place under specific historical and economic conditions of production and which produces and reproduces these conditions of production themselves, and with them the human agents of this process, their material conditions of existence and their mutual relations, that is, their particular economic form of society. For the aggregate of the relations in which the agents of this production stand to Nature and to each other, and within which they produce, is precisely society, considered from the point of view of its economic structure. Like all its predecessors, the capitalist process of production

---

[1] The joint-stock company.

develops under definite material conditions which are at the same time the bearers of definite social relations into which individuals enter in the process of producing their life's requirements. These conditions and relations are, on the one hand, prerequisites, on the other hand, results and creations, of the capitalist process of production. They are produced and reproduced by it. We have also seen that capital (the capitalist is merely capital personified and functions in the process of production as the agent of capital), in the social process of production corresponding to it, pumps a certain quantity of surplus labour out of the direct producer, the worker, surplus labour for which no equivalent is returned and which always remains essentially forced labour, no matter how much it may seem to be the result of a freely concluded contract. This surplus labour is represented by a surplus value, and this surplus value is embodied in a surplus product. Surplus labour generally, in the sense of a quantity of labour beyond that required to satisfy existing needs, there must always be. But in the capitalist system as in the slave system, etc., it has an antagonistic form and is complemented by the complete idleness of a section of society. A certain quantity of surplus labour is required in order to meet various contingencies, as well as for the necessary, progressive expansion of the process of reproduction (called accumulation from the point of view of the capitalist) in accordance with the development of needs and the increase of population. It is one of the civilizing aspects of capital that it imposes this surplus labour in a manner and under conditions which are more favourable to the development of the productive forces, and of social relations, and to the creation of the elements for a new and higher social structure than was the case in the preceding forms of slavery, serfdom, etc. Thus it leads on the one hand to a stage in which coercion and the monopolization of social development (including its material and intellectual advantages) by one section of society at the expense of the other section are eliminated; on the other hand it creates the material requirements and the germ of conditions which, in a higher form of society, make it possible to combine this surplus labour with a greater reduction of the time devoted to material labour. For, according to the development of the productive power of labour, the amount of surplus labour may be large in a short working day and relatively small in a long working day.

Capital III
VA III/2, pp. 871–3

Most writers who have attacked Adam Smith's theory of productive and unproductive labour, regard consumption as the necessary stimulus to production, and employers who live upon revenues, the unproductive workers, as being just as productive as the productive workers themselves, because they extend the limits of material consumption and consequently of production.

In general, however, from the viewpoint of bourgeois economics, these were mere apologetics either for the idle rich and the " unproductive workers," or for " powerful governments " which spent money hand over fist in order to increase the national debt, to create new sinecures in the State and rich livings in the Church. For these "unproductive workers," whose services are calculated among the expenses of the idle rich, all have this in common : that while producing only " immaterial products " they consume " material products," that is, the products of the productive workers. Other economists, Malthus among them, concede the distinction between productive and unproductive workers but prove to the industrial capitalist that the second are as necessary as the first, even for the production of material wealth.

TM I, pp. 376–7

According to Storch,[1] doctors produce health (but also illness), professors and writers produce enlightenment (but also obscurantism), poets, painters etc., produce good taste (but also lack of taste), moralists produce good manners, priests produce worship, the labour of the sovereign produces security, etc. . . . One could just as well say that illness produces doctors, stupidity produces professors and writers, lack of taste produces poets and painters, immorality produces moralists, superstition produces priests, and general insecurity produces sovereigns. This way of saying that all these activities and services produce a real or imaginary use value has been seized upon by Storch's successors in order to demonstrate that these workers are productive workers in Adam Smith's sense of the term, i.e. not that they directly create products but that they contribute to producing the products of material labour and therefore produce wealth.

TM I, p. 384

A philosopher produces ideas, a poet verses, a parson sermons, a professor text-books, etc. A criminal produces crime. But if the relationship between this latter branch of production and the whole productive activity of society is examined a little more closely one is forced to abandon a number of prejudices. The criminal produces not only crime but also the criminal law; he produces the professor who delivers lectures on this criminal law, and even the inevitable text-book in which the professor presents his lectures as a commodity for sale in the market. There results an increase in material wealth, quite apart from the pleasure which . . . the author himself derives from the manuscript of this text-book.

Further, the criminal produces the whole apparatus of

[1] Heinrich Storch (1766–1835), a Russian economist whose *Cours d'économie politique*, St Petersburg 1815, was a criticism of Adam Smith and especially of the latter's discussion of unproductive labour.

the police and criminal justice, detectives, judges, executioners, juries, etc., and all these different professions, which constitute so many categories of the social division of labour, develop diverse abilities of the human spirit, create new needs and new ways of satisfying them. Torture itself has provided occasions for the most ingenious mechanical inventions, employing a host of honest workers in the production of these instruments.

The criminal produces an impression now moral, now tragic, and renders a " service " by arousing the moral and æsthetic sentiments of the public. He produces not only text-books on criminal law, the criminal law itself, and thus legislators, but also art, literature, novels and the tragic drama, as *Œdipus* and *Richard III*, as well as Mullner's *Schuld* and Schiller's *Räuber*, testify. The criminal interrupts the monotony and security of bourgeois life. Thus he protects it from stagnation and brings forth that restless tension, that mobility of spirit without which the stimulus of competition would itself become blunted. He therefore gives a new impulse to the productive forces. Crime takes off the labour market a portion of the excess population, diminishes competition among workers, and to a certain extent stops wages from falling below the minimum, while the war against crime absorbs another part of the same population. The criminal therefore appears as one of those natural " equilibrating forces " which establish a just balance and open up a whole perspective of " useful " occupations. The influence of the criminal upon the development of the productive forces can be shown in detail. Would the locksmith's trade have attained its present perfection if there had been no thieves? Would the manufacture of banknotes have arrived at its present excellence if there had been no counterfeiters? Would the microscope have entered ordinary commercial life (cf. Babbage) had there been no forgers? Is not the development of applied chemistry as much due to the adulteration of wares, and to the attempts to discover it, as to honest productive effort? Crime, by its ceaseless development of new means of attacking property calls into existence new measures of defence, and its productive effects are as great as those of strikes in stimulating the invention of machines.

Leaving the sphere of private crime, would there be a world market, would nations themselves exist, if there had not been national crimes? Is not the tree of evil also the tree of knowledge, since the time of Adam?

In his *Fable of the Bees* (1708) Mandeville already demonstrated the productivity of all the English occupations, and anticipated our argument.

" What we call Evil in this World, Moral as well as Natural, is the grand Principle that makes us sociable Creatures, the solid Basis, the Life and Support of all Trades and Employments without Exception: That there we must look for the true Original of all Arts and Sciences, and that the Moment Evil ceases, the Society must be spoiled if not totally dissolved."

Mandeville simply had the merit of being infinitely more audacious and more honest than these narrow-minded apologists for bourgeois society.

TM I, pp. 385-7

III. THE IDEOLOGY OF CAPITALISM

THE apparent absurdity which transforms all the various interrelationships of men into the single relationship of utility, an apparently metaphysical abstraction, follows from the fact that in modern civil society all relationships are in practice subordinated to the single abstract relationship of money and speculation. This theory made its appearance, with Hobbes and Locke, at the time of the first and second English revolutions, the first blows with which the bourgeoisie conquered political power for itself. With the economic writers it is, of course, at a still earlier period, an implicit assumption. The real science of this theory of utility is political economy; in the Physiocrats it receives a genuine content, for they were the first to present political economy in a systematic way. In Helvétius and Holbach there is already an idealization of this theory, which accurately reflects the oppositional attitude of the bourgeoisie before the French Revolution. Holbach represents every activity of individuals in their reciprocal intercourse, e.g. speech, love, etc., as a relation of utility and exploitation. The real relations, which are here presupposed, are therefore speech, love, etc., i.e. specific manifestations of specific individual qualities. These relations are thus not allowed to have their *own significance* but are depicted as the expression and representation of a third relation which underlies them, *utility or exploitation*. This *paraphrase* only ceases to be senseless and arbitrary when these individual relations no longer have value on their own account, as personal activity, but only as a disguise . . . for a real third purpose and relationship, which is called the relation of utility. The linguistic masquerade only has sense when it is the conscious or unconscious expression of a real masquerade. In this case the relation of utility has a very definite meaning, namely that I profit myself when I harm someone else (*exploitation de l'homme par l'homme*). Further, in this case, the profit which I gain from a relation is altogether alien to this relation, as we saw earlier in the case of natural abilities, since from every ability there is demanded a product which has nothing in common with it. It is a relation determined by social conditions and this is the relation of utility. All this is actually the case for the bourgeois. Only one relationship counts for him; that of exploitation. Other relationships only count in so far as he can subsume them under this relationship, and even when he is confronted with relationships which cannot be directly subsumed under this one, at least he subordinates them in illusion. The material expression of this exploitation is money, which represents the value of all objects, men and social relations. For the rest, it can be seen at first glance that it is out of the real relations of intercourse, in which I stand to other men, and not at all out of reflection and will, that the category of utility is abstracted. The real relations are then asserted as the reality derived from this category, a wholly speculative method. In the same way and with the same justification Hegel represented all relations as relations of the objective spirit. Holbach's theory is therefore the historically justified, philosophical, illusion about the rising bourgeoisie in France, whose desire for exploitation could still be represented as the desire for the full development of the individual in a form of social intercourse liberated from the old feudal bonds. Emancipation as the bourgeoisie understood it, competition, was in any case the only possible way in the eighteenth century to open up a new path of free development for individuals. The theoretical enunciation of this consciousness of bourgeois practice, the consciousness of reciprocal exploitation as the general relationship of individuals to one another, was also a clear and bold advance, a secular enlightenment, compared with the political, patriarchal, religious and "cosy" façade for exploitation under feudalism; a façade which corresponded with the existing form of exploitation and was systematized in particular by the writers of the absolute monarchy.

.   .   .   .   .

The progress of the theory of utility and exploitation and its different phases are correlated with the different periods of development of the bourgeoisie. In Helvétius and Holbach, so far as real content was concerned, it had not gone far beyond paraphrasing the expressions of writers from the period of absolute monarchy. It was a new form of expression, more a wish to reduce all relationships to the relationship of exploitation, and to explain social intercourse from material needs and the modes of satisfying them, than the achievement of this aim. The task was only formulated. Hobbes and Locke had before their eyes the earlier development of the Dutch bourgeoisie (both of them lived for a time in Holland), as well as the first political events by which the bourgeoisie in England emerged from its local and provincial limits, and a relatively advanced stage of manufacture, maritime commerce, and colonization. In particular, this was true of Locke, who wrote during the period in which the joint-stock companies, the English banking system, and England's maritime supremacy were established. Thus, in these writers, and especially in Locke, the theory of exploitation is still directly bound up with an economic content. Helvétius and Holbach had before them, apart from the English theory and the previous development of the Dutch and English bourgeoisie, the French bourgeoisie still struggling for freedom of development. In particular, the universal commercial spirit of the eighteenth century had seized all classes in France, in the form of speculation. The financial affairs of the government and the consequent discussions of taxation already engaged the attention of the whole of France. Moreover, Paris was in the eighteenth century the only world city, a city in which personal intercourse between individuals of all countries took place. These features, together with the more universal outlook of Frenchmen generally, gave the theory of Helvétius and Holbach a unique universal aspect, but at the same time eliminated from it the positive economic content which it still retained among the English writers. A theory which, among the English writers, was the simple recognition of a fact, became in the French writers a philosophical system. This universality, stripped of its positive content, as it appears in Helvétius and Holbach, is essentially different from the totality, rich in content, which first appears with Bentham and Mill. The former corresponds with the struggling, still undeveloped bourgeoisie, the latter with the dominant, developed bourgeoisie. The content of the theory of exploitation which Helvétius and Holbach had neglected was, contemporaneously with the latter, developed and systematized by the Physiocrats. Since however they based themselves on the undeveloped economic conditions of France, where feudalism, which made landownership the most important feature, was still unbroken, they remained entangled in the feudal outlook and explained landownership and agricultural labour as the productive force which determines the whole structure of society. The later development of the theory of exploitation in England was accomplished by Godwin, and above all by Bentham, who reintroduced the economic content of the theory which had been neglected by the French writers. This took place at the same time as the bourgeoisie in England and in France asserted itself. Godwin's *Political Justice* was written during the period of the " Terror," while Bentham's principal works appeared during and after the French Revolution and contemporaneously with the development of large-scale industry in England. The complete union of the theory of utility with political economy is found in Mill.

Political economy, which in earlier periods had been treated by financiers, bankers and merchants, i.e. by people who were directly concerned with economic affairs, or by individuals of universal culture, such as Hobbes, Locke, and Hume, for whom its significance was that of a branch of encyclopædic knowledge, was first raised to the level of a special science by the Physiocrats, and has since been treated as such. As a special science political economy absorbed the remaining political, juridical relations into itself only so far as they could be reduced to economic relations. This subsumption of other relations under the economic relation was however recognized to be only one side of such relations, which were also accorded an independent significance outside the sphere of political economy. The complete subsumption of all existing relations under the relation of utility, the apotheosis of this relation of utility as the sole content of all other relations, first appears in Bentham, when, after the French Revolution and the development of large-scale industry, the bourgeoisie ceases to be a particular, limited class and emerges as the class whose demands are the demands of the whole of society.

After the sentimental and moralizing paraphrases, which formed the whole content of the theory of utility among the French, had been exhausted, there remained for the further development of this theory only a single question to answer: How are individuals and relationships to be used, to be exploited? The answer to this question had meanwhile already been given in political economy; the only possible advance now lay in the incorporation of this economic content. Bentham accomplished this advance. In political economy, however, it was already asserted that the principal relations of exploitation were independent of the will of individuals, were on the whole determined by production and were found already in existence by the individuals. There remained, therefore, for the theory of utility, no other area of speculation but the situation of individuals with regard to these major relationships, the private exploitation of an existing world by these individuals. Bentham and his school devoted much moral reflection to this problem. The whole criticism of the existing world by the theory of utility thus received a limited field of expression. Entangled in the conditions of the bourgeoisie, there remained for criticism only those relationships which had survived from a previous period and which stood in the way of bourgeois development. As a result, the theory of utility certainly analysed the connection of all the existing relationships with the economic one, but only in a limited fashion. The theory of utility has from the outset the character of a theory of general utility; this character acquired significance only with the incorporation of economic relations, especially the division of labour and exchange. Within the division of labour the private activity of the individual becomes of general utility; Bentham's general utility reduces itself to this latter, which is supposed to exist in competition. By the incorporation of economic relations such as rent, profit and wages, the specific relations of exploitation of the various social classes were brought in, since the type of exploitation depends upon the life situation of the exploiter. Up to this time, the theory of utility could attach itself to specific social facts; its further scrutiny of the types of exploitation ended in pious phrases. The economic significance gradually changes the theory of utility into a mere apology of what exists; into a demonstration that under the existing conditions the present relations between men are the most advantageous and in the general interest. It has this character in all the recent economists.

GI (1845–6)
MEGA I/5, pp. 387–92

IV. CAPITALISM AND HUMAN ALIENATION

POLITICAL economy begins with the fact of private property; it does not explain it. It conceives the processes of private property, as these occur in reality, in general and abstract formulas which then serve it as laws. It does not understand these laws; that is, it does not show how they arise out of the nature of private property. Political economy provides no explanation of the basis of the distinction of labour from capital, of capital from land. When, for example, the relation of wages to profit is defined, this is explained in terms of the interests of capitalists; in other words, what should be explained is assumed. Similarly, competition is referred to at every point, and is explained in terms of external conditions. Political economy tells us nothing about the extent to which these external and apparently accidental conditions are simply the expression of a necessary development. We have seen how exchange itself seems an accidental fact. The only moving forces which political economy recognizes are the *lust for gain* and the *war between seekers after gain, competition.*

Just because political economy fails to understand the interconnections within this movement, it was possible to oppose the doctrine of competition to that of monopoly, the doctrine of freedom of the crafts to that of the guilds, the doctrine of the division of landed property to that of great estates, for competition, freedom of the crafts, and the division of landed property were conceived only as accidental consequences brought about by will and force, rather than as necessary, inevitable, and natural consequences of monopoly, the guild system, and feudal property.

EPM (1844)
MEGA I/3, pp. 81–2

. . . political economy considers the *proletarian*, i.e. the individual who, without capital or ground rent, lives entirely by his labour (a narrow, abstract labour), only as a *worker*.   It is able, therefore, to assert that the proletarian, just like a horse, need only receive so much as enables him to work.   It does not consider him in his leisure time, as a human being, but leaves such consideration to the magistrate, doctors, religion, statistical tables, politics, and the parish beadle.

Let us now place ourselves at a level above that of political economy, and try to answer, from the preceding arguments given almost in the words of the economists, two questions: (1) What is the significance, in the development of humanity, of this reduction of the greater part of mankind to mere abstract labour?   (2) What errors do the reformers commit who want either to *raise* wages in order to improve the condition of the working class, or (like Proudhon) want to consider *equal* wages as the aim of the social revolution?

Labour appears in political economy only in the form of *acquisitive activity*.

EPM (1844)
MEGA I/3, pp. 45-6

The relation of the worker to work also produces the relation of the capitalist (or whatever one likes to call the lord of labour) to work. *Private property* is therefore the product, the necessary result, of *alienated labour*, of the external relation of the worker to Nature and to himself. . . .

We have, however, derived the concept of *alienated labour* (*alienated life*) from political economy, from an analysis of the *movement of private property*.   But the analysis of this concept shows that although private property appears to be the basis and cause of alienated labour, it is rather a consequence of the latter, just as the gods are *fundamentally* not the cause but the product of confusions of human reason. At a later stage there is, however, a reciprocal influence.

EPM (1844)
MEGA I/3, pp. 91-2

Every alienation of man from himself and from Nature appears in the relation which he postulates between other men and himself and Nature.   Thus religious alienation is necessarily exemplified in the relation between laity and priest, or, since it is here a question of the spiritual world, between the laity and a mediator.   In the real world of practice, this self alienation can only be expressed in the real, practical relation of man to his fellow men.   The medium through which alienation occurs is itself a practical one. Through alienated labour, therefore, man not only produces his relation to the object, and to the process of production as alien and hostile men; he also produces the relation of other men to his production and his product, and the relation between himself and other men.

EPM (1844)
MEGA I/3, p. 91

However, alienation shows itself not merely in the result, but also in the *process, of production,* within *productive activity* itself. . . .

In what does this alienation of labour consist?   First, that the work is *external* to the worker, that it is not a part of his nature, that consequently he does not fulfil himself in his work but denies himself, has a feeling of misery, not of well-being, does not develop freely a physical and mental energy, but is physically exhausted and mentally debased.   The worker therefore feels himself at home only during his leisure, whereas at work he feels homeless.   His work is not voluntary but imposed, *forced labour*.   It is not the satisfaction of a need, but only a *means* for satisfying other needs.

Its alien character is clearly shown by the fact that as soon as there is no physical or other compulsion it is avoided like the plague. Finally, the alienated character of work for the worker appears in the fact that it is not his work but work for someone else, that in work he does not belong to himself but to another person.

Just as in religion the spontaneous activity of human fantasy, of the human brain and heart, reacts independently, that is, as an alien activity of gods or devils, upon the individual, so the activity of the worker is not his spontaneous activity. It is another's activity, and a loss of his own spontaneity.

EPM (1844)
MEGA I/3, pp. 85–6

The more the worker expends himself in work, the more powerful becomes the world of objects which he creates in face of himself, and the poorer he himself becomes in his inner life, the less he belongs to himself. It is just the same as in religion. The more of himself man attributes to God, the less he has left in himself. The worker puts his life into the object, and his life then belongs no longer to him but to the object. The greater his activity, therefore, the less he possesses. What is embodied in the product of his labour is no longer his. The greater this product is, therefore, the more he himself is diminished. The *alienation* of the worker in his product means not only that his labour becomes an object, takes on its own existence, but that it exists outside him, independently, and alien to him, and that it stands opposed to him as an autonomous power. The life which he has given to the object sets itself against him as an alien and hostile force.

EPM (1844)
MEGA I/3, pp. 83–4

The object produced by labour, its product, now stands opposed to it as an *alien being*, as a *power independent* of the producer. The product of labour is labour which has been embodied in an object, and turned into a physical thing; this product is an *objectification* (*Vergegenständlichung*) of labour. The performance of work is at the same time its objectification. This performance of work appears, in the sphere of political economy, as a *vitiation* of the worker, objectification as a *loss* and as *servitude to the object*, and appropriation as *alienation*.

EPM (1844)
MEGA I/3, p. 83

Political economy conceives the *social life of men*, their active *human* life, their many-sided growth towards a communal and genuinely human life, under the form of *exchange* and *trade*. *Society*, says Destutt de Tracy, is *a series of multilateral exchanges*. It *is* this movement of multilateral integration. According to Adam Smith, *society* is a *commercial enterprise*. Every one of its members is a *salesman*. It is evident how political economy establishes an *alienated* form of social intercourse, as the *true and original* form, and that which corresponds to human nature.

Economic Studies from Marx's Notebooks (1844–45)
MEGA I/3, pp. 536–7

Mill's description of *money* as the *intermediary* of exchange is an excellent conceptualization of its nature. The nature of money is not, in the first place, that in it property is alienated but that the *mediating activity* of *human* social action by which man's products reciprocally complete each other, is *alienated* and becomes the characteristic of a *material thing*, money, which is external to man. When man exteriorizes this mediating activity he is active only as an exiled and dehumanized being; the *relation* between things, and human activity with them, becomes the activity of a being outside and above man. Through this *alien intermediary*—whereas man himself should be the intermediary between men— man sees his will, his activity and his relation to others as a power which is independent of him and of them. His slavery therefore attains its peak. That this *intermediary* becomes a *real god* is clear, since the intermediary is the *real power* over that which he mediates to me. His cult becomes an end in itself. The objects, separated from this inter- mediary, have lost their value. Thus they only have value in so far as they represent it, whereas it seemed originally that it only had value in so far as it represented them. This reversal of the original relationship is inevitable. This *intermediary* is thus the exiled, alienated *essence* of private property, *exteriorized* private property, just as it is the *alienated exchange* of human production with human pro- duction and the *alienated* social activity of man. All the qualities involved in the production of this activity, which really belong to man, are attributed to the intermediary. Man himself becomes poorer, that is, separated from this intermediary, as the intermediary becomes *richer*.

Economic Studies from Marx's Notebooks (1844–45)
MEGA I/3, p. 531

Money, since it has the *property* of purchasing everything, of appropriating objects to itself, is therefore the *object par excellence*. The universal character of this *property* corre- sponds to the omnipotence of money, which is regarded as an omnipotent essence . . . money is the *pander* between need and object, between human life and the means of subsistence. But *that which* mediates my life, mediates also the existence of other men for me. It is for me the *other* person. . . .

"Gold? yellow, glittering, precious gold? No, gods,
I am no idle votarist: roots, you clear heavens!
Thus much of this will make black white; foul, fair;
Wrong, right; base, noble; old, young; coward, valiant.
. . . . Why, this
Will lug your priests and servants from your sides;
Pluck stout men's pillows from below their heads:
This yellow slave
Will knit and break religions; bless th'accurst;
Make the hoar leprosy ador'd; place thieves,
And give them title, knee, and approbation,
With senators on the bench: this is it
That makes the wappen'd widow wed again;
She, whom the spital-house and ulcerous sores
Would cast the gorge at, this embalms and spices
To th'April day again. Come, damned earth,
Thou common whore of mankind, that putt'st odds
Among the rout of nations, I will make thee
Do thy right nature."

      (*Timon of Athens*, Shakespeare)
           EPM (1844)
         MEGA I 3, pp. 145–6

Shakespeare attributes to money two qualities:

1. It is the visible deity, the transformation of all human and natural qualities into their opposite, the universal confusion and inversion of things; it brings incompatibles into fraternity.

2. It is the universal whore, the universal pander between men and nations.

The power to confuse and invert all human and natural qualities, to bring about fraternization of incompatibles, the *divine power* of money, resides in its *essence* as the alienated and exteriorized species-life of men. It is the alienated *power of humanity*.

What I as a *man* am unable to do, what therefore all my individual faculties are unable to do, is made possible for me by means of *money*. Money therefore turns each of these faculties into something which in itself it is not, into its *opposite*.

           EPM (1844)
         MEGA I/3, pp. 147–8

The division of labour implies from the outset the division of the *prerequisites of labour*, tools and materials, and thus the partitioning of accumulated capital among different owners. This also involves the separation of capital and labour and the different forms of property itself. The more the division of labour develops and accumulation increases, the more sharply this differentiation emerges.

Two facts are revealed here. In the first place, the productive forces appear to be completely independent and severed from the individuals and to constitute a self-subsistent world alongside the individuals. The reason for this is that the individual, whose forces they are, themselves exist separated and in opposition to one another, while on the other hand these forces are only real forces in the intercourse and association of these individuals. Thus there is on the one hand a sum of productive forces which have, as it were, assumed a material form and which are for the individuals concerned the forces, not of these individuals, but of private property, and consequently of the individuals only in so far as they are owners of private property. Never, in any earlier period, did the productive forces assume a form so indifferent to the intercourse of individuals as individuals, because in these periods their intercourse was still limited. On the other hand, confronting these productive forces is the majority of individuals from whom these forces have been sundered and who, robbed in this way of all the real substance of life, have become abstract individuals, but who by this very fact are enabled to enter into relation with each other as individuals.

The only connection which they still have with the productive forces and with their own existence, labour, has lost for them any semblance of personal activity, and sustains their life only while stunting it. While in the earlier periods personal activity and the production of material life were separated in that they devolved upon different persons, and while the production of material life because of the limitations of the individuals themselves was still regarded as a subordinate kind of personal activity, they now diverge to such an extent that material life generally appears as the aim while the production of this material life, labour (which is now the only possible but, as we have seen, negative form of personal activity) appears as the means.

GI (1845–6)
MEGA I/5, pp. 56–7

. . . the mutual relations of the producers, within which the social character of their labour affirms itself, take the form of a social relation between the products.

The mystery of the commodity form, therefore, consists in the fact that in it the social character of men's labour appears to them as an objective characteristic, a social natural quality of the labour product itself, and that consequently the relation of the producers to the sum total of their own labour is presented to them as a social relation, existing not between themselves, but between the products of their labour. Through this transference the products of labour become commodities, social things whose qualities are at the same time perceptible and imperceptible by the senses. In the same way the light from an object is perceived by us not as the subjective excitation of our optic nerve, but as the objective form of something outside the eye itself. But, in the act of seeing, there is at all events, an actual passage of light from one thing to another, from the external object to the eye. There is a physical relation between physical things. But it is different with commodities. The commodity form, and the value relation between the products of labour which stamps them as commodities, have absolutely no connection with their physical properties and with the material relations arising therefrom. It is simply a definite social relation between men, that assumes, in their eyes, the fantastic form of a relation between things. To find an analogy, we must have recourse to the nebulous regions of the religious world. In that world the productions of the human brain appear as independent beings endowed with life, and entering into relation both with one another and with the human race. So it is, in the world of commodities, with the products of men's hands. This I call the fetishism which attaches itself to the products of labour, so soon as they are produced as commodities, and which is therefore inseparable from the production of commodities.

This fetishism of commodities has its origin, as the foregoing analysis has already shown, in the peculiar social character of the labour that produces them.

Capital I (1867)
VA I, pp. 77–8

We have seen that the money-form is only the reflection, in a single commodity, of the value relations between all commodities. That money is a commodity is, therefore, a new discovery only for those who, when they analyse it, start from its fully developed form. The process of exchange gives to the commodity which is converted into money, not its value, but its specific value-form. By confounding these two distinct things some writers have been led to hold that the value of gold and silver is imaginary. The fact that money can, in certain functions, be replaced by mere symbols of itself, gave rise to that other mistaken notion, that it is itself a mere symbol. Nevertheless, behind this error lurked a presentiment that the money-form of an object is not an inseparable part of that object, but is simply the form under which certain social relations manifest themselves. In this sense every commodity is a symbol, since, in so far as it is a value, it is only the material envelope of the human labour spent upon it. But while it is asserted that the social characteristics assumed by objects, or the material forms assumed by the social qualities of labour on the basis of a definite mode of production, are mere symbols, it is at the same time asserted that these characteristics are arbitrary fictions produced by human imagination. This was the mode of explanation in favour during the eighteenth century. Unable to account for the origin of the puzzling forms assumed by the social relations between men, people sought to deprive them of their strange appearance by ascribing to them a conventional origin.

Capital I (1867)
VA I, pp. 96–7

It follows, from the relation between alienated labour and private property, that the emancipation of society from private property, from servitude, takes the political form of the *emancipation of the working class*, not in the sense that only the latter's emancipation is involved, but because this emancipation includes the emancipation of humanity as a whole. For all human servitude is involved in the relation of the worker to production, and all the types of servitude are only modifications or consequences of this relation.

EPM (1844)
MEGA I/3, pp. 92–3

V. SOCIAL CLASSES AND CLASS CONFLICT

THE owners of mere labour-power, the owners of capital, and the landowners, whose respective sources of income are wages, profit, and rent of land, or in other words, wage-labourers, capitalists and landowners, form the three great classes of modern society based on the capitalist mode of production.

The economic structure of modern society is indisputably most highly and classically developed in England. But even here the class structure does not appear in a pure form. Intermediate and transitional strata obscure the class boundaries even in this case, though very much less in the country than in the towns. However, this is immaterial for our analysis. We have seen that the constant tendency, the law of development of the capitalist mode of production, is to separate the means of production increasingly from labour, and to concentrate the scattered means of production more and more into large aggregates, thereby transforming labour into wage-labour and the means of production into capital. There corresponds to this tendency, in a different sphere, the independent separation of landed property from capital and labour, or the transformation of all landed property into a form which corresponds with the capitalist mode of production.

The first question to be answered is—what constitutes a class? The answer can be found by answering another question: What constitutes wage-labourers, capitalists and landlords as the three great social classes?

At first glance it might seem that the identity of revenues and of sources of revenue is responsible. The classes are three great social groups whose components, the individual members, live from wages, profit and rent respectively, that is, from the utilization of their labour-power, capital and landed property.

However, from this point of view, doctors and officials would also form two distinct classes, for they belong to two different social groups, and the revenues of the members of each group come from the same source. The same would also be true of the infinite distinctions of interest and position which the social division of labour creates among workers as among capitalists and landowners; in the latter case, for instance, between owners of vineyards, farms, forests, mines, and fisheries. . . .

(*Manuscript ends*)

Capital III
VA (III/2), pp. 941-2

It is not a *radical* revolution, *universal human* emancipation, which is a Utopian dream for Germany, but rather a partial, *merely* political revolution which leaves the pillars of the building standing. What is the basis of a partial, merely political revolution? Simply this; *a fraction of civil society* emancipates itself and achieves a dominant position, a certain class undertakes, from its *particular situation*, a general emancipation of society. This class emancipates society as a whole, but only on condition that the whole of society is in the same situation as this class, for example, that it possesses or can acquire money or culture.

No class in civil society can play this part unless it can arouse, in itself and in the masses, a moment of enthusiasm in which it associates and mingles with society in general, identifies itself with it, and is felt and recognized as the *general representative* of this society. Its aims and interests must genuinely be the aims and interests of society itself, of which it becomes in fact the social head and heart. It is only in the name of general interests that a particular class can claim general supremacy. In order to attain this liberating position and the political direction of all spheres of society, revolutionary energy and consciousness of its own power do not suffice. For a *popular revolution* and the *emancipation of a particular class* of civil society to coincide, for *one* class to represent the whole of society, another class must concentrate in itself all the evils of society, a particular class must embody and represent a general obstacle and limitation. A particular social sphere must be regarded as the *notorious crime* of the whole society, so that emancipation from this sphere appears as a general emancipation. For *one* class to be the liberating class *par excellence*, it is essential that another class should be openly the oppressing class. The negative significance of the French nobility and clergy produced the positive significance of the bourgeoisie, the class which stood next to them and opposed them.

But every class in Germany lacks the logic, insight, courage and clarity, which would make it a negative representative of society. Moreover, there is also lacking in every class the generosity of spirit which identifies itself, if only for a moment, with the popular mind, that genius which pushes material force to political power, that revolutionary daring which throws at its adversary the defiant phrase, *I am nothing and I should be everything*. The essence of German morality and honour, in classes as in individuals, is a *modest egoism* which displays and allows others to display, its own narrowness. The relation between the different spheres of German society is therefore not dramatic, but epic. Each of these spheres begins to be aware of itself and to establish itself at the side of the others, not from the moment when it is oppressed, but from the moment that circumstances, without any action of its own, have created a new sphere which it can in turn oppress. Even *the moral sentiment of the German middle class* has no other basis than the consciousness of being the representative of the narrow and limited mediocrity of all the other classes. It is not therefore only the German kings who ascend their thrones *mal à propos*; each sphere of civil society suffers a defeat before gaining the victory; it erects its own barrier before having destroyed the barrier which opposes it; it displays the 'narrowness of its views before having displayed their generosity, and thus every opportunity of playing an important role has passed before it properly existed, and each class, at the very moment when it begins its struggle against the class above it, remains involved in a struggle against the class beneath. For this reason, the princes are in conflict with the monarch, the bureaucracy with the nobility, the bourgeoisie with all of them, while the proletariat is already beginning its struggle with the bourgeoisie. The middle class hardly dares to conceive the idea of emancipation from its own point of view before the development of social conditions, and the progress of political theory, show that this point of view is already antiquated, or at least disputable.

In France it is enough to be something in order to desire to be everything. In Germany no one has the right to be anything without first renouncing everything. In France partial emancipation is a basis for complete emancipation. In Germany complete emancipation is a *conditio sine qua non* for any partial emancipation. In France it is the reality, in Germany the impossibility, of a progressive emancipation which must give birth to complete liberty. In France every class of the population is *politically idealistic* and considers itself first of all, not as a particular class, but as the representative of the general needs of society. The role of *liberator* can therefore pass successively in a dramatic movement to different classes in the population, until it finally reaches the class which achieves social freedom, no longer assuming certain conditions external to man, which are none the less created by human society, but organizing all the conditions of human life on the basis of social freedom. In Germany, on the contrary, where practical life is as little intellectual as intellectual life is practical, no class of civil society feels the need for, or the ability to achieve, a general emancipation, until it is forced to it by its *immediate* situation, by *material* necessity and by its *fetters themselves*.

Where is there, then, a *real* possibility of emancipation in Germany?

This is our reply. A class must be formed which has *radical chains*, a class in civil society which is not a class of civil society, a class which is the dissolution of all classes, a sphere of society which has a universal character because its sufferings are universal, and which does not claim a *particular redress* because the wrong which is done to it is not a *particular wrong* but *wrong in general*. There must be formed a sphere of society which claims no *traditional* status but only a *human* status, a sphere which is not opposed to particular consequences but is totally opposed to the assumptions of the German political system, a sphere finally which cannot emancipate itself without emancipating itself from all the other spheres of society, without therefore emancipating all these other spheres, which is, in short, a *total loss* of humanity and which can only redeem itself by a *total redemption of humanity*. This dissolution of society, as a particular class, is the *proletariat*.

The proletariat is only beginning to form itself in Germany as a result of the industrial movement. For what constitutes the proletariat is not *naturally existing* poverty, but poverty *artificially produced*, is not the mass of people mechanically oppressed by the weight of society but the mass resulting from the *disintegration* of society, and above all from the disintegration of the middle class. Needless to say, however, the numbers of the proletariat are also increased by the victims of natural poverty and of Teutonic-Christian serfdom.

When the proletariat announces the *dissolution of the existing social order*, it only declares the *secret of its own existence*, for it constitutes the *effective* dissolution of this order. When the proletariat demands the *negation of private property* it only lays down as a *principle for society* what society has already made a principle *for the proletariat* and what the *latter* involuntarily embodies already as the negative result of society. Thus the proletarian has the same right, in relation to the new world which is coming into being, as the *German king* has in relation to the existing world when he calls the people *his* people or a horse *his* horse. In calling the people his private property, the king simply declares that the owner of private property is king.

Just as philosophy finds its *material* weapons in the proletariat so the proletariat finds its *intellectual* weapons in philosophy. And once the lightning of thought has penetrated deeply into this virgin soil of the people, the *Germans* will emancipate themselves and become *men*.

Let us sum up these results. The emancipation of Germany is only possible *in practice* if one adopts the point of view of that theory according to which man is the highest being for man. Germany will not be able to emancipate itself from the *Middle Ages* unless it emancipates itself at the same time from the *partial* victories over the Middle Ages. In Germany *no* type of enslavement can be abolished unless *all* enslavement is destroyed. Germany, which likes to get to the bottom of things, can only make a revolution which upsets the whole order of things. *The emancipation of Germany will be an emancipation of man.* *Philosophy* is the *head* of this emancipation and the *proletariat* is its *heart*. Philosophy can only be realized by the abolition of the proletariat, and the proletariat can only be abolished by the realization of philosophy.

KHR (1844)

MEGA I/1/1, pp. 617–21

The proletariat goes through various stages of development. With its birth begins its struggle with the bourgeoisie. At first the contest is carried on by individual labourers, then by the workpeople of a factory, then by the operatives of one trade, in one locality, against the individual bourgeois who directly exploits them. They direct their attacks not against the bourgeois conditions of production, but against the instruments of production themselves; they destroy imported wares that compete with their labour, they smash to pieces machinery, they set factories ablaze, they seek to restore by force the vanished status of the workman of the Middle Ages.

At this stage the labourers still form an incoherent mass scattered over the whole country, and broken up by their mutual competition. If anywhere they unite to form more compact bodies, this is not yet the consequence of their own active union, but of the union of the bourgeoisie, which class, in order to attain its own political ends, is compelled to set the whole proletariat in motion, and is moreover yet, for a time, able to do so. At this stage, therefore, the proletarians do not fight their enemies, but the enemies of their enemies, the remnants of absolute monarchy, the landowners, the non-industrial bourgeois, the petty bourgeoisie. Thus the whole historical movement is concentrated in the hands of the bourgeoisie; every victory so obtained is a victory for the bourgeoisie.

But with the development of industry the proletariat not only increases in number; it becomes concentrated in greater masses, its strength grows and it feels that strength more. The various interests and conditions of life within the ranks of the proletariat are more and more equalized, in proportion as machinery obliterates all distinctions of labour, and nearly everywhere reduces wages to the same low level. The growing competition among the bourgeois, and the resulting commercial crises, make the wages of the workers ever more fluctuating. The unceasing improvement of machinery, ever more rapidly developing, makes their livelihood more and more precarious; the collisions between individual workmen and individual bourgeois take more and more the character of collisions between two classes. Thereupon the workers begin to form combinations (trades unions) against the bourgeois; they club together in order to keep up the rate of wages; they found permanent associations in order to make provision beforehand for these occasional revolts. Here and there the contest breaks out into riots.

Now and then the workers are victorious, but only for a time. The real fruit of their battles lies, not in the immediate result, but in the ever expanding union of the workers. This union is helped on by the improved means of communication that are created by modern industry, and that place the workers of different localities in contact with one another. It was just this contact that was needed to centralize the numerous local struggles, all of the same character, into one national struggle between classes. But every class struggle is a political struggle. And that union, to attain which the burghers of the Middle Ages, with their miserable highways, required centuries, the modern proletarians, thanks to railways, achieve in a few years.

This organization of the proletarians into a class, and consequently into a political party, is continually being upset again by the competition between the workers themselves. But it ever rises up again, stronger, firmer, mightier. It compels legislative recognition of particular interests of the workers, by taking advantage of the divisions among the bourgeoisie itself. Thus the Ten Hours Bill in England was carried.

Altogether, collisions between the classes of the old society further in many ways the course of development of the proletariat. The bourgeoisie finds itself involved in a constant battle. At first with the aristocracy; later on, with those portions of the bourgeoisie itself, whose interests have become antagonistic to the progress of industry; at all times with the bourgeoisie of foreign countries. In all these battles it sees itself compelled to appeal to the proletariat, to ask for its help, and thus, to drag it into the political arena. The bourgeoisie itself, therefore, supplies the proletariat with its own elements of political and general education, in other words, it furnishes the proletariat with weapons for fighting the bourgeoisie.

Further, as we have already seen, entire sections of the ruling classes are, by the advance of industry, precipitated into the proletariat, or are at least threatened in their conditions of existence. These also supply the proletariat with fresh elements of enlightenment and progress.

Finally, in times when the class struggle nears the decisive hour, the process of dissolution going on within the ruling class, in fact within the whole range of old society, assumes such a violent, glaring character, that a small section of the ruling class cuts itself adrift, and joins the revolutionary class, the class that holds the future in its hands. Just as, therefore, at an earlier period, a section of the nobility went over to the bourgeoisie, so now a portion of the bourgeoisie goes over to the proletariat, and in particular, a portion of the bourgeois ideologists, who have raised themselves to the level of comprehending theoretically the historical movement as a whole.

CM (1848)
MEGA I/6, pp. 533–5

Large-scale industry assembles in one place a crowd of people who are unknown to each other. Competition divides their interests. But the maintenance of their wages, this common interest which they have against their employer, brings them together again in the same idea of resistance—

combination. Thus combination has always a double aim, that of putting an end to competition among themselves, to enable them to compete as a whole with the capitalist. If the original aim of resistance was that of maintaining wages, to the extent that the capitalists, in their turn, unite with the aim of repressive measures, the combinations, at first isolated, become organized into groups, and in face of the unity of the capitalists, the maintenance of the combination becomes more important than upholding the level of wages. This is so true that English economists have been astonished to observe the workers sacrificing a substantial part of their wages in favour of the associations, which in the eyes of the economists were only established to defend wages. In this struggle—a veritable civil war—all the elements for a future battle are brought together and developed. Once arrived at this point the association takes on a political character.

Economic conditions had in the first place transformed the mass of the people into workers. The domination of capital created the common situation and common interests of this class. Thus this mass is already a class in relation to capital, but not yet a class for itself. In the struggle, of which we have only indicated a few phases, this mass unites and forms itself into a class for itself. The interests which it defends become class interests. But the struggle between classes is a political struggle.

In the bourgeoisie, two stages can be distinguished; that in which it formed itself into a class under the feudal system and absolute monarchy, and that in which, already formed into a class, it overthrew feudalism and the monarchy, in order to turn society into bourgeois society. The first of these stages was the longest and required the greatest efforts. The bourgeoisie also began with partial combinations, directed against the feudal lords.

Many researches have been undertaken to trace the

historical stages through which the bourgeoisie passed, from the Commune up to its constitution as a class. But when it is a question of gaining a clear understanding of the strikes, combinations, and other forms in which the proletarians are achieving, before our eyes, their organization as a class, some are seized with genuine fear, while others display a *transcendental* disdain.

PP (1847)
MEGA I/6, pp. 226-7

The lower strata of the middle class—the small tradespeople, shopkeepers, and retired tradesmen generally, the handicraftsmen and peasants—all these sink gradually into the proletariat, partly because their diminutive capital does not suffice for the scale on which modern industry is carried on, and is swamped in the competition with the large capitalists, partly because their specialized skill is rendered worthless by new methods of production. Thus the proletariat is recruited from all classes of the population.

CM (1848)
MEGA I/6, p. 533

The small-holding peasants form a vast mass, the members of which live in similar conditions but without entering into manifold relations with one another. Their mode of production isolates them from one another instead of bringing them into mutual intercourse. . . . In so far as millions of families live under economic conditions of existence that separate their mode of life, their interests and their culture from those of the other classes, and put them in hostile opposition to the latter, they form a class. In so far as there is merely a local interconnection among these small-holding peasants, and the identity of their interests begets no community, no national bond and no political organization among them, they do not form a class.

18th Brumaire (1852)

The immediate result of machinery is to augment surplus-value and the mass of products in which surplus-value is embodied. And, as the substances consumed by the capitalists and their dependants become more plentiful, so these social strata increase in numbers. Their growing wealth, and the relatively diminished number of workmen required to produce the necessaries of life lead both to the rise of new and luxurious wants, and to new means of satisfying those wants. . . .

Lastly, the extraordinary productiveness of modern industry, accompanied as it is by a more extensive and a more intensive exploitation of labour-power in all other spheres of production, allows of the unproductive employment of a larger and larger part of the working class, and the consequent reproduction, on a constantly extending scale, of the ancient domestic slaves under the name of a "servant class," including men-servants, women-servants, lackeys, etc. According to the census of 1861, the population of England and Wales was 20,066,224; of these 9,776,259 were males and 10,289,965 females. If we deduct from this population all who are too old or too young for work, all unproductive women, young persons and children, the "ideological" classes, such as government officials, priests, lawyers, soldiers, etc., further, all who have no occupation but to consume the labour of others in the form of rent, interest, etc., and, lastly, paupers, vagabonds, and criminals, there remain in round numbers eight millions of the two sexes of every age, including in that number every capitalist who is in any way engaged in industry, commerce, or finance. . . .

All the persons employed in textile factories and in mines,

taken together, number 1,208,442; those employed in textile factories and metal industries, taken together, number 1,039,605; in both cases less than the number of modern domestic slaves. What a splendid result of the capitalist exploitation of machinery!

Capital I (1867)
VA I, pp. 468–70

This circumstance, that a man without wealth, but with energy, strength of character, ability and business sense, is able to become a capitalist, is greatly admired by the economic apologists of capitalism, since it shows that the commercial value of each individual is more or less accurately estimated under the capitalist mode of production. Although this situation continually brings an unwelcome number of new soldiers of fortune into the field, and into competition with the existing individual capitalists, it also consolidates the rule of capital itself, enlarges its basis, and enables it to recruit ever new forces for itself out of the lower layers of society. In a similar way the circumstance that the Catholic Church in the Middle Ages formed its hierarchy with the best brains from among the people, without regard to estate, birth or wealth, was one of the principal means of consolidating priestly rule and the subordination of the laity. The more a ruling class is able to assimilate the most prominent men of the dominated classes the more stable and dangerous is its rule.

Capital III
VA III/2, pp. 648–9

What (Ricardo) forgets to mention is the continual increase in numbers of the middle classes, ... situated midway between the workers on one side and the capitalists and landowners on the other. These middle classes rest with all their weight upon the working class and at the same time increase the social security and power of the upper class.

TM II/2, p. 368

Up to 1846 the Tories passed as the guardians of the traditions of Old England. They were suspected of admiring in the British Constitution the eighth wonder of the world, to be *laudatores temporis acti*, enthusiasts for the throne, the High Church, the privileges and liberties of the British subject. The fatal year, 1846, with its repeal of the Corn Laws, and the shout of distress which this repeal forced from the Tories, proved that they were enthusiasts for nothing but the rent of land, and at the same time disclosed the secret of their attachment to the political and religious institutions of Old England. These institutions are the very best institutions, with the help of which the *large landed property*— the landed interest—has hitherto ruled England, and even now seeks to maintain its rule. The year 1846 brought to light in its nakedness *substantial class interest* which forms the *real base* of the Tory party. The year 1846 tore down the traditionally venerable lion's hide, under which Tory class interest had hitherto hidden itself. The year 1846 transformed the Tories into *Protectionists*. Tory was the sacred name, Protectionist is the profane one; Tory was the political battle-cry, Protectionist is the economical shout of distress; Tory seemed an idea, a principle; Protectionist is an interest. Protectionists of what? Of their own revenues, of the rent of their own land. Then the Tories, in the end, are Bourgeois as much as the remainder, for where is the Bourgeois who is not a protectionist of his own purse? They are distinguished from the other Bourgeois, in the same way as the rent of land is distinguished from commercial and industrial profit. Rent of land is conservative, profit is progressive; rent of land is national, profit is cosmopolitical; rent of land believes in the State

Church, profit is a dissenter by birth. The repeal of the
Corn Laws of 1846 merely recognized an already accomplished fact, a change long since enacted in the elements of
British civil society, viz. the subordination of the landed
interest under the monied interest, of property under commerce, of agriculture under manufacturing industry, of the
country under the city. Could this fact be doubted since
the country population stands, in England, to the town's
population in the proportion of one to three? The substantial foundation of the power of the Tories was the rent
of land. The rent of land is regulated by the price of food.
The price of food, then, was artificially maintained at a
high rate by the Corn Laws. The repeal of the Corn Laws
brought down the price of food, which in its turn brought
down the rent of land, and with sinking rent broke down the
real strength upon which the political power of the Tories
reposed.

What, then, are they trying to do now? To maintain a
political power, the social foundation of which has ceased to
exist. And how can this be attained? By nothing short of
a *Counter-Revolution*, that is to say, by a reaction of the State
against Society. They strive to retain forcibly institutions
and a political power which are condemned from the very
moment at which the rural population found itself out-
numbered three times by the population of the towns.
And such an attempt must necessarily end with their destruction; it must accelerate and make more acute the social
development of England; it must bring on a crisis.

The Tories recruit their army from the farmers, who have
either not yet lost the habit of following their landlords as
their natural superiors, or who are economically dependent
upon them, or who do not yet see that the interest of the
farmer and the interest of the landlord are no more identical
than the respective interests of the borrower and of the
usurer. They are followed and supported by the Colonial

Interest, the Shipping Interest, the State Church Party, in short, by all those elements which consider it necessary to safeguard their interests against the necessary results of modern manufacturing industry, and against the social revolution prepared by it.

Opposed to the Tories, as their hereditary enemies, stand the *Whigs*, a party with whom the American Whigs have nothing in common but the name.

The British Whig, in the natural history of politics, forms a species which, like all those of the amphibious class, exists very easily, but is difficult to describe. Shall we call them, with their opponents, Tories out of office? or, as continental writers love it, take them for the representatives of certain *popular* principles? In the latter case we should get embarrassed in the same difficulty as the historian of the Whigs, Mr Coke, who, with great naïvete, confesses in his *History of Parties* that it is indeed, a certain number of " liberal, moral and enlightened principles " which constitutes the Whig party, but that it was greatly to be regretted that during the more than a century and a half that the Whigs have existed, they have been, when in office, always prevented from carrying out these principles. So that in reality, according to the confession of their own historian, the Whigs represent something quite different from their professed " liberal and enlightened principles." Thus they are in the same position as the drunkard brought up before the Lord Mayor, who declared that he represented the Temperance principle, but from some accident or other always got drunk on Sundays.

But never mind their principles; we can better make out what they are in historical fact; what they carry out, not what they once believed, and now what they want other people to believe with respect to their character.

The Whigs as well as the Tories, form a fraction of the large landed property of Great Britain. Nay, the oldest,

richest and most arrogant portion of English landed property
is the very nucleus of the Whig party.

What, then, distinguishes them from the Tories? The
Whigs are the *aristocratic representatives* of the Bourgeoisie, of
the industrial and commercial middle class. Under the
condition that the Bourgeoisie should abandon to them, to
an oligarchy of aristocratic families, the monopoly of
government and the exclusive possession of office, they
make to the middle class, and assist it in conquering, all
those concessions which in the course of social and political
development have shown themselves to have become *unavoidable* and *undelayable*. Neither more nor less. And as
often as such an unavoidable measure has been passed, they
declare loudly that herewith the end of historical progress
has been obtained; that the whole social movement has
carried its ultimate purpose, and then they " cling to
finality." They can support more easily than the Tories, a
decrease of their rental revenues, because they consider
themselves as the heaven-born farmers of the revenues of the
British Empire. They can renounce the monopoly of the
Corn Laws, as long as they maintain the monopoly of government as their family property. Ever since the "glorious
revolution " of 1688 the Whigs, with short intervals, caused
principally by the first French revolution and the consequent
reaction, have found themselves in the enjoyment of the
public offices. Whoever recalls to his mind this period of
English history, will find no other distinctive mark of Whig-
dom but the maintenance of their family oligarchy. The
interests and principles which they represent besides, from
time to time, do not belong to the Whigs; they are forced upon
them by the development of the industrial and commercial
class, the Bourgeoisie. After 1688 we find them united with
the Bankocracy, just then rising into importance, as we find
them in 1846, united with the Millocracy. The Whigs as
little carried the Reform Bill of 1831, as they carried the

Free Trade Bill of 1846. Both Reform movements, the political as well as the commercial, were movements of the Bourgeoisie. As soon as either of these movements had ripened into irresistibility; as soon as, at the same time, it had become the safest means of turning the Tories out of office, the Whigs stepped forward, took up the direction of the Government, and secured to themselves the governmental part of the victory. In 1831 they extended the political portion of reform as far as was necessary in order not to leave the middle class entirely dissatisfied; after 1846 they confined their free trade measures so far as was necessary, in order to save to the landed aristocracy the greatest possible amount of privileges. Each time they had taken the movement in hand in order to prevent its forward march, and to recover their own posts at the same time.

It is clear that from the moment when the landed aristocracy is no longer able to maintain its position as an independent power, to fight, as an independent party, for the government position, in short, that from the moment when the Tories are definitively overthrown, British history has no longer any room for the Whigs. The aristocracy once destroyed, what is the use of an aristocratic representation of the Bourgeoisie against this aristocracy?

It is well known that in the Middle Ages the German Emperors put the just then arising towns under Imperial Governors, " *advocati*," to protect these towns against the surrounding nobility. As soon as growing population and wealth gave them sufficient strength and independence to resist, and even to attack the nobility, the towns also drove out the noble Governors, the *advocati*.

The Whigs have been these *advocati* of the British Middle Class, and their governmental monopoly must break down as soon as the landed monopoly of the Tories is broken down. In the same measure as the Middle Class has developed its independent strength, they have shrunk down from a party to a coterie.

It is evident what a distastefully heterogeneous mixture the character of the British Whigs must turn out to be; Feudalists, who are at the same time Malthusians, money-mongers with feudal prejudices, aristocrats without point of honour, Bourgeois without industrial activity, finality men with progressive phrases, progressists with fanatical Conservatism, traffickers in homœopathical fractions of reforms, fosterers of family nepotism, Grand Masters of corruption, hypocrites of religion, Tartuffes of politics. The mass of the English people have a sound æsthetical common sense. They have an instinctive hatred against everything motley and ambiguous, against bats and Russellites. And then, with the Tories, the mass of the English people, the urban and rural proletariat, has in common the hatred against the " money-monger." With the Bourgeoisie it has in common the hatred against aristocrats. In the Whigs it hates the one and the other, aristocrats and Bourgeois, the landlord who oppresses, and the money-lord who exploits it. In the Whig it hates the oligarchy which has ruled over England for more than a century, and by which the People is excluded from the direction of its own affairs.

The Peelites (liberals and conservatives) are no party; they are merely the *souvenir* of a party man, of the late Sir Robert Peel. But Englishmen are too prosaical for a *souvenir* to form, with them, the foundation for anything but elegies. And now that the people have erected brass and marble monuments to the late Sir R. Peel in all parts of the country, they believe they are able so much the more to do without those perambulant Peel monuments, the Grahams, the Gladstones, the Cardwells, etc. The so-called Peelites are nothing but this staff of bureaucrats which Robert Peel had schooled for himself. And because they form a pretty complete staff, they forget for a moment that there is no army behind them. The Peelites, then, are old supporters of Sir R. Peel, who have not yet come to a conclusion as to what party to attach themselves to. It is evident that a similar scruple is not a sufficient means for them to constitute an independent power.

" The Elections—Tories and Whigs "

NYDT August 21, 1852

While the Tories, the Whigs, the Peelites—in fact, all the parties we have hitherto commented. upon—belong more or less to the past, the Free Traders (the men of the Manchester School, the Parliamentary and Financial Reformers), are the *official representatives of modern English society*, the representatives of that England which rules the market of the world. They represent the party of the self-conscious Bourgeoisie, of industrial capital striving to make available its social power as a political power as well, and to eradicate the last arrogant remnants of feudal society. This party is led on by the most active and most energetic portion of the English Bourgeoisie—the *manufacturers*. What they demand is the complete and undisguised ascendancy of the Bourgeoisie, the open, official subjection of society at large under the laws of modern, bourgeois production, and under the rule of those men who are the directors of that production. By Free Trade they mean the unfettered movement of capital, freed from all political, national and religious shackles. The soil is to be a marketable commodity, and the exploitation of the soil is to be carried on according to the common commercial laws. There are to be manufacturers of food as well as manufacturers of twist and cottons, but no longer any lords of the land. There are, in short, not to be tolerated any political or social restrictions, regulations or monopolies, unless they proceed from " the eternal laws of political economy," that is, from the conditions under which Capital produces and distributes. The struggle of this party against the old English institutions, products of a superannuated, an evanescent stage of social development, is resumed in the watchword: *Produce as cheap as you can, and do away with all the faux frais of production*, (with all superfluous, unnecessary expenses in production). And this watchword is addressed not only to the private individual, but to the *nation at large* principally.

Royalty, with its " barbarous splendours," its court, its civil list and its flunkeys—what else does it belong to but to the *faux frais* of production? The nation can produce and exchange without royalty; away with the crown. The sinecures of the nobility, the House of Lords?—*faux frais* of production. The large standing army?—*faux frais* of production. The State Church, with its riches, the spoils of plunder or of mendicity?—*faux frais* of production. Let parsons compete freely with each other, and every one pay them according to his own wants. The whole circumstantial routine of English law, with its Court of Chancery?—*faux frais* of production. National wars?—*faux frais* of production. England can exploit foreign nations more cheaply while at peace with them.

You see, to these champions of the British Bourgeoisie, to the men of the Manchester School, every institution of Old England appears in the light of a piece of machinery as costly as it is useless, and which fulfils no other purpose but to prevent the nation from producing the greatest possible quantity at the least possible expense, and to exchange its products in freedom. Necessarily, their last word is the *Bourgeois Republic*, in which free competition rules supreme in all spheres of life; in which there remains altogether that *minimum* only of government which is indispensable for administration, internally and externally, of the common class interest and business of the Bourgeoisie; and where this *minimum* of government is as soberly, as

economically organized as possible.   Such a party, in other
countries, would be called *democratic*.   But it is necessarily
revolutionary, and the complete annihilation of Old England
as an aristocratic country is the end which it follows up
with more or less consciousness.   Its nearest object, however,
is the attainment of a Parliamentary reform which should
transfer to its hands the legislative power necessary for such
a revolution.

But the British Bourgeois are not excitable Frenchmen.
When they intend to carry a Parliamentary reform they will
not make a Revolution of February.   On the contrary.
Having obtained, in 1846, a grand victory over the landed
aristocracy by the repeal of the Corn Laws, they were
satisfied with following up the material advantages of this
victory, while they neglected to draw the necessary political
and economical conclusions from it, and thus enabled the
Whigs to reinstate themselves into their hereditary monopoly
of government.   During all the time, from 1846 to 1852,
they exposed themselves to ridicule by their battle-cry:
Broad principles and practical (read *small*) measures.   And
why all this?   Because in every violent movement they are
obliged to appeal to the *working class*.   And if the aristocracy
is their vanishing opponent, the working class is their arising
enemy.   They prefer to compromise with the vanishing
opponent rather than to strengthen the arising enemy, to
whom the future belongs, by concessions of a more than
apparent importance.   Therefore, they strive to avoid
every forcible collision with the aristocracy; but historical
necessity and the Tories press them onwards.   They cannot
avoid fulfilling their mission, battering to pieces Old England,
the England of the Past; and the very moment when they
will have conquered exclusive political dominion, when
political dominion and economical supremacy will be
united in the same hands, when, therefore, the struggle
against capital will no longer be distinct from the struggle

against the existing Government—from that very moment will date the *social revolution of England.*

We now come to the *Chartists,* the politically active portion of the British *working class.* The six points of the Charter which they contend for contain nothing but the demand of *Universal Suffrage,* and of the conditions without which Universal Suffrage would be illusory for the working class; such as the ballot, payment of members, annual general elections. But Universal Suffrage is the equivalent of political power for the working class of England, where the proletariat forms the large majority of the population, where, in a long, though underground civil war, it has gained a clear consciousness of its position as a class, and where even the rural districts know no longer any peasants, but only landlords, industrial capitalists (farmers) and hired labourers. The carrying of Universal Suffrage in England would, therefore, be a far more socialistic measure than anything which has been honoured with that name on the Continent.

Its inevitable result, here, is *the political supremacy of the working class.*

"The Chartists"
NYDT August 25, 1852

The history of all hitherto existing society is the history of class struggles. Freeman and slave, patrician and plebeian, lord and serf, guild-master and journeyman, in a word, oppressor and oppressed, stood in constant opposition to one another, carried on an uninterrupted, now hidden, now open fight, a fight that each time ended either in a revolutionary reconstitution of society at large, or in the common ruin of the contending classes.

In the earlier epochs of history, we find almost everywhere a complicated arrangement of society into various orders, a manifold gradation of social rank. In ancient

Rome we have patricians, knights, plebeians, slaves; in the Middle Ages, feudal lords, vassals, guild-masters, journeymen, apprentices, serfs; in almost all of these classes, again, subordinate gradations.

The modern bourgeois society that has sprouted from the ruins of feudal society has not done away with class antagonisms. It has but established new classes, new conditions of oppression, new forms of struggle in place of the old ones.

Our epoch, the epoch of the bourgeoisie, possesses, however, this distinctive feature; it has simplified the class antagonisms. Society as a whole is more and more splitting up into two great hostile camps, into two great classes directly facing each other—bourgeoisie and proletariat.

CM (1848)
MEGA I/6, pp. 525–6

After presenting such profound explanations concerning the " connection of politics with social conditions " and of "class relations" with the State power, Herr Heinzen[1] exclaims triumphantly: " I have not been guilty in my revolutionary propaganda of the ' communist narrow-mindedness ' which speaks of men only in terms of class, and which incites one handicraft against another. I have left open the possibility that ' humanity ' is not always determined by ' class ' or by the ' size of one's purse.' "

" Vulgar " common sense turns class differences into differences in the size of one's purse, and class conflict into a quarrel between handicrafts. The size of one's purse is a purely quantitative difference, by which any two individuals of the *same* class may be *brought into conflict*. It is well known that the medieval *guilds* opposed each other " on the basis of *handicraft* differences." But it is equally well known that modern class differences are not in any way based upon

[1] Karl Heinzen (1809–80), a radical journalist and author of *Die preussische Bürokratie*, Darmstadt 1845.

handicraft differences, and that, on the contrary, the division of labour produces very *diverse* occupations within the *same* class.

. . . It is quite " possible " that particular individuals are not " always " influenced in their attitude by the class to which they belong, but this has as little effect upon the class struggle as the secession of a few nobles to the *tiers état* had upon the French Revolution. . . .

If Herr Heinzen, however, believes that *whole classes* which are based upon *economic* conditions independent of their will, and which as a result of these conditions are placed in a relation of material antagonism, can break away from their real relations by virtue of the quality of " humanity " which is inherent in all men, how easy it should be for a prince to raise himself above his " princedom," above his " princely handicraft," by virtue of " humanity " . . .

Thus Herr Heinzen divides Germans into princes and subjects. . . . The " narrow-minded " communists see not only the political distinction of prince and subject, but also the social distinction of classes. . . .

It is well known that, shortly after the July Revolution, the victorious bourgeoisie, in its September laws, probably also for reasons of " humanity," made the incitement of class against class a criminal offence, for which imprisonment and fines were imposed. It is also well known that the English bourgeois newspapers found no better way of denouncing the Chartist leaders and Chartist writers than by reproaching them with setting class against class. It is even known that on account of inciting class against class German writers are incarcerated in fortresses.

Is not Herr Heinzen this time talking the language of the French September laws, the English bourgeois newspapers, and the German penal code?

MK (1847)
MEGA I/6, pp. 316–18

VI. MARX'S *ENQUÊTE OUVRIÈRE* [1]

INTRODUCTORY NOTE

IN a letter to Sorge on November 5, 1880, Marx wrote that he had drawn up for Benoît Malon's *Revue Socialiste* a " Questionneur " (*sic*) of which a large number of copies had been distributed throughout France. " Shortly afterwards Guèsde came to London in order to prepare in collaboration with us (myself, Engels and Lafargue), an electoral programme for the workers, in connection with the approaching general election." [2]

The questionnaire was first published in the *Revue Socialiste* on April 20, 1880. In addition, 25,000 copies were reprinted and distributed " to all the workers' societies, to the socialist and democratic groups and circles, to the French newspapers, and to anyone else who asked for it." These copies were undated.

The text of the questionnaire is introduced by a brief preface which recalls the investigations into the conditions of the working class undertaken by the English government, and recommends a similar course of action to the French government. It exhorts the workers of town and country to reply to the questionnaire since only they can describe " with full knowledge the evils which they endure," " only they, and not any providential saviours, can energetically administer the remedies for the social ills from which they suffer." The appeal was also addressed to " socialists of all schools, who, desiring social reform, must also desire *exact* and *positive* knowledge of the conditions in which the working class, the class to which the future belongs, lives and works."

---

[1] See Hilde Weiss, "Die 'Enquête Ouvrière' von Karl Marx," in *Zeitschrift für Sozialforschung*, V/1, 1936, pp. 76–98.

[2] *Briefe an F. A. Sorge und Andere*, Stuttgart, 1906, p. 170.

The preface declares finally, that " the replies will be classified and will provide data for a series of special articles to be published in the *Revue Socialiste* and afterwards collected together in a volume."[1]

The questionnaire is in four parts and has altogether 101 questions. The first part concerns the nature of the occupation and the conditions of work; the second concerns working hours and leisure; the third concerns the terms of employment, wages, and the cost of living; and the fourth concerns the working-class struggle for the improvement of conditions.

The Questionnaire

I

1. What is your occupation?
2. Does the workshop in which you are employed belong to a capitalist or to a joint-stock company? Give the names of the capitalist employers or of the directors of the company.
3. State the number of persons employed.
4. State their ages and sex.
5. What is the minimum age at which children (boys or girls) are employed?
6. State the number of supervisors and other employees who are not ordinary wage earners.
7. Are there any apprentices? How many?
8. Are there, in addition to the workers usually and regularly employed, others who are employed at certain periods?
9. Does your employer's industry work exclusively or

---

[1] In fact, no results of the inquiry were ever published. The issue of the *Revue Socialiste* for July 5, 1880, mentioned that very few replies had been received, and asked its readers to send in their replies as quickly as possible. There was no further reference to the inquiry in subsequent issues, and the *Revue* itself ceased publication in 1881.

primarily for the local market, for the national market, or for export?

10. Is the workshop in the country or in the town? Give the name of the place where it is situated.

11. If your workshop is in the country, does your industrial work enable you to live, or do you combine it with agricultural work?

12. Is your work done by hand or with the aid of machinery?

13. Give details of the division of labour in your industry.

14. Is steam used as motive power?

15. State the number of workshops in which the different branches of the industry are carried on. Describe the special branch in which you are employed, giving information not only about the technical aspects, but also about the muscular and nervous strain involved, and the general effects of the work on the health of the workers.

16. Describe the sanitary conditions in the workshop; size of the rooms, space assigned to each worker; ventilation, temperature, whitewashing of the walls, lavatories, general cleanliness; noise of machines, metallic dust, humidity, etc.

17. Is there any municipal or governmental supervision of the sanitary conditions in the workshops?

18. In your industry, are there any harmful fumes which cause specific illnesses among the workers?

19. Is the workshop overcrowded with machines?

20. Are the machines, the transmission system, and the engines supplying power, protected so as to avoid any accidents?

21. Enumerate the accidents which have occurred in your personal experience.

22. If you work in a mine enumerate the preventive measures taken by your employer to ensure adequate

ventilation and to prevent explosions and other dangerous accidents.

23. If you are employed in a chemical works, in a factory, in the metal-working industry, or in any other industry which is particularly dangerous, enumerate the safety measures introduced by your employer.

24. How is your factory lighted (by gas, paraffin, etc.)?

25. In case of fire, are there enough emergency exits?

26. In case of accidents, is the employer obliged *by law* to pay compensation to the worker or his family?

27. If not, has he ever paid compensation to those who have met with an accident while working to enrich him?

28. Is there a medical service in your workshop?

29. If you work at home, describe the condition of your work-room. Do you use only tools, or do you use small machines? Are you helped by your children or by any other people (adults or children, male or female)? Do you work for individual clients or for a contractor? Do you deal directly with the latter, or do you deal with a middleman?

II

30. State your daily hours of work, and working days in the week.

31. State the holidays during the year.

32. What are the breaks in the working day?

33. Are meals taken at regular intervals or irregularly? Are they taken in the workshop or elsewhere?

34. Do you work during the meal breaks?

35. If steam power is used, when is the power turned on, and when is it turned off?

36. Is there any night work?

37. State the hours of work of children and of young persons below the age of 16.

38. Are there shifts of children and young persons which replace each other during the hours of work?

39. Are the laws concerning the employment of children enforced by the government or the municipality? Are they respected by the employer?

40. Are there any schools for the children and young persons employed in your trade? If there are, what are the school hours? Who runs the schools? What is taught in them?

41. When work continues day and night how are the shifts organized?

42. What is the normal increase in hours of work during periods of great industrial activity?

43. Are the machines cleaned by workers specially employed for this work, or are they cleaned gratuitously by the workers who are employed on them during the working day?

44. What are the regulations and the penalties for lateness? At what time does the working day begin, and at what time does it begin again after meals?

45. How much time do you spend in getting to work and in returning home?

III

46. What kind of work contract do you have with your employer? Are you engaged by the day, by the week, by the month, etc.?

47. What are the conditions laid down for giving or receiving notice?

48. In the event of the contract being broken, what penalty is imposed on the employer if it is his fault?

49. What penalty is imposed on the worker if it is his fault?

50. If there are apprentices, what are the terms of their contract?

51. Is your work regular or irregular?

52. In your trade, is the work seasonal, or is it, in normal times, spread more or less evenly over the year? If your work is seasonal, how do you live in the periods between working?

53. Are you paid time rates or piece rates?

54. If you are paid time rates, are you paid by the hour or by the day.

55. Is there additional pay for overtime work? What is it?

56. If you are paid piece rates, how are the rates fixed? If you are employed in an industry in which the work performed is measured by quantity or weight, as is the case in the mines, does your employer or his representatives resort to trickery in order to defraud you of a part of your earnings?

57. If you are paid piece rates, is the quality of the article made a pretext for fraudulent deductions from your wages?

58. Whether you are paid piece rates or time rates, when are you paid, or in other words how long is the credit which you extend to your master before receiving the price of the work carried out? Are you paid at the end of a week, a month, etc.?

59. Have you noticed that the delay in paying your wages makes it necessary for you to resort frequently to the pawnbroker, paying a high rate of interest, and depriving yourself of things which you need; or to fall into debt to shopkeepers, becoming their victim because you are their debtor? Do you know any instances in which workers have lost their wages through the bankruptcy of their employers?

60. Are wages paid directly by the employer, or by middlemen (sub-contractors, etc.)?

61. If wages are paid by sub-contractors, or other middlemen, what are the terms of your contract?

62. What is your daily and weekly wage rate in money?

63. What are the wages of women and children working with you in the same workshop?

64. What was the highest daily wage in your workshop during the past month?

65. What was the highest piece-rate wage . . .?

66. What was your wage during the same period, and if you have a family what were the wages of your wife and children?

67. Are wages paid entirely in money, or in some other way?

68. If you rent your dwelling from your employer, what are the conditions? Does he deduct the rent from your wages?

69. What are the prices of necessities such as:

    (a) rent of dwelling; conditions of letting; number of rooms, number of inhabitants, repairs and insurance: purchase and maintenance of furniture, heating, lighting, water;

    (b) food: bread, meat, vegetables, potatoes, etc., milk, eggs, fish, butter, oil, lard, sugar, salt, spices, coffee, chicory, beer, cider, wine, etc., tobacco;

    (c) clothing for parents and children, laundry, personal toilet, baths, soap, etc.;

    (d) various expenses: postage, loans and pawn-brokers' charges, children's school or apprentice-ship fees, papers and books, contributions to friendly societies, or for strikes, co-operatives and defence societies;

    (e) expenses, if any, caused by your work;

    (f) taxes.

70. Try to draw up a budget of the weekly and annual income and expenditure of yourself and your family.

71. Have you noticed, in your personal experience, a greater rise in the price of the necessities of life, such as food and shelter, than in wages?

72. State the fluctuations in wage rates which are known to you.

73. State the wage reductions in periods of stagnation and industrial crisis.

74. State the wage increases in so-called periods of prosperity.

75. Note the interruptions of work resulting from changes of fashion and from particular and general crises. Give an account of your own experiences of involuntary unemployment.

76. Compare *the price of the article you produce*, or of the services you provide, with the price of your labour.

77. Quote any instance you know of workers being displaced by the introduction of machinery or by other improvements.

78. With the development of machinery and the productivity of labour, has the intensity and duration of work increased or diminished?

79. Do you know of any instance of an increase of wages in consequence of the progress of production?

80. Have you ever known any ordinary workers who were able to retire at the age of 50 and to live on the money acquired in their capacity as wage earners?

81. For how many years, in your trade, can a worker of average health continue to work?

IV

82. Are there any defence organizations in your trade, and how are they conducted?   Send their statutes and rules.

83. How many strikes have occurred in your trade, in the course of your career?

84. How long did these strikes last?

85. Were they general or partial?

86. Was their aim an increase in wages, or were they organized to resist a wage reduction? Or were they concerned with the length of the working day, or caused by other factors?

87. What results did they achieve?

88. Say what you think of the actions of the *Prud'hommes* (arbitrators).[1]

89. Has your trade supported strikes by workers of other trades?

90. Give an account of the rules and penalties instituted by your employer for the government of his wage earners.

91. Have there been any combinations of employers for the purpose of imposing wage reductions, increasing working hours, or preventing strikes, or, in general, for getting their own way?

92. Do you know any instances in which the Government has misused the forces of the State, in order to place them at the disposal of employers against their employees?

93. Do you know any instances in which the Government has intervened to protect the workers against the exactions of the employers and their illegal combinations?

94. Does the Government apply against the employers the existing labour laws? Do its inspectors carry out their duties conscientiously?

95. Are there, in your workshop or trade, any friendly societies for cases of accident, illness, death, temporary incapacity for work, old age, etc.? Send their statutes and rules.

96. Is membership of these societies voluntary or obligatory? Are their funds controlled exclusively by the workers?

---

[1] The *conseil des prud'hommes* is a committee of arbitration in disputes between workers and employers.

97. If the contributions are obligatory and under the control of the employers, are they deducted from wages? Is interest paid on these contributions? Are they returned to the worker when he leaves or is dismissed? Do you know any instances in which workers have benefited from so-called retirement funds controlled by the employers, but whose capital is derived from the workers' wages?

98. Are there any co-operative societies in your trade? How are they managed? Do they employ workers from outside in the same way as the capitalists do? Send their statutes and rules.

99. Are there any workshops in your trade, in which the workers are remunerated partly by wages and partly by a so-called participation in the profits? Compare the sums received by these workers with those received by workers where there is no so-called participation in profits. State the obligations of workers living under this system. Can they go on strike? Or are they only permitted to be the humble servants of their masters?

100. What is the general physical, intellectual, and moral condition of men and women workers employed in your trade?

101. General comments.

Part Four

SOCIOLOGY OF POLITICS

I. THE STATE AND LAW

THE *Convention* had for a moment the courage to *order* the abolition of pauperism, not indeed " *immediately,*" as " A Prussian " [1] demands from his king, but only after entrusting the Committee of Public Safety with the preparation of the necessary plans and proposals, and after the latter had made use of the comprehensive investigations of poverty in France and had, through Barrière, proposed the establishment of the *Livres de la bienfaisance nationale,* etc. What was the result of the Convention's ordinance? Only that there was one more ordinance in the world, and that *one* year later the Convention was besieged by starving weavers.

Yet the Convention represented a *maximum* of *political energy, power* and *understanding.*

No government in the world has been able to make *regulations* concerning pauperism *immediately,* without first consulting its officials. The English Parliament, indeed, sent commissioners to all the European countries to gather information about the different administrative measures for the relief of pauperism. In so far as States have concerned themselves at all with pauperism, they have remained at the level of *administrative and charitable measures,* or have sunk below this level.

Can the *State* act in any other way? The *State* will never look for the cause of *social imperfections* " *in the State and social institutions themselves,*" as " A Prussian " demands of his king. Where there are political parties, each party finds the source of *such* evils in the fact that the opposing party, instead of

[1] Marx's two articles in *Vorwärts* were a critical examination of an article by Arnold Ruge, published under the pseudonym " A Prussian " in the same journal in July 1844, and discussing the political significance of the Silesian weavers' revolt and of the official measures taken to deal with pauperism. Ruge's article is reprinted in *MEGA* I/3, pp. 587–9.

itself, is at the *helm of State*.   Even the radical and revolutionary politicians look for the source of the evil, not in the
nature of the State, but in a particular *form of the State*, which
they want to replace by *another* form.

The *State* and the *structure of society* are not, from the
standpoint of *politics*, *two* different things.   The State is the
structure of society.   In so far as the State admits the existence of *social* evils, it attributes them to *natural laws* against
which no human power can prevail, or to *private life* which is
independent of the State, or to the *inadequacies of the administration* which is subordinate to it.   Thus in England poverty
is explained by the *natural law* according to which population
always increases beyond the means of subsistence.   From
another aspect, England explains *pauperism* as the consequence of the *evil dispositions of the poor*, just as the king of
Prussia explains it by the *unchristian disposition of the rich*, and
as the Convention explains it by the *sceptical, counter-revolu-
tionary outlook of the property owners*.   Accordingly, England
inflicts penalties on the poor, the king of Prussia admonishes
the rich, and the Convention beheads property owners.

In the last resort, *every* State seeks the cause in *adventitious
or intentional defects in the administration*, and therefore looks to
a *reform* of the administration for a redress of these evils.
Why?   Simply because the *administration* is the *organizing*
activity of the State itself.

The *contradiction* between the aims and good intentions of
the administration on the one hand, and its means and
resources on the other, cannot be removed by the State
without abolishing itself, for it rests upon this contradiction.
The State is founded upon the contradiction between *public*
and *private life*, between *general* and *particular interests*.   The
administration must, therefore, limit itself to a *formal and
negative* sphere of activity, because its power ceases at the
point where civil life and its work begin.   In face of the
consequences which spring from the unsocial character of

the life of civil society, of private property, trade, industry, of the mutual plundering by the different groups in civil society, *impotence* is the *natural law* of the administration. These divisions, this debasement and *slavery of civil society*, are the natural foundations upon which the *modern* State rests, just as *civil society* was the natural foundation of *slavery* upon which the State of *antiquity* rested. The existence of the State and the existence of slavery are inseparable. The State and slavery in antiquity—frank *classical* antithesis— were not more intimately *linked* than are the modern State and the modern world of commerce—sanctimonious *Christian* antithesis. If the modern State wished to end the *impotence* of its administration it would be obliged to abolish the present conditions of *private life*. And if the State wished to abolish these conditions of private life it would have also to put an end to its own existence, for it exists *only* in relation to them.

Art. I (1844)
MEGA I/3, pp. 13–15

The more powerful the State, and therefore the more *political* a country is, the less likely it is to seek the basis of *social* evils and to grasp the *general* explanation of them, in the *principle of the State* itself, that is in the *structure of society*, of which the State is the active, conscious and official expression. *Political* thought is really *political* thought in the sense that the thinking takes place within the framework of politics. The clearer and more vigorous political thought is, the *less* it is able to grasp the nature of social evils. The *classical* period of political thought is the *French Revolution*. Far from recognizing the source of social defects in the principle of the State, the heroes of the French Revolution looked for the sources of political evils in the defective social organization. Thus, for example, Robespierre saw in the coexistence of great poverty and great wealth only an obstacle to *genuine democracy*. He wished, therefore, to establish a universal *Spartan* austerity. The principle of politics is the will. The more partial, and the more per- fected, *political* thought becomes, the more it believes in the *omnipotence* of the will, the less able it is to see the *natural* and mental *limitations* on the will, the less capable it is of dis- covering the source of social evils.

Art. I (1844)
MEGA I/3, pp 15–16

It has been shown that the *recognition of the rights of man* by the *modern State*, has only the same significance as the *recognition of slavery* by the *State in antiquity*. The basis of the State in antiquity was slavery; the basis of the *modern* State is civil society and the *individual* of civil society, that is, the independent individual, whose only link with other individuals is private interest and *unconscious*, natural necessity, the *slave* of wage labour, of the *selfish* needs of himself and others. The modern State has recognized this, its natural foundation, in the universal rights of man. But it did not create it. As the product of civil society which was impelled by its own development beyond the old political shackles, it only recognized its own origins and basis in *proclaiming the rights of man*.

HF (1845)
MEGA I/3, p. 288

The basis of present-day " *public affairs*," that is, of the developed modern State, is not, as the " Critical School " thinks, the society of feudal privileges, but a society in which *privileges* have been *abolished* and *dissolved*, a developed *civil society*, where the elements of existence which were politically fettered by privilege have been freed. " *No privileged ex- clusiveness* " is not levelled against anyone, nor against public affairs. Just as free industry and free trade abolish privileged enclaves, and replace them with the individual freed from all privileges (which separate the individual from the community as a whole, but also involve him in a smaller exclusive community), the individual who is no longer related to other men by even the *appearance* of a general bond, and create a general conflict between man and man, individual and individual, so the whole of *civil society* is only this mutual conflict of all individuals who are no longer distinguished by anything but their *individuality*. It is only the universal movement of the individual life forces freed from the shackles of privilege. The opposition between the *democratic, representative State* and *civil society* is the perfection of the classical opposition between *public social life* and *slavery*. In the modern world, every individual participates *at the same time* in slavery and in social life. But the *slavery of civil society* is, *in appearance*, the greatest *liberty*, because it appears to be the realized *independence* of the individual for whom the frantic movement, released from general shackles and from the limitations imposed by man, of the vital elements of which he has been stripped, for example property, industry and religion, is a manifestation of his *own* liberty, when in reality it is nothing but the expression of his absolute enslavement and of the loss of his human nature. Here, *privilege* has been replaced by *right*.

HF (1845)
MEGA I/3, pp. 291–2

To speak precisely and in ordinary language, the members of civil society are not *atoms*. The *characteristic quality* of an atom is to have *no* qualities, and consequently no relations determined by its own *nature* with other beings outside itself. The atom has *no needs* and is *self-sufficient*; the external world is a complete *void*, has neither content, nor sense, nor meaning, precisely because the atom possesses *everything* in itself. The egoistic individual of civil society may in abstract and lifeless conceptions, inflate himself into an *atom*, that is, into a being without relations, self-sufficient, without needs, *absolutely perfect* and contented. But profane, *sensuous reality* has no concern for his imagination. The individual finds himself forced by everyone of his senses to believe in the existence of the world and of other individuals; and everything, down to his *profane* stomach reminds him daily that the *external* world is not a void, that it is, on the contrary, that which *fills* (his stomach). Every one of his activities and qualities, every one of his aspirations, becomes a *need*, a *want*, which transforms his *egoism* into a desire for things and human beings outside himself. But since the need of one individual is not self-evident to another egoistic individual who possesses the means of satisfying it, every individual finds himself obliged to create this relation in making himself so to speak the middleman between the needs of others and the objects of these needs. It is, therefore, *natural necessity*, it is the *essential qualities of man*, however alienated the form in which they appear, it is *interest*, which hold together the members of civil society, whose *real* bond is constituted by *civil* and not by *political* life. Thus it is not the *State* which holds together the *atoms* of civil society; it is the fact that these *atoms* are only *atoms* in *idea*, in the *heaven* of the imagination, and that *in reality* they are beings very different from atoms. They are not *god-like egoists* but *egoistic men*. Only *political superstition* believes at the present time that civil life must be held together by the State, when in reality the State is upheld by civil life.

HF (1845)
MEGA I/3, p. 296

Napoleon represented the last struggle of *revolutionary terrorism* against *civil society* and its policy, which was likewise established by the Revolution. Certainly Napoleon already understood the nature of the *modern State*; he recognized that it was based on the free development of civil society, on the free play of private interests, etc. He decided to acknowledge this basis and to protect it. He was not a visionary revolutionary. But Napoleon still regarded the *State* as an *end in itself*, and civil society only as a treasurer, a *subordinate* who was allowed to have no *will of his own*. He practised *terrorism* by substituting *permanent war* for *permanent revolution*. He satisfied to the full French national egoism, but he demanded in return the sacrifice of civil affairs, pleasure, wealth, etc., every time the political aim of conquest required it. He suppressed, in true despotic fashion, the liberalism of its daily practice, and he did not spare the most essential *material* interests of this society, commerce and industry, whenever they clashed with his own political interests. He added a contempt for businessmen to his contempt for *ideologists*. In internal affairs also, he fought against those, in civil society, who opposed the idea of the State as an end in itself. Thus he declared, in the *Conseil d'Etat*, that he would not allow the large landowners to decide to cultivate their estates or not according to their own whim. Thus, also, he had a project for nationalizing *road transport*, in order to subordinate commerce to the State. It was French traders who prepared the event which gave the first blow to Napoleon's power. Parisian speculators, by provoking an artificial famine, obliged the Emperor to postpone for two months the opening of the Russian campaign and thus to begin it when the year was too far advanced.

The liberal bourgeoisie, which was confronted by renewed revolutionary terrorism in the person of Napoleon, was next confronted, in the shape of the Restoration and the Bourbons, by counter-revolution. Finally, in 1830, the bourgeoisie achieved its aims of 1789, but with a difference. The liberal bourgeoisie, having *completed* its *political* education, no longer saw in the constitutional representative State its ideal State, or regarded itself as pursuing the salvation of the world and general human aims. It recognized there, on the contrary, the *official* expression of its own *exclusive* power and the *political* recognition of its *private* interests.

The history of the French Revolution begun in 1789 did not end in 1830 when one of its elements, filled with the consciousness of its own *social* importance, gained the victory.

HF (1845)
MEGA I/3, pp. 299–300

Just because individuals seek *only* their particular interest, which for them does not coincide with their common interest (for the " general good " is an illusory form of community life), the common interest is imposed as an interest " alien " to them, and " independent " of them, as itself in turn a particular " general " interest; or else the individuals must encounter each other in this discord, as in democracy. On the other hand, the *practical* struggle of these particular interests, which are always *really* in conflict with the community and illusory community interests, makes *practical* intervention and control necessary through the illusory " general " interest in the form of the State. The social power, i.e. the multiplied productive force, which results from the co-operation of different individuals as it is determined by the division of labour, appears to these individuals, since their co-operation is not voluntary but natural, not as their own united power but as an alien force existing outside them, of whose origin and purpose they are ignorant, and which they therefore cannot control, but which, on the contrary, passes through its own proper series of phases and stages, independent of the will and the action of man, even appearing to govern this will and action.

GI (1845–6)
MEGA I/5, pp. 23–4

Since the State is the form in which the individuals of a ruling class assert their common interests, and in which the whole civil society of an epoch is epitomized, it follows that the State acts as an intermediary for all community institutions, and that these institutions receive a political form. Hence the illusion that law is based on will, and indeed on will divorced from its real basis—on *free* will. Similarly, law is in its turn reduced to the actual laws.

Civil law develops concurrently with private property out of the disintegration of the natural community. Among the Romans the development of private property and civil law had no further industrial and commercial consequences because their whole mode of production remained unchanged. Among modern peoples, where the feudal community was disintegrated by industry and trade, a new phase began with the rise of private property and civil law, which was capable of further development. The first town which carried on an extensive trade in the Middle Ages, Amalfi, also developed at the same time maritime law. As soon as industry and trade developed private property further, first in Italy and later in other countries, the perfected Roman civil law was at once taken up again and raised to authority. When, subsequently, the bourgeoisie had acquired so much power that the princes took up their interests in order to overthrow the feudal nobility by means of the bourgeoisie, there began in all countries—in France in the sixteenth century—the real development of law, which in all countries except England proceeded on the basis of the Roman Code. Even in England, Roman legal principles had to be introduced for the further development of civil law (especially in the case of personal movable property). It should not be forgotten that law has not, any more than religion, an independent history.

GI (1845–6)
MEGA I/5, pp. 52–3

Nothing could be more comical than Hegel's analysis of private property in land. According to him, man as an individual must give reality to his will as the soul of external Nature, and must therefore take possession of Nature as his private property. If this were the destiny of " the individual," of man as an individual, it would follow that every human being must be a landowner in order to realize himself as an individual. Free private property in land, a very recent product, is not, according to Hegel, a definite social relation, but a relation of man as an individual to Nature, " the absolute right of appropriation which man has over all things " (Hegel, *Philosophy of Right*, Berlin, 1840). So much is at once evident, that the individual cannot maintain himself as a landowner by his mere " will " against the will of another individual who likewise wants to incarnate himself in the same piece of land. It requires many other things besides the good will. Furthermore it is quite impossible to understand where " the individual " sets the limits for the realization of his will, whether his will should realize itself in a whole country, or whether it requires a whole collection of countries by whose appropriation I might " manifest the supremacy of my will over the thing." Here Hegel breaks down completely: "The appropriation is of a very individual kind; I do not take possession of more than I touch with my body, but the second point is at the same time that external things have a greater extension than I can grasp. While I thus have possession of a thing, something else is likewise in touch with it. I exercise my appropriation by my hand but its scope may be extended " (ibid.). But this other thing is again in contact with still another, and so the boundary disappears, within which my will as soul can flow into the soil. " If I own anything, my reason at once passes on to the idea that not only this property, but also the thing it touches, is mine. Here positive right must fix its boundaries, for nothing more can be deduced from the concept" (ibid.). This is an extraordinarily naïve confession of " the concept," and it proves that this conception, which from the outset makes the blunder of regarding as absolute a particular legal conception of landed property which belongs to bourgeois society, does not understand anything of the real forms of this property. This implies at the same time an avowal that " positive law " can and must, change its affirmations in accordance with the needs of social, i.e. economic, development.

Capital III
VA III/2, p. 664, note 26

In historical fact the theorists who considered *force* as the basis of law were directly opposed to those who saw *will* as the basis of law. . . . If force is taken to be the basis of law, as by Hobbes, law and legislative enactments are only a symptom or expression of *other* conditions upon which the State power rests. The material life of individuals, which certainly does not depend on their mere " will," their mode of production and their form of intercourse, which reciprocally influence each other, are the real basis of the State. This material life is, at every stage in which the division of labour and private property are still necessary, quite independent of the *will* of individuals. These real conditions are not created by the State power; they are rather the power which creates it. The individuals who rule under these conditions, quite apart from the fact that their power has to constitute itself as a State, must give their will, as it is determined by these definite circumstances, a general expression as the will of the State, as law. The content of this expression is always determined by the situation of this class, as is most clearly revealed in the civil and criminal law. Just as the bodily weight of individuals does not depend upon their ideal will or caprice, so it does not depend on them whether they embody their own will in law, and at the same time, in accordance with individual caprice give everyone beneath them his independence. Their individual domination must at the same time form a general domination. Their individual power rests upon conditions of existence which develop as social conditions and whose continuance they must show to involve their own supremacy and yet be valid for all. Law is the expression of this will conditioned by their common interests. It is just the striving of independent individuals and their wills, which on this basis are necessarily egoistic in their behaviour to each other, which makes self denial through law and regulation essential, or rather self denial in exceptional cases and maintenance of their interest in general. . . . The same holds good for the subject classes, on whose will the existence of law and the State is equally little dependent. For instance, as long as the productive forces are insufficiently developed to make competition superfluous, with the consequence that competition is always reappearing, the subject classes would be willing the impossible if they " willed " to abolish competition and with it the State and law. Moreover, until conditions have developed to a point where they can produce this " will " it exists only in the imagination of the ideologists. Once conditions are sufficiently developed to produce it, the ideologist can imagine it as purely capricious and therefore conceivable at any period and under any circumstances. Crime, i.e. the struggle of the single individual against the dominant conditions, is as little the product of simple caprice as law itself. It is rather conditioned in the same way as the latter. The same visionaries who see in law the rule of an independent and general will see in crime a simple breaking of the law. The State does not rest on a dominating will, but the State which arises out of the material mode of life of individuals has also the form of a dominating will. If this will loses its domination this means not only that the will has changed but also that the material existence and life of individuals has changed despite their will. It is possible that law and legislation have an autonomous evolution but in that case they are purely formal and no longer dominating, as many striking examples in Roman and English legal history show. We have already seen how, through the activity of philosophers, a history of pure thought could arise by the separation of thought from the individuals and their actual relations which are its basis. In the present case, also, law can be separated from its real basis, and thereby we can arrive at a " ruling will " which in different periods has a different expression and which, in its creations, the laws, has its own independent history. By this means political and civil history is ideologically transformed into a history of the dominance of self-developing laws.

GI (1845–6)
MEGA I/5, pp. 307–9

The different factors of primitive accumulation may be distinguished, more or less in chronological order, with reference to Spain, Portugal, Holland, France, and England. In England at the end of the seventeenth century, they reached a systematic integration in the colonial system, the national debt, the modern system of taxation, and the protectionist system. These methods depend in part on brute force, e.g. the colonial system. But they all employ the power of the State, the concentrated and organized force of society, to hasten, hot-house fashion, the process of transformation of the feudal mode of production into the capitalist mode, and to shorten the transition. Force is the midwife of every old society pregnant with a new one. It is itself an economic power.

Capital I (1867)
VA I, p. 791

. . . it would be very difficult, if not altogether impossible, to establish any principle upon which the justice or expediency of capital punishment could be founded, in a Society, glorying in its civilization. Punishment in general had been defended as a means either of ameliorating or of intimidating. Now what right have you to punish me for the amelioration or intimidation of others? And besides, there is history—there is such a thing as statistics—which prove with the most complete evidence that since Cain the world has neither been intimidated nor ameliorated by punishment. Quite the contrary. From the point of view of abstract right, there is only one theory of punishment which recognizes human dignity in the abstract, and that is the theory of Kant, especially in the more rigid formula given to it by Hegel. Hegel says : " Punishment is the *right* of the criminal. It is an act of his own will. The violation of right has been proclaimed by the criminal as his own right. His crime is the negation of right. Punishment is the negation of this negation, and consequently an affirmation of right, solicited and forced upon the criminal by himself."

There is no doubt something specious in this formula, inasmuch as Hegel, instead of looking upon the criminal as the mere object, the slave of justice, elevates him to the position of a free and self-determined being. Looking, however, more closely into the matter, we discover that German idealism here, as in most other instances, has but given a transcendental sanction to the rules of existing society. Is it not a delusion to substitute for the individual with his real motives, with multifarious social circumstances pressing upon him, the abstraction of " free-will "—one among the many qualities of man for man himself? This theory, considering punishment as the result of the criminal's own will, is only a metaphysical expression for the old " jus talionis," eye against eye, tooth against tooth, blood against

blood. Plainly speaking, and dispensing with all paraphrases, punishment is nothing but a means of society to
defend itself against the infraction of its vital conditions,
whatever may be their character. Now, what a state of
society is that which knows of no better instrument for its
own defence than the hangman, and which proclaims
through the " leading journal of the world " its own
brutality as eternal law?

Mr A. Quételet, in his excellent and learned work,
l'Homme et ses Facultés, says: " There is a budget which
we pay with frightful regularity—it is that of prisons,
dungeons and scaffolds. . . . We might even predict how
many individuals will stain their hands with the blood of
their fellow-men, how many will be forgers, how many will
deal in poison, pretty nearly the same way as we may foretell
the annual births and deaths."

And Mr Quételet, in a calculation of the probabilities of
crime published in 1829, actually predicted with astonishing
certainty, not only the amount but all the different kinds of
crimes committed in France in 1830. That it is not so
much the particular political institutions of a country as the
fundamental conditions of modern *bourgeois* society in
general, which produce an average amount of crime in a
given national fraction of society, may be seen from the
following tables, communicated by Quételet, for the years
1822-24. We find in a number of one hundred condemned criminals in America and France:

Age	Philadelphia	France
Under twenty-one years . .	19	19
Twenty-one to thirty . . .	44	35
Thirty to forty	23	23
Above forty	14	23
	100	100

Now, if crimes observed on a great scale thus show, in
their amount and their classification, the regularity of

physical phenomena—if, as Mr Quételet remarks, " it would be difficult to decide in respect to which of the two (the physical world and the social system) the acting causes produce their effect with the utmost regularity "—is there not a necessity for deeply reflecting upon an alteration of the system that breeds these crimes, instead of glorifying the hangman who executes a lot of criminals to make room only for the supply of new ones?

" Capital Punishment "
NYDT February 18, 1853

II. DYNAMICS OF REVOLUTION

PROLETARIAT and wealth are antinomies. As such they form a whole. They are two forms of the world of private property. The problem is to discover the place which each of them occupies in the antinomy. It is not sufficient to say that they are two sides of a single whole.

Private property, as private property, as wealth, is forced to *maintain* itself and consequently to *maintain* its opposite, the proletariat. It is the *positive* side of the antinomy, satisfied private property.

The proletariat, on the contrary, is forced, as proletariat, to work for its own abolition, and thus for the abolition of the condition which makes it a proletariat—private property. It is the *negative* side of the antinomy, private property in a state of unrest, dissolved and in process of dissolution.

The possessing class and the proletarian class express the same human alienation. But the former is satisfied with its situation, feels itself well established in it, recognizes this self-alienation as *its own* power, and thus has the *appearance* of a human existence. The latter feels itself crushed by this self-alienation, sees in it its own impotence and the reality of an inhuman situation. It is, to use an expression of Hegel's, " in the midst of degradation the *revolt* against degradation," a revolt to which it is forced by the contradiction between its *humanity* and its situation, which is an open, clear and absolute negation of its humanity.

Within the framework of alienation, therefore, the property owners are the *conservative* and the proletarians the *destructive* party.

It is true that, in its economic development, private property advances towards its own dissolution; but it only

231

does this through a development which is independent of itself, unconscious and achieved against its will—solely because it produces the proletariat *as* proletariat, poverty conscious of its moral and physical poverty, degradation conscious of its degradation, and for this reason trying to abolish itself. The proletariat carries out the sentence which private property, by creating the proletariat, passes upon itself, just as it carries out the sentence which wage-labour, by creating wealth for others and poverty for itself, passes upon itself. If the proletariat triumphs this does not mean that it becomes the absolute form of society, for it is only victorious by abolishing itself as well as its opposite. Thus the proletariat disappears along with the opposite which conditions it, private property.

If socialist writers attribute this world-historical role to the proletariat this is not at all, as the " Critical School " pretends to believe, because they regard the proletarians as *gods*. On the contrary, in the fully developed proletariat, everything human is taken away, even the *appearance* of humanity. In the conditions of existence of the proletariat are condensed, in their most inhuman form, all the conditions of existence of present-day society. Man has lost himself, but he has not only acquired, at the same time, a theoretical consciousness of his loss, he has been forced, by an ineluctable, irremediable and imperious *distress*— by practical *necessity*—to revolt against this inhumanity. It is for these reasons that the proletariat can and must emancipate itself. But it can only emancipate itself by destroying its own conditions of existence. It can only destroy its own conditions of existence by destroying *all* the inhuman conditions of existence of present-day society, conditions which are epitomized in its situation. It is not in vain that it passes through the rough but stimulating school of *labour*. It is not a matter of knowing what this or that proletarian, or even the proletariat as a whole, *conceives* as its aims at any particular moment. It is a question of knowing *what* the proletariat *is*, and what it must historically accomplish in accordance with its *nature*. Its aim and its historical activity are ordained for it, in a tangible and irrevocable way, by its own situation as well as by the whole organization of present-day civil society. It is unnecessary to show here that a large part of the English and French proletariat has already become *aware* of its historic mission, and works incessantly to clarify this awareness.

HF (1845)

MEGA I/3, pp. 205-7

Political emancipation is, at the same time, a *dissolution* of the old society, upon which the sovereign power, the alienated political life of the people, rests. Political revolution is a revolution of civil society. What was the nature of the old society? It can be characterized in one word: *feudalism*. The old civil society had a *directly political* character, i.e. the elements of civil life, such as property, the family, and types of occupation, had become, in the form of lordship, caste and guilds, elements of political life. They determined, in this form, the relation of the individual to the State as a whole, i.e. his *political* situation, or in other words, his separation and exclusion from the other elements of society. For this organization of national life did not constitute property and labour as social elements; it rather succeeded in *separating* them from the body of the State and made them *distinct* societies within society. Nevertheless, at least in the feudal sense, the vital functions and conditions of civil society remained political. They excluded the individual from the body of the State, and transformed the *particular* relation which existed between his corporation and the State into a general relation between the individual and social life, just as they transformed his **civil** activity and situation into a general activity and situation. As a result of this organization, the State as a whole and its consciousness, will and activity, the general political power, also necessarily appeared as the *private* affair of a ruler and his servants, separated from the people.

The political revolution which overthrew this power of the ruler, and made State affairs the affairs of the people, which made the political State a matter of general concern, i.e. a real State, necessarily shattered everything, classes, corporations, guilds, privileges, which expressed the separation of the people from community life. The political revolution therefore *abolished* the *political character of civil society*. It dissolved civil society into its basic elements, on the one hand *individuals*, on the other hand the *material and cultural elements* which formed the life experience and the civil situation of these individuals. It set free the political spirit, which had become, so to speak, dissolved, fragmented, and lost in the various culs de sac of feudal society; it reassembled these scattered fragments, liberated the political spirit from its connection with civil life and made of it the community sphere, the general sphere of the people, theoretically independent of these particular elements of civil life. A specific activity and situation in life no longer had any but an individual significance. They no longer constituted the general relation between the individual and the State as a whole. Public affairs as such became the general affair of each individual, and political functions became general functions.

But this perfection of the idealism of the State was at the same time the accomplishment of the materialism of civil society. The bonds which had restrained the egoistic spirit of civil society were removed along with the political yoke. Political emancipation was at the same time an emancipation of civil society from politics and from even the *appearance* of a general content.

Feudal society was dissolved into its basic elements, *man*, into *egoistic* man who was its real foundation.

Man in this aspect, the member of civil society, is now the foundation and the condition of the *political* State. The State recognized him as such in the rights of man.

But the liberty of egoistic man, and the recognition of this liberty, is rather the recognition of the *frenzied* movement of the cultural and material elements which form its content.

Thus, man was not liberated from religion; he received religious liberty. He was not liberated from property; he received the liberty to own and acquire property. He was not liberated from the egoism of business; he received the liberty to engage in business.

The *formation of the political State* and the dissolution of civil society into independent *individuals*, whose relations are regulated by *law*, as the relations of men in the corporations and guilds were regulated by *privilege*, is accomplished by *one and the same act*. Man as a member of civil society, *non-political* man, necessarily appears as the *natural* man. The *droits de l'homme* appear as *droits naturels* because *conscious activity* is concentrated on *political action*. *Egoistic* man is the *passive, given* result of the dissolution of society, an object of *immediate apprehension*, and therefore a *natural object*. The *political revolution* dissolves civil society into its elements without *revolutionizing* these elements themselves or subjecting them to criticism. This revolution regards civil society, the sphere of human needs, of labour, of private interests and of civil law, as the *basis of its own existence*, as a self-subsistent *condition* and thus as its *natural basis*. Finally, man as a member of civil society is identified with *man as such*, *homme* as distinct from *citoyen*, because he is man in his sensuous, individual and *immediate* existence, whereas *political* man is only abstract, artificial man, man as an *allegorical, moral* being. Thus man as he really is, is seen only in the form of *egoistic* man, and man in his *true* nature only in the form of the *abstract citizen*.

This abstract notion of political man is excellently formulated by Rousseau, " Whoso would undertake to give institutions to a People must work with full consciousness that he has set himself to *change*, as it were, the very stuff of *human nature*; to *transform* each individual who, in isolation, is a complete but solitary whole, into a *part* of something greater than himself, from which, in a sense, he derives his life and his being; to substitute a *communal and moral* existence for the purely physical and independent life with which we are all of us endowed by Nature. His task, in short, is to take from *a man his own proper powers*, and to give him in exchange powers foreign to him as a person, which he can use only if he is helped by the rest of the community " (*Contrat Social*, Book II).

Every emancipation is a *restoration* of the human world and of human relationships to *man himself*.

Political emancipation is a reduction of man, on the one hand to a member of civil society, to an *independent* and *egoistic* individual, on the other, to a *citizen*, to a moral person.

Human emancipation will only be complete when the real, individual man has absorbed in himself the abstract citizen, when as an individual man, in his everyday life, in his work, and in his relationships, he has become a *social being*, and when he has recognized and organized his own powers (*forces propres*) as *social* powers, and consequently no longer separates this social power from himself as *political* power.

JF (1843)

MEGA I/1/1, pp. 596–9

The more developed and universal is the *political* thought of a people, the more the *proletariat*—at least at the beginning of the movement—wastes its forces on foolish and futile up-risings which are drowned in blood. Because the proletariat thinks politically it sees the source of bad social conditions in *will*, and all the means of improvement in *force* and the *overthrow* of a particular form of State. Consider, for example, the first outbreaks of the *French* proletariat. The workers of Lyons believed that they were pursuing only political aims, that they were only soldiers of the Republic, when in reality they were the soldiers of socialism. In this way their *political* understanding obscured from them the roots of their social misery, it distorted their insight into their real aims and *eclipsed* their *social instinct*.

Art. II (1844)
MEGA I/3, p. 20

The *social life* from which the worker is *shut out* is a social life very different in kind and extent from that of the *political* sphere. This social life, from which *his own labour* excludes him, is *life* itself, physical and cultural life, human morality, human activity, human enjoyment, real *human* existence. Human life is the *true social life* of man. As the irremediable exclusion from this life is much more complete, more unbearable, dreadful and contradictory, than the exclusion from political life, so is the ending of this exclusion, and even a limited reaction, a *revolt* against it, more funda-mental, as *man* is more fundamental than the *citizen*, *human life* more than *political life*. The *industrial* revolt may thus be *limited* but it has a *universal* significance; the *political* revolt may be universal, but it conceals under a *gigantic* form a *narrow* spirit.

Art. II (1844)
MEGA I/3, p.21

A *social* revolution has thus a *universal* aspect, because, though it may occur in only *one* manufacturing district, it is a human protest against an inhuman life, because it begins from the *single real individual*, and because the *social life*, against his exclusion from which the individual reacts, is the *real* social life of man, a really *human* life. The *political aspect* of a revolution consists in the movement of the politically uninfluential classes to end their *exclusion* from *political life and power*. Its standpoint is that of the State, an *abstract* whole, which *only* exists by virtue of its separation from real life, and which is *unthinkable* without the *organized* opposition between the universal idea and the individual existence of man. A revolution of a *political* kind also organizes, therefore, in accordance with this *narrow* and *discordant* outlook, a ruling group in society at the expense of society.

Art. II (1844)
MEGA I/3, p. 22

A "*social*" revolution with a *political* aspect is either a contradiction in terms, if " A Prussian " means by social revolution a social revolution *as distinct from* a political one, and yet attributes to this social revolution a political rather than a social aspect. Or else a "*social revolution with a political aspect*" is simply a *paraphrase* of what used to be called simply a "*political revolution*" or "*revolution*" *tout court*. Every revolution breaks up the *old society*; to this extent it is *social*. Every revolution overthrows *the existing ruling power*; to this extent it is *political*.

Art. II (1844)
MEGA I/3, p. 22

Revolution in general—the *overthrow* of the existing ruling power and the *dissolution* of existing social relationships—is a *political act*. Without *revolution socialism* cannot develop. It requires this *political act* as it needs the *overthrow* and the *dissolution*. But as soon as its *organizing activity* begins, as soon as its *own purpose* and *spirit* come to the fore, socialism sheds this *political* covering.

Art. II (1844)
MEGA I/3, pp. 22-3

An oppressed class is a vital condition of every society based on class antagonism. The emancipation of the oppressed class therefore necessarily involves the creation of a new society. For an oppressed class to be able to emancipate itself, it is essential that the existing forces of production and the existing social relations should be incapable of continuing to exist side by side. Of all the instruments of production, the greatest productive force is the revolutionary class itself. The organization of the revolutionary elements as a class presupposes that all the productive forces which could develop within the old society are in existence.

Does this mean that the downfall of the old society will be followed by a new class domination, expressing itself in a new political power? No. The condition for the emancipation of the working class is the abolition of all classes, just as the condition for the emancipation of the third estate, of the bourgeois order, was the abolition of all estates and orders.

The working class, in the course of its development, will substitute for the old civil society an association which will exclude classes and their antagonism, and there will no longer be any political power, properly so-called, since political power is precisely the official expression of the antagonism in civil society.

In the meantime, the antagonism between the proletariat and the bourgeoisie, is a class struggle, whose most complete expression is a total revolution. Is it astonishing, moreover, that a society founded on the *opposition* of classes, should end in a brutal *contradiction*, in a hand to hand struggle, as its last act?

Let us not say that the social movement excludes a political movement. There is no political movement which is not at the same time social. It is only in an order of things where there are no longer classes and class antagonism, that *social evolution* will cease to involve *political revolution*. Until then, the last word of social science, on the eve of every general reconstruction of society, will always be:

> *Le combat ou la mort ; la lutte sanguinaire ou le néant.*
> *C'est ainsi que la question est invinciblement posée.*[1]

George Sand

PP (1847)
MEGA I/6, pp. 227-8

If the proletariat destroys the political rule of the bourgeoisie, that will only be a temporary victory, only an element in the service of the *bourgeois revolution* itself, as in 1794, so long as in the course of history, in its " movement," the material conditions are not yet created which make necessary the abolition of the bourgeois mode of production and thus the definitive overthrow of bourgeois political rule.   The reign of terror in France could only serve, therefore, to clear away from the soil of France through its powerful blows, the remnants of feudalism. The anxious and considerate bourgeoisie would never have completed this task in decades.   The bloody action of the people thus only prepared the way for it.   Similarly, the collapse of the absolute monarchy would have been temporary, had not the economic conditions for the rule of the bourgeois class already ripened.   Men do not build themselves a new world out of the fruits of the earth, as *vulgar* superstition believes, but out of the historical accomplishments of their declining civilization.   They must, in the course of their development, begin by themselves *producing* the *material* conditions of a new society, and no effort of mind or will can free them from this destiny.

MK (1847)
MEGA I/6, p. 306

----

[1] Battle or death; bloody struggle or extinction.   It is thus that the question is irresistibly put.

Part Five

FUTURE SOCIETY

FUTURE SOCIETY

WHEN one studies the materialist theories of the original goodness of man, the equality of intellectual endowment among men, the omnipotence of education, experience and habit, the influence of external circumstances upon man, the great importance of industry, the value of pleasure, etc., there is no need for extraordinary penetration to discover what necessarily connects them with communism and socialism. If man derives all his knowledge from the sensible world and from his experience of the sensible world, then this is to say that the empirical world should be arranged in such a way that man experiences and assimilates there what is really human, that he experiences himself as man. If enlightened self-interest is the principle of all morality it is necessary for the private interest of each man to coincide with the general interest of humanity. If man is not free, in the materialist's sense, that is, if he is not negatively free to avoid this or that event, but is positively free to express his true individuality, then rather than punishing individuals for their crimes we should destroy the social conditions which engender crime, and give to each individual the scope which he needs in society in order to develop his life. If man is formed by circumstances, these circumstances must be humanly formed. If man is, by nature, a social being, he only develops his real nature in society, and the power of his nature should be measured not by the power of private individuals but by the power of society.

HF (1845)

MEGA I/3, pp. 307–8

Communism is the *positive* abolition of *private property*, of *human self-alienation*, and thus, the real *appropriation* of *human* nature, through and for man. It is therefore the return of man himself as a *social*, that is, really human, being, a complete and conscious return which assimilates all the wealth of previous development. Communism as a complete naturalism is humanism, and as a complete humanism is naturalism. It is the *definitive* resolution of the antagonism between man and Nature, and between man and man. It is the true solution of the conflict between existence and essence, between objectification and self-affirmation, between freedom and necessity, between individual and species. It is the solution of the riddle of history and knows itself to be this solution.

EPM (1844)
MEGA I/3, p. 114

Religion, the family, the State, law, morality, science, art, etc., are only *particular* forms of production and come under its general law. The positive abolition of *private property*, as the appropriation of human life, is *thus the positive* abolition of all alienation, and thus the return of man from religion, the family, the State, etc., to his *human*, i.e. *social*, life. Religious alienation only occurs in the sphere of *consciousness*, in the inner life of man, but economic alienation is that of *real life*, and its abolition therefore affects both aspects. Of course, the development in different nations has a different origin according to whether the actual life of the people is more in the realm of mind or in the external world, whether it is a *real* or *ideal* life.

EPM (1844)
MEGA I/3, p. 115

Where the division of landed property takes place, therefore, the only alternatives are to return to an even more hateful form of monopoly, or to envisage a negation or abolition of the division of landed property. This latter course is not, however, a return to feudal property, but the abolition of private property in land altogether. The first abolition of monopoly is always a generalization and extension of it. The abolition of monopoly which has attained its widest and most inclusive existence, is its complete destruction. Association, applied to the land, has the advantages from an economic point of view of large-scale ownership, and at the same time achieves the original tendency of the division of land, namely equality. Association further restores the intimate relationship of man to the land, in a rational way instead of through serfdom, overlordship and a foolish mystique of property. The land ceases to be an object of sordid speculation, and through freedom of work and enjoyment becomes once again the real, personal property of men.

EPM (1844)
MEGA I/3, p. 78

We have seen how, on the assumption that private property has been positively abolished, man produces man, himself and then other men, how the object which is the direct activity of his personality, is at the same time his existence for other men, and their existence for him. Similarly, the material of labour, and man himself as a subject, are the point of origin as well as the result of this movement (and because there must be this *point of origin*, private property is a historical *necessity*). Therefore, the *social* character is the universal character of the whole movement; as society itself produces *man* as *man*, so it is *produced* by him. Activity and mind are *social* in their content, as well as in their *origin*; they are *social* activity and *social* mind. The *human* significance of Nature only exists for *social* man, because only in this case is Nature a *bond* with other *men*, the basis of his existence for others and of their existence for him. Only then is Nature the *basis* of his own *human* existence, and a vital part of human reality. The *natural* existence of man has become his *human* existence and Nature itself has become, for him, human. Thus *society* is the accomplished union of man with Nature, the veritable resurrection of Nature, the realized naturalism of man and the realized humanism of Nature.

EPM (1844)
MEGA I/3, pp. 115–16

Since, however, for socialist man the whole of *what is called world history* is nothing but the creation of man by human labour, and the emergence of Nature for man, he therefore has the evident and irrefutable proof of his *self-creation*, of his own *origins*. Once the *essence* of man and of Nature, man as a natural being and Nature as a human reality, has become evident in practical life, in sense experience, the search for an *alien* being, a being outside man and Nature (a search which is an avowal of the unreality of man and Nature) becomes impossible in practice. *Atheism*, as a denial of this unreality, is no longer meaningful, for atheism is a *denial of God*, and seeks to assert by this denial the *existence of man*. Socialism no longer requires such a roundabout method; it begins from the *theoretical and practical sense perception* of man and Nature as real existences. It is a *positive* human *self-consciousness*, no longer a self-consciousness attained through the negation of religion, just as the real life of man is positive and no longer attained through the negation of private property (*communism*). Communism is the phase of negation of the negation, and is consequently, for the next stage of historical development, a *real* and necessary factor in the emancipation and rehabilitation of man. *Communism* is the necessary form and the active principle of the immediate future, but communism is not itself the aim of human development or the final form of human society.

EPM (1844)
MEGA I/3, pp. 125–6

Thus, according to our conception, all the conflicts of history have their origin in the contradiction between the productive forces and the mode of intercourse. It is not necessary that this contradiction should, in order to produce conflicts in one country, be brought to a head in that particular country. . . . This contradiction between the productive forces and the mode of intercourse which, as we saw, has appeared several times in previous history, without however endangering its basis, necessarily exploded in a revolution on each occasion. It assumed at the same time a variety of subsidiary forms, as an aggregate of conflicts, conflicts between different classes, battles of ideas, etc., political struggles, etc. From a narrow point of view, one of these subsidiary forms may be selected and regarded as the basis of the revolution, and this is all the more easy to do in that the individuals who began the revolution themselves had illusions about their activity, illusions which corresponded to their level of culture and to the stage of historical development.

The transformation of personal powers (relationships) into material powers through the division of labour cannot be undone again merely by dismissing the idea of it from one's mind, but only by the action of individuals who re-establish their control over these material powers and abolish the division of labour. This is not possible without a community. Only in association with others has each individual the means of cultivating his talents in all directions. Only in a community therefore is personal freedom possible. In the previous substitutes for community, in the State, etc., personal freedom existed only for those individuals who grew up in the ruling class and only in so far as they were members of this class. The illusory community in which, up to the present, individuals have combined, always acquired an independent existence apart from them, and since it was a union of one class against another it represented for the dominated class not only a completely illusory community but also a new shackle. In a genuine community individuals gain their freedom in and through their association.

GI (1845–6)
MEGA I/5, pp. 63–4

It follows from the whole preceding analysis that the communal relationship into which the individuals of a class entered, and which was determined by their common interests over against a third party, was always a community to which these individuals belonged only as average individuals, only in so far as they lived within the conditions of existence of their class. It was a relationship in which they participated not as individuals but as members of a class. But with the community of revolutionary proletarians, who establish their control over the conditions of existence of themselves and the other members of society, it is just the reverse; the individuals participate as individuals. It is just this combination of individuals (assuming, of course, the advanced level of modern productive forces) which brings the conditions for the free development and activity of individuals under their own control, conditions which were formerly abandoned to chance and which had acquired an independent existence over against the separate individuals. This independence resulted from the separation of individuals, and from the forced character of their combination, which was determined by the division of labour, and which had become an alien constraint. Combination as it has previously existed (not voluntarily as is suggested in Rousseau's *Social Contract*, but necessarily) was based on these conditions (compare for instance the formation of the North American State and the South American republics) in which the individuals were at the mercy of chance. This right to the undisturbed enjoyment of chance, within determining conditions, has hitherto been called personal freedom. These conditions are, of course, only the productive forces and forms of intercourse at any particular time.

If this development of individuals in the conditions of existence common to the estates and classes which historically succeed each other, and in the general conceptions which are forced upon them, is considered from a philosophical viewpoint, it is easy to imagine that the species, or mankind, has evolved in these individuals, or that they evolved man. In this way history can be given some hard knocks. The different estates and classes can then be conceived as specific instances of a general phenomenon, as sub-varieties of a species, or as phases in the development of mankind.

This subsumption of individuals under definite classes cannot be abolished until a class has been formed which no longer has a particular class interest to assert against the ruling class.

The starting point of individuals was always themselves, but of course themselves as they were in their given historical conditions and relationships, not " pure " individuals in the sense of the ideologists. But in the course of historical development, and precisely as a result of the assumption of independence by social relationships, which is the inevitable outcome of the division of labour, there emerges a distinction between the personal life of the individual and his life as it is determined by some branch of labour and the conditions pertaining to it. . . . In a system of estates (and still more in the tribe) this is still concealed: for instance, a nobleman always remains a nobleman, a commoner always a commoner, irrespective of his other relationships, a quality inseparable from his individuality. The distinction between the personal and the class individual, the accidental nature of conditions of life for the individual, appears only with the emergence of class, which itself is a product of the bourgeoisie. This accidental nature is only engendered and developed by the competition and conflict between individuals themselves. In theory, therefore, individuals appear to have greater freedom under the rule of the bourgeoisie than before; in reality of course they are less free, because they are more subject to the power of things. . . . For the proletarians . . . the condition of their own lives, labour, and with it all the conditions of existence of modern society, have become something accidental, over which the individual proletarians have no control and over which no *social* organization can give them control. The contradiction between the personality of the individual proletarian and the condition of life imposed on him, his labour, becomes evident to himself, for he is sacrificed from his youth onwards and has no opportunity of achieving within his own class the conditions which would place him in another class. Thus, while the runaway serfs only desired the freedom to develop and gain recognition for their actual conditions of existence, and therefore in the end only arrived at free labour, the proletarians, if they are to achieve recognition as persons, will be obliged to abolish their own former conditions of existence, which are at the same time those of society as a whole, that is, to abolish labour. They are, consequently, in direct opposition to the State as the form in which the members of society have so far found their collective expression, and in order to develop as persons they must overthrow the State.

GI (1845–6)
MEGA I/5, pp. 64–7

Finally, let us consider, by way of change, a community of free individuals, carrying on their work with the means of production in common, in which the labour-power of all the different individuals is consciously applied as the combined labour-power of the community. All the characteristics of

Robinson Crusoe's labour are here repeated, but with this difference, that they are social, instead of individual. Everything produced by him was exclusively the result of his own personal labour, and therefore simply an object of use for himself. The total product of our community is a social product. One part serves as fresh means of production and remains social. But another part is consumed by the members as means of subsistence, and has consequently to be distributed among them. The mode of this distribution will vary with the productive organization of the community, and the degree of historical development attained by the producers. We will assume, but merely for the sake of a parallel with the production of commodities, that the share of each individual producer in the means of subsistence is determined by his labour-time. Labour-time would, in that case, play a double part. Its apportionment in accordance with a definite social plan maintains the proper proportion between the different kinds of work to be done and the various wants of the community. On the other hand, it also serves as a measure of the individual's share in the common labour, and of his share in that part of the total product destined for individual consumption. The social relations of the individual producers, both to their labour and to its products, are in this case perfectly simple and intelligible, and that with regard not only to production but also to distribution.

Capital I (1867)
VA I, p. 84

Modern industry never looks upon or treats the existing form of a production process as final. The technical basis of industry is therefore revolutionary, while all earlier modes of production were essentially conservative. By means of machinery, chemical processes and other methods, it leads to continual changes not only in the technical basis of production, but also in the function of the labourer, and in the social combinations of the labour-process. At the same time, therefore, it revolutionizes the division of labour within the society, and incessantly transfers masses of capital and of workpeople from one branch of production to another. Large-scale industry, by its very nature therefore necessitates changes in work, variability of function, universal mobility of the labourer; on the other hand, in its capitalistic form, it reproduces the old division of labour with its ossified particularities. We have seen how this insurmountable contradiction robs the worker's situation of all peace, permanence and security; how it constantly threatens, by taking away the instruments of labour, to snatch from his hands his means of subsistence, and, by suppressing his particular sub-divided task, to make him superfluous. We have seen, too, how this contradiction works itself out through incessant sacrifices by the working class, the most reckless squandering of labour-power, and the devastations caused by social anarchy. This is the negative side. But though changes of work at present impose themselves after the manner of an overpowering natural law, and with the blindly destructive action of a natural law that meets with resistance at all points, large-scale industry, through its very catastrophes, imposes the recognition, as a fundamental law of production, of changes in work, and consequently the versatility of the worker. It becomes a question of life and death for society to adapt the mode of production to the normal functioning of this law. Large-scale industry, indeed, compels society, under penalty of death, to replace the miserable reserve army of labour which capital keeps at its disposal for its varying needs in the way of exploitation, by the complete adaptability of individuals to the changing demands for different kinds of work. In this way, the detail-worker of today, the limited individual, the mere bearer of a particular social function, will be replaced by the fully developed individual, for whom the different social functions he performs are but so many alternative modes of activity.

One step already spontaneously taken towards effecting this revolution is the establishment of technical and agricultural schools, and of *écoles d'enseignement professionel*, in which the children of the working men receive some instruction in technology and in the practical handling of the various implements of labour. Though the Factory Acts, the first concessions wrung from capital, are limited to combining elementary education with work in the factory, there can be no doubt that when the working class comes into power, as inevitably it must, technical instruction, both theoretical and practical, will take its proper place in the working-class schools. Nor is there any doubt that such revolutionary ferments, the final aim of which is the abolition of the old division of labour, are diametrically opposed to the capitalist mode of production, and to the economic condition of the labourers which corresponds to it. But the development of the contradictions within a historical form of production is the only way in which they can be resolved and a new form established.

Capital I (1867)
VA I, pp. 512-14

. . . large-scale industry, in overturning the economic foundation on which the traditional family and the family labour corresponding to it was based, had also dissolved all traditional family ties. The rights of children had to be proclaimed. . . . It was not, however, the misuse of parental authority that created the capitalistic exploitation, whether direct or indirect, of children's labour; but, on the contrary, it was the capitalistic mode of exploitation which, by sweeping away the economic basis of parental authority, made its exercise degenerate into a misuse of power.

However terrible and disgusting, under the capitalist system, the dissolution of the old family ties may appear, nevertheless, large-scale industry, by assigning as it does an important part in the process of production, outside the domestic sphere, to women, to young persons, and to children of both sexes, creates a new economic basis for a higher form of the family and of the relations between the sexes. It is, of course, just as absurd to regard the Teutonic-Christian form of the family as absolute and final as it would be to apply that character to the ancient Roman, the ancient Greek, or the Eastern forms which, moreover, taken together form a series in historical development. Moreover, it is obvious that the fact of the collective working group being composed of individuals of both sexes and all ages, must necessarily, under suitable conditions, become a source of humane development; although in its spontaneously developed, brutal capitalist form, where the labourer exists for the process of production, and not the process of production for the labourer, it is a pestilential source of corruption and slavery.

Capital I (1867)
VA I, pp. 514–16

The realm of freedom only begins, in fact, where that labour which is determined by need and external purposes, ceases; it is therefore, by its very nature, outside the sphere of material production proper. Just as the savage must wrestle with Nature in order to satisfy his wants, to maintain and reproduce his life, so also must civilized man, and he must do it in all forms of society and under any possible mode of production. With his development the realm of natural necessity expands, because his wants increase, but at the same time the forces of production, by which these wants are satisfied, also increase. Freedom in this field cannot consist of anything else but the fact that socialized mankind, the associated producers, regulate their interchange with Nature rationally, bring it under their common control, instead of being ruled by it as by some blind power, and accomplish their task with the least expenditure of energy and under such conditions as are proper and worthy for human beings. Nevertheless, this always remains a realm of necessity. Beyond it begins that development of human potentiality for its own sake, the true realm of freedom, which however can only flourish upon that realm of necessity as its basis. The shortening of the working day is its fundamental prerequisite.

Capital III
VA III/2, pp. 873-4

The " free State "—what is this ?

It is by no means the aim of the workers, who have freed themselves from the narrow outlook of humble subjects, to set the State free. In the German Empire the " State " is almost as " free " as in Russia. Freedom consists in transforming the State from an organ dominating society into one completely subordinate to it, and even at the present time the forms of State are more free or less free to the extent that they restrict the " freedom of the State."

CGP (1875)

" Present-day society " is capitalist society, which exists in all civilized countries, more or less free from medieval adjuncts, more or less modified by the special historical development of each country, and more or less developed. On the other hand, the " present-day State " changes with a country's frontier. It is different in the Prusso-German Empire from what it is in Switzerland, it is different in England from what it is in the United States. " *The* present-day State " is, therefore, a fiction.

Nevertheless, the different States of the different civilized

countries, in spite of their manifold diversity of form, all
have this in common, that they are based on modern bourgeois society, only one more or less capitalistically developed.
They have, therefore, also certain essential features in
common. In this sense it is possible to speak of the " present-
day State," in contrast with the future, in which its present
root, bourgeois society, will have died away.

The question then arises: What changes will the State
undergo in communist society? In other words, what
social functions will remain there which are analogous to
the present functions of the State? This question can only
be answered scientifically, and one does not get a flea-hop
nearer to the problem by any number of juxtapositions of
the word ' people ' with the word ' State.'

Between capitalist and communist society lies the period
of the revolutionary transformation of the one into the other.
There corresponds to this also a political transition period
in which the State can be nothing but *the revolutionary
dictatorship of the proletariat.*

CGP (1875)

What we have to deal with here is a communist society,
not as it has *developed* on its own foundation, but, on the
contrary, just as it *emerges* from capitalist society ; and which
is thus in every respect, economically, morally and intellec-
tually, still stamped with the birth-marks of the old society
from whose womb it emerges. Accordingly, the individual
producer receives back from society—after the deductions
have been made—exactly what he contributes to it. What
he has contributed to it is his individual quantum of labour.
For example, the social working day consists of the sum of the
individual hours of work; the individual labour-time of the
individual producer is the part of the social working day
contributed by him, his share in it. He receives a certificate from society that he has furnished such and such an

amount of labour (after deducting his labour for the common funds), and with this certificate he draws from the social stock of means of consumption as much as costs the same amount of labour. The same amount of labour which he has given to society in one form he receives back in another.

Here obviously the same principle prevails as that which regulates the exchange of commodities, as far as this is exchange of equal values. Content and form are changed, because under the altered conditions no one can give anything except his labour, and because, on the other hand, nothing can pass into the ownership of individuals except individual means of consumption. But, as far as the distribution of the latter among the individual producers is concerned, the same principle prevails as in the exchange of commodity-equivalents: a given amount of labour in one form is exchanged for an equal amount of labour in another form.

Hence, *equal right* here is still in principle—*bourgeois right*, although principle and practice are no longer at loggerheads, whereas the exchange of equivalents in commodity exchange only exists *on the average* and not in the individual case.

In spite of this advance, *equal right* is still burdened with bourgeois limitations. The right of the producers is *proportional* to the labour they supply; the equality consists in the fact that measurement is made with an *equal standard*, labour.

But one man is superior to another physically or mentally and so supplies more labour in the same time, or can labour for a longer time; and labour, to serve as a measure, must be defined by its duration or intensity, otherwise it ceases to be a standard of measurement. The *equal* right is an unequal right for unequal labour. It recognizes no class differences, because everyone is only a worker like everyone else; but it tacitly recognizes unequal individual endowment, and thus natural privileges in respect of productive capacity. *It is, therefore, in its content, a right of inequality, like every right.* Right by its very nature can consist only in the application of an equal standard; but unequal individuals (and they would not be different individuals if they were not unequal) can only be assessed by an equal standard in so far as they are regarded from a single aspect, from one particular side only, as for instance, in the present case, they are regarded *only as workers*, and nothing more is seen in them, everything else being ignored. Further, one worker is married, another not; one has more children than another, and so on. Thus, with an equal performance of labour, and hence an equal share in the social consumption fund, one individual will in fact receive more than another, one will be richer than another, and so on. To avoid all these defects, right instead of being equal would have to be unequal.

But these defects are inevitable in the first phase of communist society as it is when it has just emerged after prolonged birth-pangs from capitalist society. Right can never be higher than the economic structure of society and the cultural development conditioned by it.

In a higher phase of communist society, when the en-slaving subordination of the individual to the division of labour, and with it the antithesis between mental and physical labour, has vanished; when labour is no longer merely a means of life but has become life's principal need; when the productive forces have also increased with the all-round development of the individual, and all the springs of co-operative wealth flow more abundantly—only then will it be possible completely to transcend the narrow outlook of bourgeois right and only then will society be able to inscribe on its banners: From each according to his ability, to each according to his needs!

CGP (1875)

APPENDIX

SELECTED BIBLIOGRAPHY [1]

Date	Title	First Published	Principal English Translations
1841	Doctoral dissertation, *Differenz der demokritischen und epikureischen Naturphilosophie*	*Mehring* [2] With preparatory writings, etc., in *MEGA* I/1	—
1842–3	Articles in the *Rheinische Zeitung*	Partly in *Mehring* Completely in *MEGA* I/1	—
1842–3	*Kritik des Hegelschen Staatsrecht*	*MEGA* I/1	—
1843	Articles in *Anekdota* (ed. by Arnold Ruge)	*Mehring* *MEGA* I/1	—
1844	Articles in *Deutsch-Französische Jahrbücher* ("Zur Kritik der Hegelschen Rechts-Philosophie: Einleitung," "Zur Judenfrage," etc.)	*Mehring* *MEGA* I/1	Some in H. J. Stenning, *Selected Essays*, 1926 Extracts in *BR* [3]

[1] This Bibliography lists Marx's principal writings in chronological order, with the dates of original publication and of the main English translations. Articles in newspapers and reviews are included under the year of publication, with the date of subsequent publication in book form. For a complete bibliography, with an Introduction giving details of the publication of Marx's writings, see M. Rubel, *Bibliographie des Oeuvres de Karl Marx*, Rivière, Paris 1956.

[2] F. Mehring, *Aus dem literarischen Nachlass von Karl Marx, Friedrich Engels und Ferdinand Lassalle*, Stuttgart 1902.

[3] *BR* refers to new translations in the present book.

Date	Title	First Published	Principal English Translations
1844	Articles in *Vorwärts*, Paris	Partly in *Mehring*	Some in Stenning, *op. cit.*
	[Economic and Philosophical manuscripts]	Completely in *MEGA* I/3	Extracts in *BR*
		MEGA I/3	Extracts in *BR*
1844-5	[Economic Notebooks]	*MEGA* I/3	Extracts in *BR*
1845	*Die heilige Familie*	Frankfurt 1845	Extracts in Stenning, *op. cit.*
		Reprinted in *MEGA* I/3	Extracts in *BR*
1846	*Die Deutsche Ideologie* (with Engels)	First complete in *MEGA* I/5	*German Ideology, Pts. I and III*, ed. R. Pascal, 1938
			Extracts from Pts. I, II, and III in *BR*
1847	*Misère de la philosophie*	Paris, 1847	*Poverty of Philosophy*, trans. Henry Quelch, 1900
		Reprinted in *MEGA* I/6	Extracts in *BR*
1847-8	Articles in *Deutsche-Brüsseler-Zeitung* (esp. " Die moralisie-rende Kritik und die kritische Moral ")	Partly in *Mehring*	Part of " Die moralisierende Kritik . . etc." in Stenning, *op. cit.*
		Completely in *MEGA* I/6	Extracts in *BR*

1848	*Manifest der Kommunistischen Partei* (with Engels)	London, 1848 Reprinted in *MEGA* I/6	Trans. by Helen MacFarlane, published in the *Red Republican*, 1850 Authorized English trans. by Samuel Moore, with introduction and notes by Engels, 1888 Trans. by E. and C. Paul, with D. Riazanov's *Historical Introduction*, 1930 Edition published by the Labour Party, with a long introduction by H. J. Laski, under the title *Communist Manifesto : Socialist Landmark*, 1948
	Lohnarbeit und Kapital	In *Neue Rheinische Zeitung*, April 1849 Reprinted in *MEGA* I/6 with a manuscript on wage-labour written in 1847	*Wage-Labour and Capital*, trans. by J. L. Joynes, 1885 Several later translations Extracts in *BR*
1850	*Die Klassenkämpfe in Frankreich, 1848–50*	In *Neue Rheinische Zeitung—Politisch—ökonomische Revue* Reprinted in 1895 with a preface by Engels	*The Class-Struggles in France*, 1924

Date	Title	First Published	Principal English Translations
1852	Der achtzehnte Brumaire des Louis Napoleon	In Die Revolution (J. Weydemeyer's review, published in New York)	The Eighteenth Brumaire of Louis Bonaparte, trans. by Daniel de Leon, 1898
			Extracts in BR
1857–8	[Economic manuscripts]	Grundrisse der Kritik der politischen Ökonomie (Rohentwurf). Anhang 1850–59, Moscow 1939 and 1941	Trans. of the "Introduction" of 1857 (see next entry)
			Extracts in BR
1859	Zur Kritik der politischen Ökonomie	Berlin, 1859	A Contribution to the Critique of Political Economy, trans. by N. I. Stone, 1909. This is a translation from Kautsky's edition, and includes the 1857 "Introduction"
		Reprinted, with Marx's unpublished "Introduction" written in 1857, by K. Kautsky, Stuttgart 1907. The "Introduction", with other manuscripts has been reprinted in Grundrisse, etc. (see previous entry)	Extracts in BR
1860	Herr Vogt	London, 1860	
		Reprinted, with an appendix by Engels, Leipzig 1927	

1865	*Value, Price and Profit*	(An address given in English) First published by Eleanor Marx-Aveling, London 1898	
1867 onwards	*Das Kapital*	Vol. I. Hamburg 1867 2nd rev. edn., ibid., 1872–3 3rd and 4th edns. corrected by Engels, 1883 and 1890	*Capital : a Critical Analysis of Capitalist Production* (2 vols.), trans. from the 3rd German edn. by Samuel Moore and Edward Aveling, and edited by Engels, 1887
			Capital, trans. from the 4th German edn. by E. and C. Paul, with an introduction by G. D. H. Cole, 1928
			Extracts in *BR*
		Vol. II. Published by Engels, Hamburg 1885	*The Process of Circulation of Capital,* trans. by E. Untermann, 1907
			Extracts in *BR*
		Vol. III. Published by Engels, 1893–4	*The Process of Capitalist Production as a Whole,* trans. by E. Untermann, 1909
			Extracts in *BR*

Date	Title	First Published	Principal English Translations
1867 onwards	*Das Kapital*	[Manuscripts on "Theories of Surplus Value," which Marx intended to use for a fourth volume.] Published by K. Kautsky as *Theorien über den Mehrwert* (3 vols.), Stuttgart, 1905–10	*Theories of Surplus Value*, selections trans. by G. A. Bonner and E. Burns, 1953
			A History of Economic Theories. Trans. of Vol. I of Kautsky's edn. by T. McCarthy, 1952
			Extracts in *BR*
1871	*The Civil War in France*	(In English.) London, 1871	
1875	[Critique of the Gotha Programme]	Published by Engels in *Neue Zeit*, 1891	*Critique of the Gotha Programme*, ed. by C. P. Dutt, 1938
			Extracts in *BR*
1880	"Enquête Ouvrière"	In *Revue Socialiste*, April 1880	In full, with an introductory note, in *BR*
Correspondence	Correspondence between Marx and Engels	Partly by Bebel and Bernstein, Stuttgart 1914	Selection in *The Correspondence of Marx and Engels, 1846–1895*, trans. and edited by Dona Torr, 1934
		Completely in *MEGA* III/Vols. 1–4	

NOTE. A large part of Marx's correspondence has been published, but most of it has not been translated into English. There are, however, English translations of some important letters to Weydemeyer, Kugelmann, Annenkov, and others. See *Karl Marx and Friedrich Engels : Selected Works*, Vol. II, London 1950, and Dona Torr, op. cit.

INDEX

Catalog

If you are interested in a list of fine Paperback
books, covering a wide range of subjects
and interests, send your name and address,
requesting your free catalog, to:

McGraw-Hill Paperbacks
330 West 42nd Street
New York, New York 10036